"There's a wealth of material here and sound advice that could help save a lot of people a lot of pain.

"Joni Greenwalt is a survivor in a growing nationwide conflict, the often bitterly fought Homeowner Association wars. In a breezy, one-neighbor-to-another style, she tells how to prevail against the Covenant Police, how to turn around a poorly run or dictatorially managed association, and what questions to ask BEFORE buying a home in an association-governed neighborhood. Reader beware: You'll read homeowner horror stories that'll make your hair curl."

John Grossmann, Author of Trouble on the Home Front?
Mountain Lake, New Jersey

"An excellent, well-researched analysis of the aggravations that can arise from the enforcement of protective covenants. I recommend that all who work with or are subject to covenants study this book with the thought of avoiding grief and expensive litigation. It will make living under the control of covenants a much more pleasant experience."

Nathan Baum, Attorney
Baum and Gustafson, Denver, Colorado

"Most who deal with homeowner associations approach the dilemmas strictly from a technical standpoint. Either they have forgotten or they were never aware of the entire picture. A much needed book."

Del Brown,
San Dimas, California

"This will open everyone's eyes to the need for cooperation and understanding between board members and homeowners. Any board member who seriously desires having a good association should read this book."

Steve Smalley,
Colorado Management Company

"An extremely informative book presented with sprinkles of humor thrown in on a very serious and important subject. As a Professional Registered Parliamentarian I work with homeowner associations. I understand the problems that members face."

Lou Fasulo,
Golden, Colorado

"Absolutely priceless information for those living in a covenants-controlled community or those contemplating a move to this type of neighborhood."

Norman and Audrey Rebsamen,
St. Louis, Missouri

"I have had so many nightmarish experiences with my association I was going to move. After reading these inspiring and forceful ideas, I'm going to stay and stand up for my rights."

Margaret Grassmann,
Sun City West, Arizona

"Put this on the must read list for lawyers, developers, management companies, board members, and real estate brokers. In 20 years as a Realtor® I've sold many condos and townhomes, always cautioning my buyers to read their declarations, etc. Until I read this book I didn't know how really important that advice was!"

Joyce Frink,
Vice president of an association, Lakewood, Colorado

Homeowner Associations
A Nightmare or a Dream Come True?

Homeowner Associations
A Nightmare or a Dream Come True?

Do you thrive or barely survive in a community governed by an association? With humor and down-to-earth facts, this guide offers real-life scenarios and solutions.

Joni Greenwalt

Resident and the president of a homeowner association in a happy community

Cassie Publications, Inc.

Published by Cassie Publications, Inc.

- Illustrations: Shannon Keegan
- Page Design: Ultimax, Inc.
- Cover Design: Ultimax, Inc.
- Photograph: Ryan Shacklett
- Principal Editor: Harriett Graves

Printed in the United States of America

Library of Congress Catalog Card Number: 97-92365

ISBN 0-9659166-0-X

Homeowner Associations
A Nightmare or a Dream Come True?
First Printing 1998
Second Printing 2001 Revised

This book does not attempt to answer all questions about all situations you may encounter. There is no intention to give legal advice. Contact legal counsel for advice on specific circumstances. While all particulars included have been prepared from current, reliable sources, none are guaranteed.

Cassie Publications, Inc.
P.O. Box 261368
Denver, CO 80226
303-422-6277 or Toll Free 888-683-9550
www.homeownerassoc.com

Contents

Acknowledgments — 11

1. From Hostility to Happiness — 13
> Then Hostile Happenings Started to Happen
> Terrible Trash Terrorizes
> Sometimes Things Happen Because They Need to Happen
> Time to Organize a Coup d'État
> Our Community Is Now Running Smoothly

2. Your Dream to Live in a Community Controlled by Covenants — 23
> The Dream
> The Nightmare
> The Dream Comes True
> What if a Neighbor Drizzles on My Dream?
> An Outlook That Truly Allows Dreams to Come True

3. The Benefits of Covenants-controlled Communities, According to Advertising — 29
> Which Way to Utopia?
> Covenants Aren't the Magic Wand That Bestows Happiness
> The Boring, But Necessary Basics
   Is It a Bird, a Plane, a Condo, or a . . . ?
> What Is a Covenants-controlled Community?
> Thirty-year Old Whiskers Are Growing on Today's Docs
> Fuzzy Mold Is Taking Hold

4. Real Case Scenarios, Comments, and Suggested Solutions — 43
> Rules Can Be Changed
> A Suggested Solution to a Silly Problem
> Pride of Ownership Cannot Be Legislated

5. So What's New? Isn't Life About Taking Responsibility? — 75
> Get Involved!
> It's about HOA Fees
> Speaking of Money

6. Required Reading Isn't Enough — 83
> Required Reading — the Documents
> Know Who's in Charge — the Enforcers
> If You're Considering a Move to a Covenants-controlled "Dreamland"
> If You Happen to Get Romanced into a Sub-happy Community
> How to Organize Your Coup d'État
> Don't Leave Without a Signed Proxy!
> You Don't Have to Be a Homeowner to Organize a Coup

7. So You Want to Be on the Board? Who Are You?   **99**
- ❯ The Profile of Those Who Belong on the Board
- ❯ The Profile of Those Who Do *Not* Belong on the Board
- ❯ More About Votes and Proxies
- ❯ The Power of Votes and Proxies Can Authorize a Dictatorship
- ❯ Same Scenario — Different Dictators
- ❯ What's in a Name?
- ❯ Words <u>Do</u> Have Power
- ❯ Management Companies
- ❯ Is the Board of Directors Real or Let's Pretend?

8. How to Get Special Assessments and Increase Dues   **119**
- ❯ Getting Bids — a Sketch of What Can Happen
- ❯ How *Not* to Keep Dues Low
- ❯ Beware of Phony Low Dues
-    Beware of Excessively High Dues

9. If You Feel Like Road Kill, You Have a Problem   **137**
- ❯ Recognize the Real Problem, Is It Them or You?
- ❯ Dumb and Dumber Moments
- ❯ Expect Neighborliness, Be Neighborly — Not Nosy

10. I Address the Bench   **147**
- ❯ From Developer to Disaster
- ❯ From Developer to Dream
- ❯ Benefits the Legal Profession Offers — According to Rumor
- ❯ Now Choose the Right Attorney
- ❯ Is the Fox in Charge of Guarding the Chicken Coop?
- ❯ Another Culprit at the Base of HOA Problems Is Exposed

11. You're on the Board. Now What Do You Do?   **171**
- ❯ Use Ethics, Empathy, and Compassion
- ❯ Turning BADs Back into DABs
- ❯ You'll Never Reach the Peak Going Down Hill
- ❯ If You're at the Peak, Stay There

General Summary — Living in a community governed by an association can be pleasant and rewarding   **I**

Summary and Additional Suggested Details for Developers, the Legal Profession, Document Modification, and Legislation   **II**

Homeowners' Questionnaire   **V**

A Brief Guide to Parliamentary Procedure   **VI**

Sample Rules and Regs   **IX**

Index   **XIII**

About the Author   **XXI**

This book is dedicated to . . .

Everybody who aspires to live happily within a community under the authority of an association and to those who respect constitutional rights for all.

Acknowledgments of my heartfelt appreciation go to . . .

- Shannon Keegan for the illustrations
- Ultimax, Inc. for the cover design
- Ryan Shacklett for the photography
- Harriett Graves, Joanne Lowrey, Algird Pocius, Harriet Strobel, plus 16 more extraordinarily helpful people for their painstaking editing
- Steven Greenwalt, Joe Turnbough, and Howard Wisher for lifesaving computer technology
- All the newspaper journalists for their articles about difficulties within associations
- Jim Winzenburg, attorney, for his guidance and permission to print excerpts from *Boardroom Discussion*
- To Dr. Wayne Dyer, I offer my sincere gratitude for all the priceless wisdom he has gleaned from a multitude of sources and shared through his audio tapes, books, and seminars. He has been my number one mentor for over 20 years.
- To my husband, John Meury, I give a colossal "THANK YOU." This would have been an impossible task without his legwork, loving support, patience, encouragement, back rubs, and meals.

From Hostility to Happiness

Bang, bang, bang, bang. Four shots rang out. Only superficial wounds were inflicted. Clarification of those shots is on the next page.

Throughout the nation there are some communities with homeowner associations that are very *friendly and neighborly*. I know because I live in one.

Regrettably, there are also some that are absolutely *rude and hostile*. I know because I used to live in one of those. *It's the same place — I haven't moved!*

The events follow

When I bought my townhome August 1, 1988 I had been a real estate agent for nine years. Many of the homes I had sold were in communities controlled by covenants. My advice to my clients: thoroughly investigate the community, carefully read the documents, and get involved with the association. Don't assume George and Georgette are taking care of everything properly.

I thought I knew what thorough investigation really meant. As most buyers do, I merrily fell in love with the ambiance and the layout of the home. All I checked was how often the board could raise the dues, how much they were allowed to raise them, and the history of such raises. In the excitement of finding a home, it's tempting to do the same or less.

I not only admit my stupidity — the following events verify it!

Sometimes it takes a while for the real stuff to smack the fan

I followed some of my own advice. I got involved. I attended every association meeting.

On the surface everything appeared to be just fine. There was no management company, just three friendly board members.

The ensuing miserable and ultimately victorious events follow — my experiences of turning hostility back to happiness.

Set the stage

Stories started coming to me about an ill-tempered faction of four homeowners who had assumed the role of the community's chronic complainers. Hereafter, the cranks will fondly be identified as "The Clan." I was told that The Clan had absolutely terrorized everyone who had ever been on the board. It was reported that since the beginning of the complex every board of directors had received at least one complaining letter every month.

Honestly, I couldn't believe The Clan could be as bad as their reputation. Ha!

▸ THEN HOSTILE HAPPENINGS STARTED TO HAPPEN

There were only landscaping stones in two prominent locations on my property. Not being a fan of rocks, I got written permission from the board to replace the stones with environmentally friendly vegetation.

As I was removing the rocks, a member of the architectural control committee told me, in a pleasant, cookie-baking, grandmotherly way to cease and desist. Cookie-baking grandmother indeed! She turned out to be the leader of The Clan.

The president of the association witnessed the entire rock-shebang. She came to my home and said, "Continue to remove the rocks. It's okay, you have our written permission." The rocks were removed and the plants were planted.

Right after my "rock-riot" the president resigned only a few months into her three-year term. She was intimidated by the fear that she might be sued if she crossed another T the wrong way. It seems that permission to remove rocks was crossing a T a little askew.

The order of events

The water in the entire complex was shut off for a few hours. The significance of that incident is explained shortly.

There were 39 occupied homes, plus 12 vacant lots that were owned by the developer.

At the 1990 annual meeting in January we were to vote for the positions of president and vice president. Usually only one position is open each year. That year one member was up for reelection and another board member had moved out of the complex.

There were 14 homeowners at the meeting. *There were 18 votes for two of The Clan!* How could that be? Bang, bang, bang, bang! Four shots rang out!

One member of The Clan's foursome had *secured the developer's 12 proxy votes,* one vote for each vacant lot. She *had 13 votes — add three more* from the other clan members — then *add two more from a couple of clan sympathizers. A total of 18 votes for The Clan.* A fairly hefty count with only 14 homes represented. The token votes from the remaining eight homeowners were absolutely worthless. The intentions of the majority were completely bypassed.

The Clan had just effectively "elected" two members of The Clan.

The newly "elected" president, the leader of The Clan, had suspected the reason for our brief period of no water was from non-payment of the water bill. She also suspected that the secretary/treasurer's fingers had become a little sticky with the association's bank account.

She was right. Over $14,000 had dribbled away a few hundred dollars at a time. The association's account had dwindled to less than $20.

Only one signature was required on the checks. The secretary/treasurer handled the bills, wrote the checks, and signed the checks. There was no bond or liability insurance coverage to protect the HOA (homeowner association) against embezzlement. That was not a solid plan.

The HOA had to issue a $350 special assessment immediately to each homeowner to replace the vaporized funds. The developer was assessed one-quarter of that amount for each of his 12 vacant lots. He only paid one-quarter of the monthly association dues. It always seemed to me to be a double standard that the developer had one full vote for each lot, but only paid one-quarter of the monetary assessments.

Due to the efforts of the president, the secretary/treasurer was prosecuted by the county. She was ordered to make monthly payments to our association until the missing funds were completely replaced or she would go directly to jail. It took three years, but we did get all the money back from the dollar-dipping check writer.

A third member of The Clan was appointed by the board as the new secretary/treasurer. Now we had a matched set.

The newly *"elected"* board hired a management company. The owner of the company, with clipboard in hand, made weekly treks throughout the complex. She systematically searched out and documented, in the style of Sherlock Holmes with his magnifying glass, any infractions of the rules. She would peer into backyards owned by the homeowners — not common area — and **make note of everything.** It seemed as though fining homeowners, especially those the board didn't like, was recreational entertainment. We now had the covenants police.

The Clan, with the help of the management company, produced a monthly newsletter that always highlighted the **COVENANT OF THE MONTH.** The newsletters also featured such "warm fuzzy" announcements as **NO TOYS IN THE FRONT YARDS** and . . .

FINES INCREASE
Effective June 15, 1990, the amount of the fine for violation of the covenants governing the association will be $25 for the second offense. The first offense is a warning letter. For the third offense the fine will be $50. The fourth offense will carry a fine of $100.

That tidbit came from what was to be their final newsletter.

▶ TERRIBLE TRASH TERRORIZES

Before The Clan was *"elected"* to the board, when they were just the community complainers, one of their favorite subjects was the placement of the homeowners' trash containers.

Most residents kept their trash containers neatly tucked up by their garage. Traditionally that practice had been accepted since the first unit was built in 1985.

A few residents, including The Clan, kept their containers inside their garage or those few fortunate enough to have a side yard, placed them there.

Because of The Clan's constant trash-container complaints, the previous board had that ambiguous covenant interpreted by two attorneys. Both attorneys said containers placed next to the garage were in compliance with the covenant.

The Clan had an interpretation all their own.

They wanted **all trash containers totally out of sight. They dictated that all containers either be stored . . .**

●   **. . . in the garage**

I was one of many homeowners who objected to keeping our trash containers in our garages. We explained that the only room in our one-car garages for the container was in front of the car. That plan necessitated moving the car each time the trash container was put in or out of the garage. Plus, it created an unhealthy environment. The entrance from the garage is directly into the kitchen area. That practice is not allowed in restaurants. It is no less of an odoriferous, unsanitary problem for private homes.

●   **. . . or in the backyard or side yard**

For many that plan didn't solve the problem of moving the car for trash container ingress and egress. Some backyards are land locked by the adjoining neighbors' yards. The only entrance is from the home or the back door of the garage. The back doors of the garages are too narrow to accommodate the size of the trash containers.

Our backyards are small, so those of us with no side yard would have to have our trash container near the patio — right under our noses. "Everyone come over for a barbecue and smell my trash."

‣ *SOMETIMES THINGS HAPPEN BECAUSE THEY NEED TO HAPPEN*

I was in the process of protesting the county's property tax value of my home. Since the documentation required to lower my tax valuation would be the same for every home in my complex, I volunteered to let other homeowners "ride" on my documentation if they supplied me with their pertinent information. Interestingly, we discovered that The Clan had already protested their tax valuation, but never offered to share their documentation with one other homeowner.

I asked the board and the management company for a phone list so I could call my neighbors to determine who wanted to pursue getting their property tax valuations lowered. Both the management company and the board refused to give a list to me.

When a neighbor, a past board member, gave an old list to me The Clan had an attorney send a letter to him mandating that he *never* give a phone list to anyone ever again!

I was trying to help the homeowners. I had no plans of using the list to make obscene or harassing phone calls. You can bet if my purpose had been to sniff out homeowner infractions and create fines, the board would have given a current phone list to me in a heartbeat.

We now furnish a neighborhood directory. It includes every resident's name and address, and the phone numbers of those who have given their permission to publish their phone number.

Back to the pulse of the matter: the first homeowner who brought her necessary property tax information to me voluntarily voiced her extreme unhappiness with the new governing of our community. Not overly delighted with it myself, as other homeowners supplied their tax valuation information to me, I asked, "How do you feel about the way the board governs our community?"

Coincidences are miracles in which God prefers to remain anonymous.

Responses from the residents to that question

"I feel as if I just lost my freedom."

"It's too bad, but now it's like *them against us*."

"What do they want, their own little perfect world where no one can do *anything* without asking them?"

"If they want to tell me how to live, they can *[expletive deleted]* well make my house payments."

"Covenants and bylaws should be used as a guideline tempered with common sense and compassion. Sure, I don't want someone's dead car jacked up for a month with parts lying all over the yard. But, someone having the hood up on his car for an hour or two, while he changes filters or plugs, doesn't seem like the end of the world to me."

"It may have been legal, but not ethical or moral the way they got elected to be in the power seats. It's terrible! Don't they care about any one else?"

"I want a home, not an institution."

"They represent themselves — not us, not the best interests of everyone — just their own. I'm moving."

"I feel like I am living under Hitler!"

"If this is a retirement community, they should tell you before you buy." [It isn't a retirement community.]

"I feel as though someone is always watching me to see if I'm going to do something wrong so they can fine me."

"I can't live this way. If I can't sell, I'll give it back to HUD!"

"I've lived here since these were built and it didn't used to be this way — it's like living in a police state."

"I'm afraid to open mail from the association until my husband gets home."

"It's like living in a concentration camp!"

"What do they mean I can't work on my car? Do they mean I can't change my own spark plugs any more?"

"Well, the only thing I can say is they only care about themselves. If they like it, they think everyone else *has* to like it too. They are all single with no children at home, one car, and narrow minds."

"I take care of my front lawn and it's right outside my front door, but my kids can't even play with their toys on it? That, to me, is downright ridiculous."

"I already have a mother."

"Move, never — kill, maybe!"

"This is getting to be like a trailer park."

I'm not quite certain what that last statement means.

Did you feel the *sheer pain* as you read each homeowner's misery? Did you *sense the lack of pride of ownership?* Did you think *any* of those homeowners felt they were enjoying the benefits they had seen advertised about the joys of living in a community controlled by covenants?

Every time a neighbor made a declaration of discontentment, I wrote the statement down and put an asterisk by that neighbor's name on the notorious phone list. For the two who were "on the fence" I put a question mark. Until I took that survey, every unhappy homeowner felt like the Lone Ranger — alone in their anguished search for justice.

Out of 39 homeowners the final score showed that 33 were miserable. Including spouses, that 33 represented over 50 residents. It made no sense for 50 to continue suffering for the pleasure of four.

A moment of levity

It was time for schools to close for summer vacation when all that fracas was happening. A little light bulb flashed over my head. I knew at every high school there would be a mountain of real estate For Sale signs stacked in front of each school. Students "borrow" the signs to offer the school For Sale and the stack of signs builds. I suggested to one resident that we go pick up four signs and in the middle of the night plant them in front of the homes of the members of The Clan. Then a huge, brilliant light bulb flashed — better yet, let's get 35 signs and plant them in front of every home *except* the members of The Clan. We did neither, but the fantasy was sheer ambrosia. A little chuckle never hurts.

A position of strict enforcement not only endangers happiness, it has the potential to kill!

One bachelor gentleman was so frightened of possible consequences that he changed a flat tire in his garage with the door closed! When one of the residents found out about it she was quick to tell him, "Don't ever do that again, Larry. What if the car had fallen on you? There would be no way for anyone to know until we smelled your dead body!"

Oppression has a way of causing revolutions.

❯ TIME TO ORGANIZE A COUP D'ÉTAT

A neighbor (the one who had given the infamous phone list to me) and I met with an attorney three months after The Clan's self-election. We were advised we could organize a coup and petition the board to bring the matter to a vote of the homeowners to dislodge all of them from the board. Since our annual meeting was nine months away, our petition also called for a special meeting to be scheduled.

We asked each disgruntled (asterisked) homeowner to sign the petition. At the same time we insisted that each homeowner sign a proxy.

You may feel "insisted" is a pretty pushy word. It isn't pushy. It's a very necessary attitude. We explained that it was a one-time-only effort by us and we were not going to the meeting one vote short!

If they were truly fed up with the current situation, they had three options: they could cooperate by signing a proxy, remain miserable, or *they* could organize a petition to call a special meeting to replace the board.

We supplied each homeowner with the names of the five organizers of the coup to give them a choice as to whom they assigned their proxy. The bubonic plague wouldn't have stopped one of us from attending that meeting.

We contacted the developer and requested he **not** give his 12 proxies to anyone ever again, not even to any of the five organizers! We asked him to please keep his proxies to himself if the topic was of no concern to him. We suggested if the issue was one of importance to him that he do his own voting. With only 39 units, handing one person or faction, an additional 12 votes threw the whole voting process out of kilter. That imbalance made it impossible to serve the true needs of the majority of homeowners.

Until the meeting, we had no clue whether the developer would honor our request. He did!

Two days before the petition was presented to the board I received a warning letter to put my trash container in my garage or backyard. Other homeowners received the same edict. The date of the special meeting was racing against the ticking of the penalty-process-clock. The special meeting won the race — the trash containers remained in place and none of us ever paid a fine!

After receiving the petition, The Clan went around to homeowners and asked, "Why are you doing this?" Each homeowner would essentially reply, "Because your rigid, self-serving attitude is tearing the community apart and making all of us miserable." It isn't as though that was an entirely new thought that The Clan had never heard before. They had heard similar and worse statements screamed at them at association meetings.

The homeowners' responses fell on the board's deaf ears.

The special meeting . . .

. . . started with the president asking the same overworked question again. She added that they were absolutely dismayed at the homeowners wanting to remove them from the board. Obviously not one of them had *paid any attention to the consistent answers* given by the homeowners. They didn't want to hear what they didn't want to hear.

The silence was so deep you could hear hair growing. Then big mouth me (fully knowing better) couldn't keep my toothy orifice shut any longer. I said, "You've been told the answer over and over. Why do you keep asking the same question? Didn't you hear the answers or were you using selective hearing?"

By the end of the special meeting . . .

. . . there were three new faces on the board — all *elected* by the homeowners.

I didn't run for office at that special meeting because I held so many proxies which had been given to me by petition signers. I didn't want to be guilty of a procedure even similar to the one used by The Clan to elect themselves.

The time frame

What was supposed to have been a three-year term for the president, a two-year term for the vice president, and a one-year term for the secretary/treasurer, we reduced to six-month terms.

The Clan was three months into their "elected" reign when we started the go-away process. That process took another three months.

Our revolution was well timed. In their brief reign of terror The Clan was as busy as little beavers putting a lot more plans on their drawing board that they were proposing to perpetrate on the community. To name two: no street parking and a limit of two cars per household.

The Clan was not completely defused yet. They quickly slipped right back into their original and exclusive positions as the community's chronic complainers.

Subsequent board members *served their time,* but avoided making affirmative decisions that would have been beneficial for the majority of homeowners. They gave knee jerk reactions against decisions that might have the potential of raising the ire of The Clan and produce still more complaints. They were afraid of The Clan!

That didn't solve a thing. It only encouraged more complaints because The Clan smelled the fear. They maintained their control from behind the scenes. The association was caught in a vicious circle.

I was appointed as vice president, June 1991, when one member of the new board moved. A year later, the president moved and I was given the position of president by the other two board members. I have been elected, *really elected,* two times since.

❯ OUR COMMUNITY IS NOW RUNNING SMOOTHLY

All three current members of the board have been elected by vote of the homeowners. As the board, we aren't afraid to make decisions for the good of the community. We hadn't heard a complaint from you-know-who for several years. They just went on the warpath again! When will they learn that complaints have to be valid for the board to take action?

The past frightening imbalance of the voting scenario cannot happen to us a second time. The developer has no more proxies to give. He completed building the remaining 12 homes. All 51 homes are now occupied.

The majority of homeowners appear to be happy, as evidenced by the lack of complaints and civilized association meetings. It's the same set of rules we've always had. We didn't modify one regulation. We only reinterpreted the rules and changed the attitude toward the homeowners' rights. We also changed management companies. We don't need a Sherlock Holmes to perform weekly patrols in the hopes of inflicting penalties.

Unfortunately, there are some residents who have returned to their original misguided and contented apathy. They don't get involved in the operation of the community. They don't even offer their input by proxy, let alone attend meetings.

It seems apathetic residents need to feel like road kill before they will make an effort to be involved in their community. They just shlep around assuming everything is going just fine. They prefer someone else handle the responsibilities. They don't offer feedback or even a cordial, "Thanks for spending your time, with no pay, to keep our community in balance and blissful." I have the uneasy feeling that we, the board of directors, won't hear one word from any of them until they encounter a poison dart in the middle of their petunia patch.

There's more to the story

Sometime after The Clan was dethroned, my husband and I requested and received approval from the architectural committee and the other two board members to place a privacy fence enclosure around our trash receptacle. The enclosure matched the fencing in the complex, camouflaged the trash container, and prevented the wind from tipping it over.

Shortly after we finished our project we received a "tear the trash enclosure down in ten (10) days or contact the city prior to . . ." letter. The city had received anonymous complaints about the enclosure.

Two city officials came to inspect our "monstrosity." One of the officials instantly said, "Why on earth would anyone object to this? It's pretty. I'd like one myself."

Some people spend their recreational time creating problems for others. They regard solutions as a four-letter, obscene word.

The enclosure remained in place. When the developer completed building the remaining 12 units, he asked permission to incorporate my trash enclosure design with the new homes!

The end of 1993 . . .

The preceding incidents triggered an inspirational light bulb to go on over my head. I realized sharing my sequence of events could turn my sour lemons into sweet lemonade for others. The idea to write this book was conceived. By chance, look what appeared . . .

Thursday, January 27, 1994
Reprinted with permission of the *Rocky Mountain News*

Have the covenants police come after you?

The afternoon sun bakes your living room. You put up a nice awning. Then the covenants police come around. No awnings, they tell you.

You painstakingly build a wonderful swing set for your little one. It's costly, beautiful redwood. Then the covenants police come around. No redwood, they tell you.

Who are these people? Why, they're your neighbors and often they've volunteered for this job.

Sure, everybody wants the neighborhood to look nice. It keeps up everybody's property values, after all. But, once in a while, the covenants police seem over zealous.

If you've had an experience like this, call our COVENANTS Hotline, 555-5188, and tell us about it.

Immediately I called. I told Karen Abbott, the journalist and staff writer for Denver's *Rocky Mountain News*, that my tale was probably not like the rest of the calls she was receiving. I said, "We *had* a problem. We removed the covenants police from the board and are now a happy community."

I conveyed how we turned our hostile community into a friendly one, the episode about the enclosure for my trash container, and the fact that I was planning to write a book about happenings in communities under the rule of an association.

Karen sent a photographer to my home. I anticipated a small black and white picture would appear buried somewhere in the article. That did not turn out to be the case. There I was, in full color, at the top of the feature article sitting on my trash container placed in the notorious enclosure, similar to the picture on the cover of the book.

Appreciation

Karen offered to publish my phone number in her article, and at the same time she cautioned me. She said that to gather enough material to write a feature story usually takes printing a call-request article several times. Karen ran her call-request article only once. She couldn't return all the calls! As Karen predicted, I received a *lot* of calls from those in other communities who shared their tales of happiness, woes, and their resolutions. My sincere appreciation goes to Karen for publishing my phone number and to those who called me.

Karen's resulting article (chapter 4), the calls I received, and other newspaper articles are the major sources of the real-case scenarios in this book. (All newspaper articles are unabridged, a requirement of the permission to reprint.)

It's taken over four years to complete this book. It kept growing as I researched and discovered more pertinent information. I learned more, and more, and still yet more. I am still learning. I'm not alone. As I enlightened other real estate brokers with some of my newly acquired knowledge, they freely admitted being as unaware as I had been.

There were rewrites and continual additions as more discoveries unfolded. The first writing reflected entirely too much of my outrage at the events that had happened in my community. My wrath came back in full swing every time I wrote about the plights of others.

Book burnout struck. I set my project aside to wait until my mind would allow me to remove or soften some of my grumpy copy. Writing has proven to be very therapeutic. It's helped me put a lot of my fury to rest. You'll discover that my anger has not been entirely stilled. However, it is that very anger that will put you on guard to prevent or solve devastating events that can happen or may be happening to you at this very moment.

At times you may feel as though my aspiration is to discourage living in any community controlled by covenants and an association. That is not the case. There are many homeowner-friendly communities in this country. The accounts of grief are not meant to discourage. Rather, they are presented to suggest to those of you who are about to buy a property what to be aware of and to inform those of you who are in distress that there are remedies and that you are not isolated beings. One homeowner who was less than happy with her do-nothing board and extremely unhappy about the domineering management company said, "I'm delighted to discover that it's not just me. I'm not crazy. I'm not alone!"

Over 40 million live in such communities today. Experts predict that number will quickly double. All of us deserve to live happily in our homes.

This is neither an ABC nor a 1, 2, 3 technical book. Life and communities controlled by covenants are not in an ABC or 1, 2, 3 technical mode either. Life does not take us by the hand. Life teaches. The collection of newspaper articles and other stories reported in this book teaches that whatever dilemmas may happen there's always a resolution available. They convey real-life situations and myriad suggested practical solutions.

There are books available that approach covenants communities from a technical view (a few are suggested in Relevant reading on page XX at the end of the index). For the current statutes in your area contact your local chapter of Community Association Institute (CAI).

Your Dream to Live in a Community Controlled by Covenants

Enjoyment of life is far more rewarding than surviving from life. As illustrated in chapter 1, living in a community controlled by covenants can be a nightmare or a dream come true.

❯ THE DREAM

Does one of these scenarios fit you?

● You're a young couple. You decided buying your own home made a lot more sense than to keep pouring money into rent. Nevertheless, you didn't want a bunch of house-related tasks taking over your lives. You still wanted time to have fun. Your solution: you bought a townhome, a place where *they* take care of all the icky chores.

● You have a fantastic job. You travel all over the world. One time you even had to "tough it out" in Hawaii for a whole month! While all of that is great, you wanted *one* place you could call home. However, you read a book by Alan King titled *Anybody Who Owns His Own Home Deserves It*. It detailed all the painful obligations owning a home offers — lawn care and ad nauseum infinitum. Not being easily discouraged, you bought a townhome to satisfy your needs and eliminate the burdens.

● Your neighbor just painted his house pumpkin orange with bright green trim. You not only wanted to escape from that monstrosity, your family and your income had grown and you needed a larger home. You bought a beautiful home in a community controlled by covenants to avoid the possibility of such a colorful event ever happening to you again.

● You had "had it" by the time you finally got your divorce. You were the one who had always held up the heavy end of all the household duties. It was high time for you to go with the flow, coast a little, and finally enjoy life. Condominium living seemed like a prize idea.

● You owned your home for 20, 30 years or more. All the inherent responsibilities were getting you down. You wanted to stop pruning the roses and start smelling them. Your blue ribbon solution was to move to a cluster home in an adult community.

● You're single, have a good job, and enjoy life. You wanted to buy a home even though you didn't cherish the idea of being tied down to mowing a lawn and the thought of going home to an empty house late at night seemed a little frightening. You had always felt safe and secure in your apartment with all the people around. So, you bought a condominium.

● When your spouse died you didn't want to have to take care of all the obligations that you had once shared. Buying a townhome sounded absolutely ideal.

› THE NIGHTMARE

Maybe this nightmare didn't happen *exactly* this way, but it is a scenario of an actual situation. To get you into the picture, come on a trip of let's pretend. This is your story.

Whatever your reasons for buying a home in a community controlled by covenants, it's a reasonably safe bet that harassment by the association wasn't on your list.

You probably smiled as you moved in and visualized your decorating plans. Likely you felt on top of the world with the next stop: heaven.

The end of November you decided to announce your happiness with a "Peace on Earth, Good Will to Men" message to your neighbors by making the outside of your new abode more festive with holiday decorations. You searched numerous stores to find just the right holiday light clips that would be virtually invisible, no intention to defy any rules. Rather you made every endeavor to be tasteful. Finally you found the perfect clips — clear Lucite and tiny. Very carefully and methodically you tucked them where they would remain invisible until lights were inserted and glowing. Your intention was to leave the Lucite holders in place to use for many holiday seasons to come. Invisible? Not so to the covenants police! The association had a Sherlock Holmes on the board. His handy magnifying glass helped him locate material evidence.

On the fourth of January, you received a letter from the association pointing out that it was shameless of you to attach such an *unsightly apparatus* to your home without even stopping to ask, "May I?" from the architectural control committee or the board of directors. Further, it was nothing short of unforgivable for you to have the audacity not to remove the contraption immediately after the holiday season. You were instructed to cease, desist, and remove the unsightly attachment forthwith.

I would wager had the proper request been made to the ACC (architectural control committee) or the board of directors, the answer would have been a resounding, *"No!"* The rule they applied was probably painted with broad, ambiguous brush strokes that allowed the ACC's interpretation: to protect property values at all times, *no one* shall be allowed to install *anything* to the exterior of *any* home at *any* time for *any* reason.

You were given a 48-hour grace period to accomplish the deed or be fined $25. You were told that if it was necessary to send further notices to you, the fine would double and redouble. They wouldn't discuss it with you. They just kept sending citations and penalty notices. The final proclamation was from an attorney announcing that the association had slapped a lien on your home and filed a lawsuit against you.

Why are some people in such a hurry to jump on the "lawsuit bandwagon"? The first order of business should be honest, caring communication with the homeowner. Some states mandate a hearing with the homeowner *before issuing penalties*. At times the covenants police seem to *protect* disorder rather than *prevent* disorder.

Step out of that picture now — before the court date. Let's pretend is over. The Lucite-lugging homeowner lost in court after approximately $8,000 in attorney fees and court costs. The *repulsive*, clear Lucite, diminutive, tucked away, 5/8-inch light clips had to be removed. The homeowner moved out of that concentration camp to a community with no covenants.

I will not attempt to influence what verdict you would have given if you had been the judge in that case. In *my* book those tiny, clear Lucite clips were totally insignificant. Certainly, they were not even visible, unless one's nose was right next to the home, let alone so hideous that they threatened property values.

No one will ever find what they're not looking for. If that Sherlock Holmes would leave his magnifying glass on the shelf and the association would allow the homeowners a breath or two of dignity, they would have a much happier community. The approach they took to "solve the problem" was certainly sufficient to start the decay of happiness, neighborliness, *and* pride of ownership. They instilled the community with the fear of wondering who would be the next one on the association's "hit list." That homeowner must have felt as though he had set out for Utopia, inadvertently made a wrong turn, and landed in Purgatory.

It may be easier, but for whom?

Stringent enforcement of rules, regulations, and restrictions makes it easier for some people to make decisions. They feel these are safe conclusions because they are backed up in print. "I didn't make the rule, did you make the rule?" "No, I didn't make the rule. It had to have come down to us from Mount Sinai. I read it in the declarations, you know, the association's bible. Obviously, it would be a mortal sin not to enforce the rule to the hilt."

The association quickly justifies their actions by *pointing a finger at the rule in the declarations* as the culprit. Olympic finger pointing should be avoided. Be aware that every time you point a finger at a culprit, three fingers will always be pointing toward you (the real culprit).

Attorneys and judges employ the same *easier, point-a-finger-at-the-declarations* excuse. To embrace a doctrine that would offer citizens enough latitude for the deserved enjoyment of their homes is a principle that fits a little too loosely for most legal eagles. Verdicts against homeowners further encourage associations to flex their tough attitudes.

Homeowners' suffering isn't produced solely from a painful court resolution. Anguish is attached to every component of the entire procedure leading to the final decision. The painful plan is initiated by the association.

There is a price of ownership, but pain should not be part of that price.

A friend said to me, "I moved to this home to have more conveniences. Then I found out I had *no* conveniences."

Sometimes it's the ACC wielding the big unyielding "rule stick." When the board of directors is discussed in this book, the same information applies equally to the ACC.

❯ THE DREAM COMES TRUE

Let's play let's pretend again. This time your dream comes true in this real story.

You looked for a townhome in a community that not only allowed, but welcomed some individuality from the homeowners. You checked carefully to make certain you didn't end up in a "plastic" community. The kind of community that landscapes one home then takes a cookie cutter and stamps out the same identical design at every other home in the complex.

Associations open to community individuality usually employ common sense. They are rarely the type to pursue strict enforcement of pointless rules that serve no worthy purpose.

You did your homework in every complex that showed prospects of suiting your needs. You knew time spent to investigate could avoid a miserable case of the "If-I'd-a-just" virus.

You asked several homeowners a bundle of questions, the first step to immunization.

> Q: I'm thinking about buying a home in your community. Would you mind my asking a few questions?
>
> Q: How long have you lived here?
>
> Q: How do you feel about how your community is governed?
>
> Q: Do you have a management company?
>
> Q: How do you feel about the management company?
>
> Q: Who is in charge, the board or the management company?
>
> Q: Do you attend the association's meetings?
>
> Q: What do you like best about the community?
>
> Q: What do you like least about it?
>
> Q: If you had it to do over, would you buy a home in this community?
>
> Q: How much are the homeowners' dues and what services do they cover?
>
> Q: How often have they raised the dues?
>
> Q: Are you, your spouse, or a friend on the board of directors or architectural committee?

You evaluated the credibility of the answers relative to the homeowners' connection with the governing body.

You found the right community and you bought a home. The first thing you did was . . .

> Q: May I replace my cement patio with a redwood deck?
>
> A: Of course, you didn't really even need to ask approval for something like that. Since we own our backyards we can do almost anything as long as it won't block anyone's sunshine or view and no immediate neighbor objects.

Residents in your complex voted to retain personal responsibility of the exterior maintenance except for roofs, painting the exteriors, and mowing the front yards.

The board of directors of the association cares and understands

Everyone in your complex is happy and has true pride of ownership. Residents have the latitude that affords individuality and the board keeps up with continuing and preventive maintenance. They take care of all legitimate problems.

One neighbor had two warped boards on her fence. The ACC reminded her to replace the boards. Another neighbor had a dead tree in his yard. He was asked to plant a new one. You appreciate their attention to important aesthetic details and their lack of control-itis on issues that add to the homeowners' enjoyment and do not blemish the community.

Okay. Let's pretend time is over now. That was a picture of real life as it happens in the community where I live.

❯ *WHAT IF A NEIGHBOR DRIZZLES ON MY DREAM?*

The board is there to help homeowners solve significant problems and to keep the community running smoothly. However, the board should request any resident who has a personal complaint with a neighbor to first talk with that neighbor to work things out. For instance, I have two neighbors whose dogs used to practice marathon barking for hours on end. It only took a couple of friendly calls from me, as a neighbor not as the president, and the dogs are now kept quiet.

Homeowners and renters not only have the right, they have the responsibility to function as mature adults. Too often residents expect the board or the management company to be the buffer for every petty issue. Such residents are uneasy about speaking to their neighbor for fear they'll get angry at them. The marvelous tool of honest communication frightens them. They'd rather their neighbor be angry at the board or management company.

Boards of directors and management companies are not there to solve every pint-sized predicament. They are not landlords, baby-sitters, *or managers* of the residents.

You say, "What? Did I just read that management companies don't manage?" I say, "If the management company *is* managing, they've overstepped their bounds and the board has turned their elected powers and duties over to that company." (More in chapter 7 — *Indeed, what is a name?* and *Is the board of directors real or let's pretend?*)

All deserve to live happily in their homes — Kids too

BOARDROOM DISCUSSION
❖ Published by the LAW FIRM OF WINZENBURG, LEFF, PURVIS AND PAYNE, LLP ❖
• 1660 Lincoln Street, #1750 • Denver, Colorado 80264 • 303-863-1870
NO LEMONADE STANDS ALLOWED?   July 1992

We recently got a call from a Board President who had received complaints from Owners that a refreshment stand constructed by children was in violation of the Association's covenants.
Our recommendation: Let kids be kids!
Covenant and rule enforcement must be taken seriously, but it must also be done in a reasonable manner. We doubt any judge would fine an Owner (or Owner's children) for doing something as harmless as constructing a temporary refreshment stand.

Perhaps when those complaining owners were kids, they weren't allowed to enjoy being children. Selling lemonade is not only a sound learning experience, it's a healthy and enterprising activity for children.

▶ *AN OUTLOOK THAT TRULY ALLOWS DREAMS TO COME TRUE*

Without exception everyone who contacted me who was instrumental in changing a disagreeable to an agreeable living circumstance made common statements such as these . . .

"It's like living in a different community."

"The residents can breathe again."

"Everyone is so neighborly now."

"The meetings are now pleasant and productive. They used to be a war of words to see who could out-scream the other."

"I'm happy to have been part of my community's solution instead of moving to escape from the problem."

My purpose is to open doors to homeowners' happiness. I candidly make suggestions that do not always agree with the legal society. I have no desire to encourage anyone to stick his head or community into a legal vise. It is the reader's responsibility to investigate state statutes and the association's documents before taking any action. ***When in doubt, seek legal counsel. But, stay out of court!***

My observations come from that of a homeowner and of a board member. As I vent the pain of my past experiences upon all enforcers inflicted with "over control-itis," remember that all of this is coming from one who has been the president of her HOA for over six years. However, the memories of my neighbors' agonies when the epidemic of HOA black plague struck our complex will remain with me forever. I instantly spot the symptoms of the same disease in other communities and sense the anguish.

ALL communities could, and many do, operate with a common sense, live, enjoy, everyone-take-responsibility-for-the-neighborhood-and-their-neighbors'-feelings attitude. (Wow, that was one long adjective! I hope you had enough breath control to get past it.)

The mere fact that a community is controlled by covenants and an association does not brand it either congenial or hostile.

Don't automatically classify an association as Gestapo-like just because rules are being enforced. Associations who earn that trademark are those that use their powers to interpret and enforce insignificant rules for the pure enjoyment of controlling others.

Recognize and appreciate those associations that consistently enforce significant issues in the same manner with every resident and fulfill their fiduciary duties to keep the community running smoothly.

If you're ***considering moving to a community under the control of an association,*** learn how to identify the right community for you.

If you're ***living happily in one,*** learn how to keep it happy.

If you're ***living unhappily in one,*** learn what your choices are to thrive instead of barely survive.

Even though there are differences in specific state laws and statutes, from Maryland to California the problems and solutions are commonly shared. I've talked several times with Sam and Lois Pratt in New Jersey, who conduct research and develop proposals aimed at improving living in community associations. They report that homeowners' concerns focus on the need for more democratic governance, including fair elections, open meetings, better access to information, and fair dispute resolution procedures. These problems have the same ring as those I've heard from homeowners across the nation.

Whether the stories reported came from the 1980s or 1990s, the same stories will continue in the 2000s and 3000s if the public doesn't take positive action now to improve living in community associations.

What follows are steps to a path of happy homeownership. Ideas are extended to help reverse unpleasant community situations. Incidents and remedies apply to all communities controlled by covenants, from moderately priced to multi-million-dollar homes.

Don't settle for a lifestyle that is anything less than enjoyable.

The Benefits of Covenants-controlled Communities, According to Advertising

Covenants-controlled communities that are ruled with a harsh, unmerciful gavel are advertised with the same Madison Avenue babble and the same benevolent "purely for your benefit" language used for communities that truly are compassionate.

All types of communities are addressed in this book. Unyielding communities are given more space, as they are the ones that will inflict heartache in place of anticipated happiness.

If the majority of developments were friendly, there would be no need for this book.

The benefits, according to advertising

UTOPIAN HOMES

A carefully planned covenants-controlled community with all the necessary elements to create an environment to make your living happy, easy, and carefree! You'll enjoy a blissful lifestyle at Utopian!

COME VISIT US TODAY!

Admittedly, that is a reduced and simplified version of the advertised messages sent to us by developers/builders about their newly developed covenants-controlled communities. We, the public, assume the disclosure to be true. Creature-comfort words, such as carefree and blissful, become synonymous in our minds with covenants-controlled communities.

As we visit the developer's sales office, our vision of pure happiness is further strengthened by the community representative — the developer's sales agent.

With the blissful covenants-controlled words still buzzing around in our minds, we may find the right home in an established community (a resale, not a new home).

Whether we buy a new or a resale home, ultimate pleasure is not guaranteed by the sheer existence of covenants controlling the community.

It's true you'll seldom be tormented by a fire-engine-red home in a covenants-controlled community. That's great! The lack of homes painted bizarre colors and other offensive conditions are important factors for pleasure and protection of property values. You could find yourself in Utopia.

❯ WHICH WAY TO UTOPIA?

Karen Abbott (*Rocky Mountain News* staff writer) said, "All over metropolitan Denver, lawyers write letters and file lawsuits as neighbors feud over subdivision covenants, rules and regulations, architectural control committee decisions, and homeowner association fines." (Karen's entire article is reprinted in chapter 4.)

That doesn't read anything like the ad for blissful Utopian Homes. How can this be when the ad said that all would be happy, easy, and carefree *because* covenants control the community? Lawsuits are not generally labeled as happy, easy, or carefree.

Some developments fail to offer true comforts of living.

You can ... "Turn failure into fertilizer and use it to grow." — Benjamin Franklin

Spread properly fertilizer produces nourishing vegetables, fruits, and flowers with wondrous fragrances. Many have spread the "stuff" correctly in the right places — they have made their communities blossom and grow. They have made their recorded restrictions work for their enjoyment of living.

The catalogue of restrictions can include anything from admissible fence height, specific materials allowed to construct fences, acceptable colors of window coverings (as seen from the outside of the home), curfew hours, and statements such as *no* modification to the exterior of any home or building. Does no modification include hanging plants, bird feeders, a name plate, or a light for security reasons? Interpretations of that rule can vary from board to board. (Betty Procter's story, *A real struggle to a happy ending* in chapter 4, relates how that rule was perceived to mean *no* screen, storm, or security doors!)

The list of restrictions can be quite lengthy and ambiguous, containing a multitude of trivial issues. The longer the list, the more chance rigid, self-serving interpretations will be too confining for normal, comfortable living. Vague, immaterial rules encourage overzealous enforcers of the rules to snatch a homeowner right out of Utopia into a courtroom. That produces voluminous reports from homeowners of their unhappiness. If only such reports were merely isolated cases. Do not lose sight that fertilizer *can* produce nourishment.

❯ COVENANTS AREN'T THE MAGIC WAND THAT BESTOWS HAPPINESS

Ken said the HOA dug up his pansies because they were one-half-inch over his property line onto the common area.

M.H., who used to live in Concealed Lake said, "We moved out of Concealed Lake a few years ago because the association was totally inconsistent. But, the memories of Concealed Lake will remain with us.

"When I moved to the area the association immediately made me remove my boat from the street. Yet a neighbor was allowed to park his dump truck, for months at a time, in front of my home. The board members were friends of the owner of the dump truck.

"The only consistency was the board's inconsistency. They enforced rules only when it pleased them.

"Concealed Lake is a good name. The board hides (controls) the lake. They are supposed to give keys to homeowners who are current with their dues. They don't. Homeowners have to check a key out from the HOA to enter the lake area!

"Instead of a beach, the board chose to place large boulders around the lake to abolish using the waterfront.

"The board constantly changed the rules. Their meetings made me feel as though I'd just been run over by a train. They would announce new rules that fit their own personal agenda and add them to the existing list of antagonistic rules.

"In some ways the board showed an interest in being economical, such as organizing homeowners to keep the perimeter fence in repair. I think homeowners taking responsibility and pitching in to help keep HOA fees low is a marvelous idea.

"Then the board would do something totally out of line such as hiring an attorney to collect the association fees. *Not just delinquent fees, the regular HOA fees!* [Seems like an expensive route to take.]

"I have a couple of large dogs. One of my neighbors had a cat that walked on top of my fence. The neighbor would call the police when my dogs barked at his cat. Also, my 'friendly' neighbor would stick his head over my fence and, again, call the police about my dogs barking and charging toward the fence. I consider my dogs were being entrapped into barking and charging. The city's ordinances are totally against dog owners. They fined me every time. [A neighbor-to-neighbor conflict compounded by the city's easy decisions.]

"Restrictions depend entirely on the interpreters. Rules should not be necessary except on matters that are an infringement on your neighbors' rights and welfare. Associations should learn to talk with homeowners and work something out with them.

"We moved out of that city to a community with no covenants. We would never put ourselves in that type of miserable position again!"

————————————

Tom Jackson and his family lived in a large townhome complex in Littleton, Colorado. He noted, "'Gestapo' Management Company has made homeowners' lives miserable."

Tom said, "I received a warning letter for parking my car within 50 feet of a stop sign. Streets of the community are public and maintained by the county. I contacted the county, the sheriff's department, and every other highway department I could think of. Categorically, I was told there was no such public ordinance.

"Children used to play on my patio. I didn't want to be liable if they hurt themselves so I bordered the patio with little red scalloped bricks. It worked. The children respected the boundary.

"I received a letter from the management company telling me to remove the bricks because it was against the covenants to 'store building materials' on the patio area!

"A neighbor was instructed to remove a one-and-a-half-inch brass name plate from her door.

"I got many warning letters for violations of the covenants. I noticed the same 'violations' were ignored at other homes. My attorney said the board and the management company were being *selective* and that could be considered as harassment by the court.

"After I shared my attorney's words with the management company, the warning letters ceased.

"A petition was organized to construct a playground that had been promised to be completed long ago. The playground with a swing set, teeter-totters, and a few other playthings would have cost only about $1,000. The insurance company said that if there were no monkey bars, our current premium would not change.

"One board member embellished the playground concept to the extent of including a recreation center, tennis court, basketball court, and you name it. The new, adorned concept raised the cost to a point of making the playground economically unfeasible. To this day, there is no place for the children to play. It's still necessary for parents to drive their children to the nearest park.

"I circulated a petition to replace 'Gestapo' Management Company at the end of their contract. I contacted approximately half of the homeowners and was turned down by only two. We presented the board with the petition of approximately 200 signatures, more than the number needed.

"The board refused to recognize the petition. [Such a refusal is likely not legal, but it happens all too often.] They professed the management company was acting under instructions from the board.

"After one long screaming-match meeting, the board members were retired and reasonable board members were installed.

"'Nasty' Management Company moved over to make room for 'Closer to Caring' Management Company, Inc.

"My family and I have since moved to a single-family home with no covenants." Tom said, "I didn't mind paying the association fee to take care of lawn and exterior maintenance, trash removal, painting, and other significant services. It's that I have better ways to spend my money than to pay someone to harass me."

Tom said, "We have pride in our home. We do not need someone instructing us to show our pride in the manner *they* perceive pride. Some things are important and some things just aren't. Boards and management companies should learn that."

Peg said condo life turned out to be a shock to her system.

She said, "Some homes have garages, some don't. We have one car, one person has four. Those without garages have to park at least a half-block away. Extra parking is by permit only.

"Some people appoint themselves as judge and jury. They constantly patrol to make sure you park a half-block away from your home if you don't have a garage.

"Throw a towel on the fence — a $25 fine.

"Change a battery in your car four blocks away — $50 fine for hazardous material sitting on the commons."

Peg received a letter about not picking up after her dog defecated. [She said she always picked up her pup's stuff.] She replied to the board, "You identify my dog's poop and I'll pick it up."

Peg has moved to a home in an area not controlled by covenants, other than local county codes.

Herb Bolton bought a single-family home in 1990 in Arvada, Colorado. Herb asked his real estate agent if it was a covenants-controlled community and was told, "No, and if there *were* covenants they couldn't be enforced anyway." [Wrong!] The title company didn't find any recorded covenants, so Herb naturally assumed covenants were not an issue. [In truth, the developer recorded protective covenants in 1988.]

Herb said, "Eight months after I moved in, a neighbor asked me if I wanted to go with him to a homeowners' meeting. I said, 'A what?' I was getting a clue about the existence of covenants, but still had no knowledge of mandatory dues. Sometime in 1991 or 1992, a good year and a half to two years after the fact, a 'Covenants-controlled Community' sign was installed at the entrance.

"I finally received a notice of past-due fees, late charges, an extra $50 charge for an attorney's fee, and threat of a lien being slapped on my home." The association also tried to charged Herb for the previous owner's two or three years worth of unpaid fees. [It appears to be a case of an association not taking care of the business of informing and then taking Gestapo actions against the homeowner. Someone from the association should have, at least, called or sent a friendly letter before instigating such an unfriendly process.]

The $80 a year fee was hardly exorbitant enough to cause bankruptcy. Nonetheless, knowing about the covenants and the fee before closing would certainly have been a more agreeable chain of events.

Herb paid his past due fees, late charges, the attorney's charge, and proceeded to obtain a copy of the elusive, 11-page-thin covenants.

"After a hail storm destroyed roofs," Herb said, "the association distributed a letter obliging homeowners to use only shake shingles for replacement, 'according to the covenants'. Then it was discovered roofing materials weren't even mentioned in the covenants!"

Recently, the board requested that residents authorize more power to the association in order to put more "teeth" into the restrictions. Herb's reply to the board was, "If neighbors have problems they should just discuss it with their neighbor [Herb does that]. We don't need a community covenants police department.

"The HOA needs an attitude adjustment." [That's a start, but they need more than that, Herb.]

_____

Alice lives in a condo in Boulder, Colorado. When she called me she was on her way to a board meeting to make a protest. The association had confiscated her Weber grill and folding chairs. RULE: Nothing under the stairs. Alice said, "This is inconsistent. Others have things under their stairways.

"They gave my grill and chairs back and I haven't been bothered since."

[Alice, you are fortunate. It would be wonderful if all homeowners experienced an equally easy process when they lock horns with their association.]

_____

M.K. in Englewood, Colorado said, "I've lived here well over eight years. You sure don't need an MBA to get on the board. The board doesn't work with anyone on anything. They're just too rigid." She said, "It's been the same unacceptable board members for five years."

[Suggestion for M.K.: Get together with sympathetic neighbors to organize the election of new attitudes to the board. M.K. admitted she isn't familiar with the process to determine who becomes board members. Never assume proper procedures have been followed. When it doesn't *feel good*, it's likely fabricated procedures are being used. Homeowners must take the responsibility to read the controlling documents, dull and dim as they may be. Following the proper procedures, you and your neighbors may be able to take action to get friendly enforcers of the rules on the board.]

A resident in a Texas complex said, "People should get involved in their communities to help and care for each other. Vanity should not outweigh patience."

All is not warm, fuzzy, and well in Covenants Land

By now you're probably feeling the advertised benefits, as in the ad for Utopian Homes, *may* be a little too simplistic and syrupy sweet a description of covenants-controlled communities. You're right. Ads are guilty.

Some communities are deceptive. They appear to offer the opportunity to fly as peacefully as a butterfly and yet they bear the sting of a wasp. Beware of the sting.

- Condo **description** — Each homeowner owns the airspace of his unit and a *share of the entire land that is owned by the association.* If there are one hundred units each unit might own one-hundredth of the entire land, with no specific boundaries of ownership. All of the land is common area. Sometimes, a building and unit number and the word condo or condominium are in the legal description. Responsibility for maintenance of the exterior and interior should be detailed in the recorded documents.

- Condo *style* — Is more like an apartment building with one or more units above and/or below. Ownership is as described above.

- Townhome **description** — Attached units with no unit above or below, with a party-wall agreement for walls shared by another unit. Land ownership is, at a minimum, the land directly below the home. All other land may be common area.

- Townhome *style with a condo description* — Attached homes with no unit above or below. Ownership can vary from only airspace to ownership of the interior and exterior walls, except for the common wall(s). Common wall(s) can be "owned" with a *party-wall agreement.* Land ownership is that of a condo.

A *condo style unit cannot have a townhome legal description,* but a *townhome style can have a condo legal description.* It is the distinction of land ownership. If there are common areas or elements, covenants and an association are essential and usually mandatory.

- Single-family *detached* home — The builder determines if there will be recorded covenants and an association. Even single-family detached homes can have the same ownership as in the above condo description.

An existing single-family community could also opt to initiate covenants and form an association. The teeth of such covenants would be really dull. They would require voluntary compliance from homeowners because the covenants would not be recorded as a restriction on the deeds.

You will run into a variety of other terms such as patio and cluster homes. No matter the label of the home, the legal description and the recorded documents will specify the ownership of the land and structure.

➤ WHAT IS A COVENANTS-CONTROLLED COMMUNITY?

A neighbor told me that until she read my book, over three years after she had moved into this complex, she had not realized that ours is a covenants-controlled community because the sign at the entrance only gives the name of the complex. It doesn't state "A Covenants-controlled Community."

- **All covenants-controlled communities have restrictive covenants.**

Restrictive covenants come in a wide variety of girth, limitations, and sharp teeth. They are a collection of assorted restrictions that could include . . .

- specific colors of paint that can be used on the exterior,

- garage doors closed except when entering or exiting,
- types of fences that can or cannot be installed,
- acceptable roofing materials,
- RV and other vehicle parking restrictions,
- no for-sale or for-rent signs,
- no clotheslines,
- no birdhouse or bird feeder, and . . .
- . . . as many other items as the mind can conceive.

- **All communities with restrictive covenants and a homeowner association are covenants-controlled communities.**

Declarations, Articles of Incorporation, and Bylaws are the day-to-day governing documents in most covenants-controlled communities. The word **"Documents"** is used to relate to the entire stack of legal papers. They include the recorded restrictions and covenants, the Articles, the Bylaws, and all other relevant HOA papers. Far too often the stack is excessively thick and written in overwhelmingly complicated legalese. When is the last time you read simplified legalese?

There are two separate lawful purposes of the documents. One purpose is real estate law. The other is corporate law.

Declarations (the term used in Colorado and in many other states) deal with the real estate (the land) of the community. Declarations are restrictive covenants that are recorded deed restrictions that run with the land. They also authorize a corporation to be formed. *Declarations can be modified only under the provisions specified in the declarations.*

Authorization is given in the declarations to the board to create rules and regulations. Commonly known as Rules and Regs, they can contain some or all of the regulations written in simplified language, a more easily understandable version of the restrictions. They can also contain embellishments on the recorded restrictions. Recorded rules can be embellished. They cannot arbitrarily be diminished. However, rules can be legally diminished by modification under the guidelines in the declarations for such modification (if such guidelines exist). Sometimes the board enlists the help of the management company and or an attorney to form the Rules and Regs.

Articles of Incorporation form the corporation and generally define

- the purpose and powers of the association,
- membership in the association,
- voting rights,
- nomination and election of the directors of the association,
- the number of officers,
- the length of term of office for elected directors, and
- provisions for indemnification of directors and officers (preferable if this in the Articles, but it can be in the Bylaws).

The Articles state the corporation will be run according to a set of Bylaws.

Bylaws explain how to operate the corporation. Generally, they declare

- the purpose of the association,

- the rights of the association,
- the election of the officers and directors and their terms,
- the number of officers and directors required, with a statement how the number and terms can be amended in the bylaws,
- the powers and duties of the officers and directors,
- the proceedings of the officers and directors,
- provisions for indemnification of directors and officers (to give indemnification more teeth it's preferable to amend and put this in the Articles),
- meetings of the officers and directors and how all members are to be notified,
- procedures for meetings of the members of the association,
- parliamentary authority (more about parliamentary procedures on page VI)
- how books and records are to be handled,
- provisions for assessments,
- provisions for amendments, and
- requirements for committees.

In Colorado, and most other states, if a conflict arises between the Bylaws and the Articles, the Articles control. The Declarations control when there is a conflict with the Articles. The order of precedence may be designated in your documents. Recorded covenants should take a back-seat position to state, county, and municipal ordinances.

To simplify your reading and my writing, here are some acronyms and abbreviations (there is a full glossary on page XX):

- CCC — Covenants-controlled Community
- BOD — Board Of Directors
- HOA — HomeOwner Association (always remember that *all homeowners are members of the association*)
- DAB — Declarations, Articles of Incorporation, and Bylaws
- Decs — Declarations (the recorded restrictions on the deeds)
- Docs — Documents (the entire stack of legal documents)
- Regs — Rules and Regulations (pages IX to XII is a five-page example of Regs)

There are various other terms used to indicate the elements of the documents of CCCs such as Covenants, Conditions, and Restrictions (CC&Rs). No matter what names are given to them, all documents have the same cited purposes. They are the covenants. They are the RULES. They are the restrictions. Sometimes Covenants-controlled Communities are referred to as Common Interest Communities (CICs) and Common Interest Developments (CIDs). No matter what the label they all have restrictions and covenants. In this book, for simplification, the terms used are those listed above.

- **All communities with DABs, an HOA, and a BOD are CCCs.**

Some communities with attached homes (such as townhomes, cluster homes, and so on), single-family, detached homes, and *all* condominiums are blessed with the entire stack of documents: DABs and sometimes more. Restrictions and rules can be woven throughout *all* the documents. The list of restrictions is far more extensive and complicated than those already mentioned. The greater the thickness of the documents the more likelihood of extensive nit-picking and seriously sharp-teeth enforcement.

- **Not all CCCs with restrictive covenants have DABs, an HOA, or a BOD.**

Some communities with single-family, detached homes have a set of recorded covenants, but not recorded as a restriction on the deed. *NO* DABs. With no DABs there will probably be no BOD and no working HOA — no one in charge of enforcing the covenants.

The covenants for such communities are written to embellish zoning codes that don't quite cover certain unusual, offensive happenings. With no HOA or BOD, who is going to enforce compliance with *any* of the covenants? It certainly will not be the zoning department. Their only concern is the zoning codes. With no enforcers the covenants are altogether toothless. As the years roll by, the covenants are usually ignored and eventually forgotten.

For over 20 years, I lived in a single-family subdivision with covenants and no HOA. No problems arose until one day the neighbor behind me constructed a log cabin for storage. Even though it was new, it rivaled the appearance of being older than the log cabin in which Abraham Lincoln was born. It was less than pleasant to view.

I called the city zoning department and told the gentleman about the eyesore that didn't comply with our covenants. His reply was, "Stop looking out of that window!" So much for those covenants. A community HOA could have alleviated the problem.

Communities with DABs and a BOD that rules with a "velvet hammer" and those who rule with an "iron gavel" proclaim the same kindhearted "purely for your benefit" intention. At a quick glance, it's sometimes difficult to determine which type of community it really is.

The opportunity for happy homeownership lies in CCCs only if they have *very thin* Docs written in *real-people language* and are paired with an HOA that functions with common sense.

▶ *THIRTY-YEAR-OLD WHISKERS ARE GROWING ON TODAY'S DOCS*

With no previous experiences available to understand what the pros and cons would be to live in a community controlled by covenants, DABs were born in approximately the 1960s. Operating within the bureaucratic framework created by VA and FHA, the legal profession created the collection of standard, boilerplate, "canned" rules.

Over 30 years have passed. Developers and attorneys still use wording from the original off-the-rack rules. Case in point: Satellite dishes were huge eyesores in the 1960s and 1970s. The "No satellite dishes" archaic verbiage rule was used until Congress killed it in 1996. A multitude of other out-of-date dictums are still used in the Docs of many communities being built today.

Sometimes the documents can be modernized, as homeowners in one community did. Congress and the FCC have eliminated the no satellite problem for most communities. (That community's story, *Rules can be changed,* and *Congress and the FCC step on the "No satellite" restriction* are coming up in chapter 4.)

The primary purpose . . .

. . . of the wording in the DABs is NOT as advertised — "created exclusively for the benefit of you, the eventual homeowner." The primary purpose is for the developer to satisfy the local regulatory government's rules, regulations, and laws (zoning, planning, and building departments). Covenants and restrictions are mandatory in condominium developments.

The next purpose . . .

. . . of the wording in the DABs is to satisfy lender rules so the builder can offer financing to buyers. If the developer doesn't meet these requirements, only buyers paying all cash would be able to buy his homes. That is *NOT* a good working plan.

Lenders normally require recorded covenants for developments with common elements. The Docs specify ownership of common elements. Recorded covenants are the developers' option in developments of single-family detached homes with no common elements.

Fulfilling both purposes . . .

. . . is *absolutely necessary.*

It is *not necessary* to create a boxcar full of garbage rules that are not even required to secure the needed government and lender approvals.

The developer is focused on doing what he has to do to get his homes built. Developers save money by using the same set of Docs over and over again as they complete one development and start another. As long as the public is willing to buy homes with old, unfriendly Docs, developers will continue to take the less expensive, easier way.

Chances are close to slim and utterly none for the developer to position your end-result-bliss at the front of his mind. If he does pay an attorney to modify any of the phrasing in the boilerplate, prefab DABs, more than likely the modification will be strictly for the benefit of the developer, not for your live-happily-ever-after dream.

Furthermore, it's possible that neither the developer nor his attorney has ever *lived* in a CCC. What may seem quite practical to them on paper doesn't always work well in reality.

It's reasonable to expect that the first real interest of the developer is to get his project approved, built, sold, and move on to his next project.

It's nonetheless reasonable for homeowners to expect the enjoyment of living in their homes.

It takes more than exterior paint colors and fence heights to afford homeowners a blissful living style. Paint and fences are only the tip of a titanic iceberg.

Melt away the tip and reality may be exposed

Following is a portion of an article by Karen Abbott, staff writer for the *Rocky Mountain News*. The rest of the article is presented, with permission, in chapter 4.

February 8, 1994
Conversation heard over the backyard fence

■ "I live in a neighborhood that's got covenants against drying clothes on a line outside unless nobody else can see it. Instead of thinking that's energy-efficient, they think it's unsightly . . ." — Resident in Jefferson County, CO

Example of a tie-your-hands-behind-your-back, off-the-rack rule

---

Article X
<u>RESTRICTIONS</u>
Section 9. Miscellaneous Structures.
(d) No clotheslines, or .... shall be located on any Lot as to be
visible from a street, any other Lot, or from the Common Area.

They forgot to mention low flying jets.

Granted, *permanent* clotheslines aren't exactly aesthetic. But, where did the notion ever come from that clothes hanging on a line are unsightly? It's the lines that are unsightly, not the clothes. Clothes don't hang for hours and hours or days. Let alone for years. Couldn't they just as easily be perceived as a symbol of cleanliness? Allowing retractable clotheslines would certainly not be life threatening or a threat to property values.

If a sufficient number of residents in a complex prefer hanging their clothes on a line (it *is* energy efficient), those residents could petition the board to modify the rule if there is enough elasticity in the Docs to accommodate modification. It's certainly worth checking out.

Documents, developers, and attorneys can be friendly

As long as no conflict with state statutes is produced, **amiable, common sense rules** *can* be incorporated into a relatively slender set of Docs, rather than the all too common, fat *lawsuit time-bombs* that exist. The trend hasn't moved in that direction yet because homeowner comforts aren't always a burning concern of developers or their attorneys.

It would be a burning concern of developers if it were impossible for them to sell their homes in communities that strangle homeowners with an obese set of hostile, incomprehensible Docs.

Flinch factors would be eliminated if the Docs contained only *life-serving, significant* rules. That would help produce community harmony and property values would still be protected. It isn't necessary to include a magnitude of insignificant rules in muddled language to get local governmental departments' and mortgage lenders' approval. Docs do not have to be written in legalese.

At times it seems the purpose of legalese is to render unintelligible communication. However, even without one aforesaid or pursuant thereto, attorneys can create incoherence with quite harmless, everyday words. "Some associations' documents are completely incomprehensible, even to me, and I'm an attorney," said Florida State Representative Steve Geller. (*Woman's Day* article "Trouble on the Home Front?" November 1, 1996 by John Grossmann.)

I am also vehemently repelled by the following routine: you find a rule addressed in Article X. Article X gives details on the rule written in the usual mumbo jumbo terms and then says, ". . . except as in Sections 8 (b) and 8 (c) of this declaration, but notwithstanding any other provisions of this declaration to the contrary." At that point, you know you've just been successfully given an award-winning, royal run-around.

Most court cases are no longer heard by a jury, but rather presented directly to the judge via written briefs from the attorneys. Recently a friend told me about an attorney who is not a common, garden variety attorney. That attorney actually found a way to *simplify* his language! Hug that concept! That special attorney said he never uses legalese and writes his briefs as though he were writing a letter to a friend who has no understanding of legal terms. Imagine, no aforesaids, pursuant theretos, militates, and hereofs! I understand he wins more cases since he put that course into practice.

If an attorney can simplify for judges, who are expected to understand legalese, why can't those of us who don't have a law degree occupying wall space have the documents, the ones we are to abide by, written in clear terminology that we can easily grasp?

David Dertina, a Colorado developer, shared that he directed his attorney to make sure the entire set of Docs for his new townhome development be in authentic language for this planet. The Docs were to be no more than a *total* of forty pages or David said he would charge the attorney for each and every page over that specified total. That is a refreshing, common sense, caring approach by a developer. David firmly agrees that Docs should offer only necessary and homeowner-friendly rules. If only there were more developers like David Dertina!

Look who's in charge now . . .

Once the construction dust has settled and folks are comfortably snuggled into their homes, the developer, who has reigned over the HOA during the construction phase, steps back and blithely says, "Congratulations, homeowners. You are now completely in charge of the association. I know you'll derive nothing but pure pleasure from being in charge of your own little government."

The responsibility of the HOA has just been formally presented to the homeowners and to the new BOD to put all the rules in their proper perspective. Maybe a management company is also involved. The subject of management companies is discussed in *detail* on page 109.

Your first and immediate task . . . make absolutely certain that *all funds* including the capital reserve funds, collected by the developer, are transferred to the homeowners' newly acquired association's account. Our capital reserve fund was *not* transferred by the builder to the HOA. By the time it was discovered, the developer, even though he had a representative in the area, was 28 states away and, good luck, HOA. Past records had been lost, so proving a case would have been difficult, if not impossible. Anyway, it would have cost considerably more to litigate than would ever have been recovered in our lost capital funds.

BOARDROOM DISCUSSION
❖ Published by the LAW FIRM OF WINZENBURG, LEFF, PURVIS AND PAYNE, LLP ❖
• 1660 Lincoln Street, #1750 • Denver, Colorado 80264 • 303-863-1870
July/August, 1996

DEVELOPER BREACHES FIDUCIARY DUTY BY NOT PROPERLY FUNDING RESERVES

An Illinois Court of Appeals recently held that a condominium *developer owes a fiduciary duty to unit owners and may breach that duty by failing to fund reserves adequately.*

The Association alleged that the developer failed to fund the Association's reserves properly and did not pay the proportionate share of expenses at the time the developer controlled the board. At the end of the period of developer control, there was only $7,000 in the Association's account.

The declaration required that the board (1) establish and maintain a reasonable reserve for contingencies and replacements and (2) maintain, repair and replace the condominium's common elements.

According to the court, the developer should have known that $7,000 was not sufficient reserve for the Association.

The law in Colorado: Under CCIOA (Colorado Common Interest Ownership Act July 1, 1992), *all developer-appointed board members are required to exercise the care required of fiduciaries of unit owners. That is a very high standard. Declarant-controlled boards should be very careful to fully implement the association's documents.*

This is another thrill the developer may dump on the new guardians of the HOA. The HOA may have to undertake explaining away verbal commitments made by those in the developer's sales office that are in conflict with the Docs. At times, a salesperson doesn't care to make the effort to investigate what really is true. Sometimes he makes embellished statements to accomplish his singular purpose of making a quick sale.

It's not an original concept that a salesperson may say "yes" to whatever may fit any and all of a prospective buyer's comfort desires. I've been told that in my complex there was a throng of complaints arising from this practice. Residents filed grievances with the BOD such as "The salesman told me . . . the extra parking spaces are for guest parking only." With no statement in the recorded documents referencing the "He told me . . ." issue, the salesman's line had as much value as many other worthless sales-oriented statements.

Never be swayed by a salesperson's verbal statements. *Ask for a legible copy of the complete set of the governing documents.* **Legible and complete** *are the key words.* Many times the documents have been copied so many times that very few words are actually legible. If you don't receive everything you need, don't even consider buying in that community.

Even if it appears to be a single-family, detached home with no protective covenants or amenity fees, don't assume. Check it out. Knock on some doors and ask the homeowners if there are covenants and/or fees in the community. Ask if there is a mandatory HOA. If so, there are more questions to ask the homeowners in chapter 6. Do this vital bit of homework *before* you sign the contract to buy.

Some states require full disclosure. Some don't. Even in states that do have such a requirement, sometimes things just have a way of slipping through the cracks.

Bob Janauskas in Ocala, Florida said, "In Florida full disclosure and a Disclosure Summary are required for some deed-restricted communities but not for PUDs (Planned Unit Development) even though PUDs have common areas, covenants, dues, and HOAs."

DISCLOSURE SUMMARY FOR (*name of the Florida community*)
> 1) As purchaser of property in this community, you will be obligated to be a member of a Homeowners' Association.
> 2) There have been or will be recorded restrictive covenants governing the use and occupancy of properties in this community.
> 3) You will be obligated to pay assessments to the Association, which assessments are subject to periodic change.
> 4) Your failure to pay these assessments could result in a lien on your property.

5) There (is) (is not) an obligation to pay rent or land use fees for recreational or other commonly used facilities as an obligation of membership in the Homeowners' Association. (If such obligation exists, then the amount of the current obligation shall be set forth.) $_____

6) The restrictive covenants (can) (cannot) be amended without the approval of the Association membership.

7) The statements contained in this disclosure form are only summary in nature, and, AS A PROSPECTIVE PURCHASER, YOU SHOULD REFER TO THE COVENANTS AND THE ASSOCIATION'S GOVERNING DOCUMENTS.

(Dated and signed by the purchasers)

Such a Disclosure Summary should be required in every state to be given in every community with deed restrictions before the contract to buy is ever presented.

Bob recommends, "Once you have the documents in hand make certain that it's a community suitable to where you want to live. After all, this is probably going to be one of the largest financial investments you'll ever make. Right?"

Bob's recommendation is valid even if it isn't a new development. This is no time to merely let your buying emotions take over. Take the responsibility to take the time to do proper investigation.

I was given parental advice that redundancy helps promote action. My father said, "If you want to get a point across, say it again and then sing it." You'll hear a few more verses of this song because it will require action on your part to help effect the needed changes.

❯ FUZZY MOLD IS TAKING HOLD

It's time the outmoded, ready-made Docs take on a new look, in plain language, to promote amicable communities suitable for today's living!

There is no valid justification for any resident to be burned at the stake of trivial, antique, hostile rules!

Please take note

It is **not** my intention to declare that every CCC with an HOA and DABs is out to get you or is a booby trap about to detonate. What is important is for you to understand the disposition of your CCC.

For those who share my privilege of living in a **happy, neighborly** CCC, this book will encourage you to help *keep* your community running smoothly with your sights on the **for-the-good-of-all-concerned** perspective.

If you are in the middle of some dismal experience, this book will help you start the process to adjust your community to run smoothly with a more amiable point of view.

For those who are in the stage of contemplating a move to the advertised conveniences of a CCC, this book will assist you in locating a community that will best suit your desires and lifestyle.

CHAPTER 4

Real Case Scenarios, Comm_ents, and Suggested Solutions

As CCC stories of agony are presented in newspapers, on television, and on radio, reactions can range from, "That's ridiculous, I can't believe an association would sue for something as trivial as that," to "Good for the HOA. If you don't keep on top of the rules, you lose control."

No matter which way your reaction slants, it's hard to find correlation among these reported incidents. A total picture of living in a CCC is never painted. Using "real-world pigment," this book paints the entire picture right before your eyes. You draw your own conclusions from these real case scenarios, newspaper articles, and excerpts from the *Boardroom Discussion* newsletters.

As you read the many reports of sad incidents and lawsuits, please do not think that *all* CCCs are located in war zones or hard-hat territories. There are many happy CCCs that allow a life. If this book were filled with all happy, happy, happy, you would not learn how to avoid the potholes, pitfalls, and lawsuits.

Start with a deep breath of fresh air

The first homes in my complex were built in 1985. Other than the county convicting our past treasurer for embezzlement, the only threat of a lawsuit was our HOA going after the developer to recoup the cost of street damage caused by his heavy equipment when he completed building the last phase of the complex. Of course, he had promised faithfully, before he began building, that he would repair any damage caused by the construction. We goofed. We didn't get his promise in writing.

We settled out of court for less than we should have. At least, we didn't cost the HOA outrageous legal fees and court costs. Proving a point can be expensive. To go to court to get what you really deserve usually ends up parallel to bending down to pick up a dollar and dropping a hundred dollar bill in the process!

Karen Abbott's article . . .

February 8, 1994
Reprinted with permission of the *Rocky Mountain News*
(Note: For reasons of confidentiality, the name of my complex is fictitious.)

BIG NEIGHBOR IS WATCHING

Covenants have their place — but when enforced too zealously, the rules can make residents feel like they're living in a police state.

By Karen Abbott
Rocky Mountain News Staff Writer

♦ The neighbors were talking, out around the pool, about why the whirlpool still wasn't working.

Likely the homeowner association couldn't afford to fix it, some of them groused, because of the lawyer's bill over that atrocious pink mailbox. They didn't know the woman nearby was the mailbox owner's sister.

"They were talking about *me*," said Janis McClure of Aurora, whose mailbox once matched her pink front door. The door is still pink, but the mailbox now is white. McClure said other neighborhood mailboxes are black, redwood, blue with geese and even, in one case, shaped like a man playing a guitar. "I felt like I was being picked on," she said.

"Now it's like everything is all my fault," she said. "If they had just come and been really nice and asked me to paint my mailbox, I probably would have. They didn't have to get the attorney to write me a two-page letter."

All over metropolitan Denver, lawyers write letters and file lawsuits as neighbors feud over subdivision covenants, rules and regulations, architectural control committee decisions and homeowner association fines.

People battle bitterly about parking, pool hours, pets and what does or doesn't look nice. "There is a lot of conflict," said attorney Lynn Jordan, who represents many homeowner associations and developers.

One single mother, whose dog had given birth to a litter, was startled to find her neighbor in her backyard with a camera. "He was wondering how many dogs I had," she said. A driveway screaming match ensued. "Now, I'm like hiding every time somebody walks by," she said. "If they look in my yard I panic and run round making sure there isn't a toy or a bike out.

"Covenants are fine," she said, "but they should take into account what it does to another human being when it's handled wrong. I can't understand someone patrolling and tattling and not being willing to work it out."

Many people choose to live in covenants-controlled neighborhoods — those where all the residents must abide by certain rules, enforced by elected officers of homeowner associations or by volunteer committees — in the belief that such neighborhoods look nicer and are more pleasant to live in, which keeps up everybody's property values.

Most dwellings in metro Denver — old and new — are covered by covenants, although their strictness varies widely. Some common ones require people to clean up after their dogs; keep their garage doors shut most of the time; park their mobile homes, campers, or boats out of sight; eschew satellite dishes and antennas; and have their exterior alterations — including paint hues, fencing, roofing material, landscaping and swing sets — approved in advance by a neighborhood committee.

♦ "I wish I lived in a covenant area," said a woman who, like many who were interviewed on the subject, didn't want her name disclosed for fear of stirring up more neighborhood animosity. "Where I live in Denver, anything goes. There are people with dump trucks parked in front, junk cars parked on their front lawns. I'm seriously considering moving to a covenant-controlled area so I don't have to live in the trash."

♦ That's why Teri Low and her husband recently built a home in a covenants-controlled neighborhood in unincorporated Jefferson County. But they aren't entirely happy, either. "Some people still think they can do what they want, when they want, and it just pulls everybody else down that abides by the covenants." Teri Low said. "We've got people with chicken-wire fences and mobile homes parked on the street."

♦ But nobody's got bird feeders in one Lakewood townhouse neighborhood, where Audubon Society member Julie Young said she never would have bought if she'd known about the rule in advance. "And I can't find it in the written covenants," she said.

The first Young knew of the problem with the three bird feeders hanging inside her private, fenced patio was when she got an official notice saying they weren't allowed because they might attract squirrels. She phoned the committee member whose name was on the notice and told him, "I never lived anywhere that didn't like birds or wildlife." His response, Young said, was that he could get a permit to kill her beloved birds.

Young used to live in a mountain neighborhood where she and her husband were homeowner association officers. They had to enforce covenants when neighbors had "junk cars and that sort of thing," Young said. "But we never picked on somebody who had maybe one or two too many dogs, as long as they kept them penned up."

She thought about selling her townhouse, "I was so upset," she said. Instead, she took down her bird feeders.

♦ Bob Bronson tore down his new storage shed in Jefferson County's Willowbrook subdivision after futilely fighting the homeowner association in court. "It just ate up family time and created bad vibes," he said. "They're enormously, enormously nosy here," he said. "Not everybody who ends up on a homeowner association's board is a loser; and many people have very good motives. But some of these people need to get a life."

♦ Some people need to get copies of their neighborhood covenants and read them before they decide to move in, said a woman in the Piney Creek subdivision, an Arapahoe County neighborhood where a lawsuit has been filed over the tiny Christmas light clips attached to one home. "I get real tired of people complaining about covenants," the woman said. "Anyone who has complaints with covenants should not move into the neighborhood, or move out. There are plenty of trashy ones they can go to."

There is another option. Consider a coup instead of moving.

♦ In Arvada's Pleasant Valley Townhomes, neighbors staged a coup three years ago and, at a special meeting, voted out three board members they said were terrorizing everyone with too-strict covenants enforcement.

"People said, 'I feel like I'm in a concentration camp.'" said Joni Greenwalt, Pleasant Valley's current association's president.

One resident, who lived alone, was so afraid of opening his garage door that he changed a flat tire inside the garage with the door shut; an activity so dangerous, since no one would have known if the car had fallen on him, that other neighbors made him promise never to do it again.

Greenwalt advised residents of covenants-controlled neighborhoods, to get involved in the mini-governments that rule their neighborhoods, and to remember that new officers can be elected and rules and regulations can be amended. "They aren't handed down from Mount Sinai," she said. "I think it's time people got the message: Don't allow your homeowner association to treat you as if you're in jail."

Greenwalt is planning to write a book about how people in covenants-controlled neighborhoods can get along better and wants to hear from people with experiences in such neighborhoods. Call her at 303-422-6277.

Metropolitan Denver is not unique, in any foggy stretch of the imagination. Wherever there are CCCs there are letters from HOAs and lawyers, and there are lawsuits. Grumpy decisions are delivered by BODs, volunteer HOA committees, and judges virtually every micro-second. Some are valid. Many are not.

The following observations were formulated from information relayed in the preceding article. If all the elements from both sides of the story were available, my evaluations and suggestions could be somewhat different. To make it easier for you to identify the solutions and suggestions, I have emphasized the article and my comments with bullets (♦).

♦ **JANIS McCLURE'S TALE:** The first dilemma is the BOD's inconsistent decisions. A mailbox variance is okay for you, and you, and you; however, not for you. Table that approach. It's just plain wrong.

As president of our HOA, I receive the ***Boardroom Discussion*** newsletter, published in Denver by the law firm of Winzenburg, Leff and Mitchell, LLP. The newsletter deals exclusively with CCCs, Jim Winzenburg's specialty. Quite emphatically, they have pointed out: Thou shalt not be inconsistent or thou may be sued. Inconsistency clearly is a *very* dangerous practice.

If you are a board member, a management company working for an HOA, or a homeowner involved in your HOA, there is no charge to receive *Boardroom Discussion*. To be placed on their mailing list call 303-863-1870 or send your request to Winzenburg, Leff and Mitchell, LLP • Boardroom Discussion • 1660 Lincoln Street, #1750 • Denver, CO 80264. Generously, they state, "Feel free to copy any of these articles in your Association's newsletter." Excerpts from the newsletters are reproduced in this book with the permission of *Boardroom Discussion*. *While the newsletters are prepared by the law firm they are not intended to give legal advice. Call them or other legal counsel for advice on specific circumstances.*

Be on the alert for whimsical decisions. I do not say that to provoke lawsuits. I'm 99.99 percent opposed to that concept. Just show this chapter, or the whole book, to anyone making fickle decisions. Firmly suggest that they get their consistency ducks in a row. You can let them know that *you* have no intention of suing them. You merely want to inform them that there are other homeowners who are crankier than you and that they could be setting themselves up for one of those cranky homeowners to force the issue in court.

Janis McClure's second dilemma is that her neighbors quickly and easily labeled her as their scapegoat, the one to point a finger at as the source of *every* community woe. (They may be in training for Olympic finger pointing.) In identifying Janis as the one and only culprit, they forgot to take the responsibility of taking the time to look into the manner in which their complex was being handled. The BOD, or possibly the management company, is the real culprit. It's an extremely safe bet that when the shoe goes on the finger pointers' proverbial footsies, those same neighbors will sing a different tune and maybe even start to understand Janis' pain and bewilderment.

♦ *"I wish I . . ."* I wish living in a covenants-controlled area was always as appealing as advertised. It isn't enjoyable to face dump trucks, junk cars, and trash. Sometimes happenings in covenants-controlled areas aren't enjoyable to face either. However, if you exert every prudent precaution, you can find your Utopia in almost any price range.

♦ **TERI LOW:** She and her husband are unhappy because covenants aren't enforced. Possibly there is no HOA and, therefore, no one to enforce the covenants. If there is an HOA, get involved, Teri. Go to the meetings and identify the enforcers of the covenants or, in this case, un-enforcers of the covenants. According to *Boardroom Discussion*, covenants can sometimes be abandoned with non-enforcement.

♦ **JULIE YOUNG OF THE AUDUBON SOCIETY:** Rightfully, Julie Young feels like a mistreated creature. The response Julie received from that board or committee member, was both rude and crude. No one deserves to be treated in such a boorish manner. Being a board or committee member does not give license to walk on Julie, or anyone else. To make such ill-mannered assertions is an attempt to intimidate and make the *"problem person"* go away.

You gave up too easily, Julie. Don't blindly comply. If you can't find the rule in the Docs, insist they show you where that specific restriction is written. In fact, a copy of the specific rule in the Docs should have been given to you when they issued the official notice. If it can't be confirmed, it's probably an invisible, made-up, counterfeit rule filling a board member's weird personal objective.

♦ **BOB BRONSON OF WILLOWBROOK:** Tucked up into the foothills, Willowbrook is an extremely appealing area of upper-income, single-family homes.

Remember, Bob, residents are either blessed or stuck with the covenants once the attorney has finalized the wording and the developer accepts them.

If you went to court expecting justice to prevail, Bob, you were blowing into a stiff breeze. Court verdicts, almost without fail, support the HOA and the strict letter of the rules in Docs. That is the *safest and easiest* decision. Just follow the bouncing rules. I won't say it *never* happens, but don't ever expect a precedent-setting decision in favor of a homeowner when the case involves a community controlled by covenants. (Discussed further in chapter 10, *I address the bench.*)

First read the Docs. Then learn the characteristics of the enforcers. Always get approval, in writing, from the proper people for any and all projects. Stay out of court. Nobody wins there except the lawyers.

♦ The woman from Piney Creek who is so enamored with the strict letter of the rules in the covenants hardly seems proud enough of her stance to disclose her name. *"Some people need to get copies of their neighborhood covenants and read them before they decide to move in."*

Remember the scenario back in chapter 2 about the midget-sized Christmas light clips? It all happened in Piney Creek. Maybe Spiny Creek would be a more fitting name. Anyone want to wager with me? I'll bet she is one of the stern enforcers of Piney Creek's *rules-are-carved-in-granite-and-are-more-important-than-people* attitude and I'll lay odds there is not one mention in their covenants that would lead anyone to anticipate a problem with tiny holiday light clips attached to a home.

"I get real tired of people complaining about covenants. Anyone who has complaints with covenants should not move into the neighborhood, or move out." You know I get real tired of narrow-minded people oversimplifying the real problems of CCCs. I interpret her words to mean, "Either don't move in, keep quiet, or move out." "Don't move in" is sound advice. "Move out" encompasses a large amount of time, effort, money, and many times undue hardships. There's a small chance that none of those are significant to her. There's a big chance that they *are* significant to other people.

Homeowners' complaints are rarely just about the covenants. Their complaints are about the manner in which the covenants are enforced.

"There are plenty of trashy ones they can go to." There are plenty of HOAs with trashy attitudes, too.

Other tales Karen Abbott reported

February 8, 1994
Reprinted with permission of the *Rocky Mountain News* — part of this article is on page 38 — the rest is presented in four portions, ending on the next page.

Conversation heard over the backyard fence

■ "My neighbor reported us for parking a junk vehicle in front of our house. The homeowner association never bothered to look at it; they just sent a nasty letter and said if you don't move it the police and lawyers will be in touch. It wasn't a junk vehicle; it was a 12-year-old truck with only 40,000 miles on it, and the body was in great shape . . . If I'd known about all this before I moved in, I wouldn't have." — Rachel Aumann, Arapahoe County, CO

Rachel, your enforcers slap first and ask questions later. Or maybe they only slap and never get around to asking questions.

Good sense mandates verifying the genuineness of a complaint. Common courtesy dictates first calling the offender if the violation is authentic. Authoritative or nasty letters sent out with careless abandon set the stage for misery. Misery sets the stage for lack of pride of ownership. That sets the stage for property values heading downward.

February 8, 1994
Conversation heard over the backyard fence continued

■ "We swore we never wanted to be in another homeowner association neighborhood. The only people who volunteered for those boards were people who wanted to exercise control over other people, although they always profess these noble motives . . . And your neighbors couldn't wait to fink on you. But when we had a complaint, they wouldn't do anything about it; they [the board] said they couldn't get involved, and why not just be friendly?"
— Lu Ann Stratford, Northglenn, CO

Lu Ann, that is either another case of BOD inconsistency or yours. Maybe you're not getting involved enough with the HOA. Hopefully, you haven't been sitting back expecting things to be run magically in a congenial way with no responsibility needed on your part. Know it's *your* community. Go to the meetings. Volunteer to help make yours a pleasant community. That *may* require organizing the unhappy residents to put more qualified, caring members "on board."

Lu Ann, perhaps the BOD should have thought of the responsibilities and work involved before they offered their services as board members (more in chapter 7, *Is the board of directors real or let's pretend?*).

Don't discount this possibility either. Your issue might not be on the BOD's personal priority list. Some BODs disregard some rules. They will enforce only rules that fit their exclusive fancies and materialize additional rules out of vapor. Such materialized rules have to be officially added to the Regs and they cannot be contrary to the recorded rules in the Docs. Such BODs are inordinately insistent on the "rightness" of their interpretation of the rules and their enforcement policy. Their "rightness" fits their desires quite well.

Another possibility is that your complaint might be one in which the BOD should not get involved. Some residents expect the BOD to act as if they were landlords or headmasters. Residents expect them to solve every insignificant matter. That is *not* the BOD's job. They didn't volunteer to be the homeowners' mommy and daddy.

Lu Ann, if you want to find out where the truth really lies, if you are not already involved, get involved in your HOA.

February 8, 1994
Conversation heard over the backyard fence continued

■ "The town I grew up in was the absolute worst. Reston, VA. You couldn't have a storm door. You couldn't fly an American flag. You couldn't build a fence. You couldn't grow corn in your yard. Where I live now, it's fine. There are covenants here but nobody enforces them, and nobody's looking at their neighbors' yards. Everybody kind of minds their own business. It's nice."
— Sherry Hall, Bailey, CO

I'd never heard of a whole town being so narrow-minded. That's a real stem winder. Residents of Reston, Virginia, should have the same corrective measures available to them as dwellers *can* have in CCCs. Sherry, it may feel good after the living conditions you previously experienced. However, I would wince slightly with nobody enforcing *any* of the covenants. That practice could make a 180-degree turn and bite you in your posterior.

February 8, 1994
The end of *Conversation heard over the backyard fence*

■ "About two years ago when the Cherry Creek school district was having a bond election from the PTO at our school I got a yard sign that said vote yes on whatever the amendment was . . . I put it up in my backyard . . . which faces the entrance to our neighborhood, and promptly got a call from our association's president saying no political advertising, period. I was extremely annoyed and felt that my civil rights had been abridged. He just told me to go and look it up in my covenants, and sure enough, there it was." — Gloria Puester, Aurora, CO

"I was extremely annoyed and felt that my civil rights had been abridged." Many restrictions in CCCs *do* abridge homeowners' civil rights. Rules written by man can be changed or completely thrown away by man (by woman, too). CCCs that are saddled with too strict, outmoded, or too ridiculous rules can modify or nullify them within the provision in their Decs for modification. If your Decs don't have such a provision, change may still be possible with 100 percent approval of the lenders and the homeowners. The next story tells how one community totally revised their covenants. It took them a year and a half to accomplish the task. Who ever said life is easy?

▶ RULES CAN BE CHANGED

Michael Garard's story about his community and revising their covenants:

In the mid-1970s a builder developed an upscale custom home community controlled by covenants.

In 1978 the builder ran an advertisement that asserted:

> **Most areas suitable for a custom home offer only building sites, leaving the design and construction of a home — and the headaches — up to you. At Coventry, we do things differently. We've made it easy for you, because covenants are in place.**

Michael Garard, a resident in Coventry and broker/owner of Garard and Associates Real Estate, was a member of the volunteer panel to update the 20-year-old covenants, a one-and-a-half-year process.

Michael said, "The covenants were okay for the time they were written, but things change over 20 years.

"Because of our strong community support, we were able to use block captains and to coordinate several meetings with approximately 20 homeowners per meeting. All residents had a chance to voice their opinions.

"**Some examples of the outdated ideas the original covenants dictated:**
- Garage doors must be closed
- No vans allowed
- No satellite dishes
- No in-home businesses

"**We revised and softened the above, plus tried to give other items a more 'black and white' definition.**
- Garage doors must be closed when the garage is not in use.
- Vans are now allowed, since many family cars are mini-vans.
- Satellite dishes are allowed up to 18 inches in diameter. They are much smaller today than they were 20 years ago.
- Now you can operate a corporation with a computer and a modem from any room in your home, as long as there is no additional traffic generated to the house above normal residential traffic.

"Out of homes, we had over 80% approval of the new covenants.

"Over the years," Garard said, "the largest difficulties were related to fences, vehicles, and dog runs because the old covenants were vague and could be interpreted several ways. We fixed the wording in the new covenants.

"There is an annual meeting for all homeowners. The board of directors meet monthly. The monthly meetings are open to all homeowners.

> "The architectural committee pays attention to any remodeling, exteriors, and fences that homeowners choose to do.
>
> "Recently the association built a magnificent new playground. It took several committees and a lot of feedback from the homeowners.
>
> "Our $110-per-home monthly dues cover a 24-hour gated access entrance, plus maintenance of the pool, tennis courts, greenbelts, common areas, clubhouse, pond areas, streets; additionally, street-snow removal, watering of greenbelts, newsletters, community events, etc.
>
> "Covenants are public record and everyone agrees to them before they buy. Supportive homeowners and our covenants control has been a large factor in maintaining and increasing our property values."

That was a superb example of how changing, updating, and softening the covenants can be an extremely viable solution. Follow Michael's steps and get input from the residents to create friendly covenants that work *for* the homeowners, instead of intimidating them.

No matter how good or bad, outdated or current the covenants are, they still have to be enforced with loving care or community grief will result.

Note the remark: "Covenants are public record and everyone agrees to them before they buy." That same claim is used time and time again as someone is being harassed, fined, or sued by his HOA. Yes, the covenants are of public record and buyers should have a copy given to them before the contract becomes final. If only the solution were really that simple. Problems arise from the lack of clarity and individual interpretations of the covenants. Few, if any, read every word and there are those who don't necessarily understand half of what they've read, thanks to the LDC (Legalese Department of Chaos). There are those who read and thoroughly comprehend every word in the Docs. How do they "read" the attitudes of the BODs that will reign over the community as the years roll by?

Example of a canned, too vague or too strict, archaic rule

Article X
RESTRICTIONS

Section 4. Residential Use. Subject to Section 5 of the Article X, Lots shall be used for residential purposes only, including uses related to the convenience and enjoyment of such residential use, and *no business or profession of any nature shall be conducted on any Lot or in any structure* located thereon.

Michael didn't share the wording of the original no-business covenant in Coventry, but it's a safe bet it was verbatim to the above.

Does no "business or profession" include selling Avon, typing on a computer, making business phone calls, or a child having a paper route or occasionally earning a few dollars from baby-sitting? How far might an overly controlling HOA take that regulation?

Congress and the FCC step on the "No satellite" restriction

If Michael's single-family CCC development were modifying their Decs today, they wouldn't have to bother with the satellite problem.

The Federal Communications Commission has adopted rules concerning restrictions of viewers' ability to receive video programming signals from direct broadcast satellites (DBS), multichannel multipoint distribution (wireless cable) providers (MMDS), and television broadcast stations (TVBS).

As directed by Congress in the Telecommunications Act of 1996, August 6, the FCC eliminated the "No satellite" problem for most CCCs.

The new rule prohibits enforcement of restrictions, including residential covenants, that impair the installation, maintenance, or use of antennas designed to receive direct broadcast satellite service and video programming service via multipoint distribution services, which are one meter or less in diameter, as well as antennas designed to receive television broadcast signals. Any restriction will be considered an impairment if it unreasonably delays or prevents installation, maintenance or use of an antenna, unreasonably increases the cost, or precludes reception.

In the comments to the rule, the FCC stated that homeowner associations' procedures that require approval before installation are prohibited unless they involve safety or historic preservation objectives. To apply, the objectives must be clearly stated within the restriction. These exemptions will not apply in most association situations.

In addition, no fine or other penalty may accrue against an antenna user while a proceeding is pending to determine the validity of any restriction.

The rule applies only to an individual who owns or has exclusive use of the area in which he or she wants to install one or more antennas. However, in planned unit developments (installations on an owner's lot) and in condominiums (an installation on a limited common area, such as a balcony), cannot be completely prohibited.

Restrictions against installation in a common area are still fully enforceable. The FCC intends to continue to consider public comment concerning expansion of the rule.

CAI (Community Associations Institute) suggests that associations could decide to install one antenna, to which all individuals desiring telecommunications service could be connected.

More detailed information can be obtained by calling the FCC 202-418-0163 or by checking CAI on the Internet (address: http://www.caionline.org) and Community Associations Online (CAO). A copy of the FCC rule may be obtained from the FCC at fcc.gov or CAI's Faxback at 703-836-6904, #50. If you have any questions, please contact CAI's Public Affairs Department at 703-548-8600. Ask them for the phone number of your state's chapter.

I hope it doesn't take an act of Congress to force more palatable "rule-recipes" (groundwork guidelines) to make the Docs more appetizing to homeowners in CCCs.

Well, maybe it will come state by state through legislation

The march on stupidity has begun.

Monday, October 21, 1996
Reprinted with permission of the *Rocky Mountain News*

Covenants: altering the landscape
Proposal would trim power of subdivisions over their homeowners

By Marlys Duran
Rocky Mountain News Staff Writer

BOULDER COUNTY — Chris Lucas' three-year battle with her homeowner association got her arrested, cost thousands of dollars, and put her in counseling.

It also convinced her that individual homeowners have too few rights in disputes over subdivision covenants.

So Lucas is proposing legislation that would give homeowners additional clout, including the right to secede from a neighborhood association when differences can't be resolved.

"If there's total dissatisfaction, why should people have to move?" She said, "Why perpetuate the cost on both sides?"

Lucas also wants a "grandfathering" clause prohibiting associations from suddenly challenging conditions that have been permitted to exist for several years.

The proposal being drafted would amend the Colorado Common Interest Ownership Act, Lucas said. The law intended to balance the interests of homeowners, their associations and others who deal with subdivision regulations.

But Lucas said the law gives homeowners too little protection from boards that interpret and enforce covenants. "The way some covenants are written, your neighborhoods have it over you," she said.

Lucas' long-running battle with the Flintlock I Homeowner Association in Boulder County began with the board's decision to remove landscaping on a common area that Lucas had installed and maintained for 18 years. The situation got out of control when an association official showed up with a crew to do the work, and Lucas and her mother were arrested.

The dispute landed in court. Lucas lost after amassing several thousand dollars in legal fees. Now she wants to take the fight to the legislature.

Lucas is garnering support from other homeowners who have had costly, bitter battles with the governing boards of their neighborhood associations. She said she learned that disgruntled homeowners were coming up with similar ideas all over the metro area. "Finally we started talking and saying we need to do something," she said.

One sympathizer is Emmett Johnson, who won a court fight with the Dam East Homeowner Association in Aurora over a fence. He said the association was ordered to pay 70% of his legal expenses, but the dispute still cost him $22,000.

"The situation is pathetic," he said. "I'm completely mystified by how these things come about."

Allen and Jan Burris are being sued by the Indian Creek Ranch Improvement Association in Douglas County District Court because they have one horse too many on their property. He says more than three horses have been allowed on lots since the subdivision was created more than 20 years ago. "That's an example of why 'grandfathering' in particular is needed," he said.

If Lucas' proposals make it to the legislature, they could face formidable opposition. Subdivisions with protective covenants are "the most popular housing today. This is what people want," said Denver attorney Jerry Orten.

He is vice president of the Rocky Mountain chapter of Community Associations Institute, which provides educational, lobbying and other services for homeowner groups and professionals who work with them.

If the institute decided that Lucas' proposed legislation was a positive move for homeowners, "we would jump on the bandwagon," said president Sandra O'Bryan, a certified public accountant. But, she asked, "Is it going to solve one problem but open up others?"

Lucas' proposals also would

■ Require mandatory mediation before an association could place a lien on a homeowner's property.

■ Require homeowner groups to fully disclose their records.

■ Prohibit use of homeowners' fees for lobbying or other political purposes.

More details are in chapter 10, ***Another Culprit at the Base of HOA Problems is Exposed***. Also, a summary at the back of the book offers some suggestions for legislation.

You want to have a garage what?

> Uptight Townhomes offers the opportunity to participate in one community garage sale per year. No independent, individual garage sales are allowed. The gavel goes down — end of story.

Well, excuse the residents in Uptight Townhomes for their inconceivable desire to participate in life. Fortunately, our complex isn't shackled with that silly regulation.

Maybe I cringed too soon. Maybe the HOA just didn't realize there might be a solution.

Are you open to a suggested solution?

If no, leap to "More reports like this one would be refreshing" on page 56

If yes . . .

. . . take this brief Dec test

1) Do your Decs specifically address only one community garage sale allowed per year as opposed to individual garage sales?   ☐ Yes   ☐ No
   - If *NO,* trip down to the third question.

2) If it *is* specifically in the Decs, are you willing to find a legal way to modify the rule?   ☐ Yes   ☐ No
   - If *YES,* continue reading for one potential resolution.

3) Did you use the help of a vague, wide-open-interpret-to-your-own-desire rule in order to avoid signs remaining centuries after homeowners have closed the doors on their garage sales?   ☐ Yes   ☐ No
   - If *YES,* keep going, you're on the right train.

4) Do your Decs allow you to set fines on new items of violation?   ☐ Yes   ☐ No
   - If your answer is *YES,* you know what to do. Come with me to the suggested solution to a silly problem.
   - If *NO,* you may be out of luck. Either skip to *More reports like this one would be refreshing* or, if you really want to help spread joy, check with your helpful attorney to see if there just might be a legal way to accomplish a happy end result for your neighborhood.

▶ *A SUGGESTED SOLUTION TO A SILLY PROBLEM*

- Consider a $5 deposit for each sign and keeping the deposit for each bedraggled garage sign left over 48 hours after closing shop.
- Make posting the address, dates, and times a requirement on all signs. Without compliance the garage sale will be shut down immediately without pausing at Go.

Sound too time consuming to gather up the leftover signs? Mildly meditate for a moment the possibility of announcing the following in large, bold print in the next newsletter. The complex will pay children, adults, dogs, ducks, or any other creature with feet, fur, fuzz, feathers, fins, or foliage who register as a bonafide dead-sign bounty hunter.

TRANQUIL TOWNHOMES NEWSLETTER

GARAGE SALES PERMITTED

Register now as a Bounty Hunter
for
OLD GARAGE SALE SIGNS

To have a garage sale . . .
- Address, dates, and times must be on all signs. Without the necessary data the garage sale will be immediately closed.
- A $5 deposit must be paid to the HOA ten days before the garage sale for each sign posted in the complex. Location of each sign must be registered with the office.
- There is a protected period of 48 hours after closing the garage sale. Four dollars of the deposit will be returned to the resident for each sign turned in to the HOA. The HOA will retain $1 for bookkeeping and handling.
- Within the period of 49 to 72 hours after the garage sale $4 will be paid for each sign turned in to the HOA by registered **Bounty Hunters.**
- Maintenance will remove signs remaining after 73 hours and the entire $5 will be retained by the HOA.

How to be a registered Bounty Hunter . . .
- Register with the HOA.
- Bounty will be paid only during the 49-to-72-hour period. The hunter will automatically be permanently removed as a bonafide dead-sign bounty hunter if sign(s) are turned in during the 48-hour protected period.

That can be a newly found, healthy summertime activity for children. It could even offer the prospect to adult residents to earn a few extra dollars. It definitely offers a viable solution to restoring individuality to the complex and injects some festivity into the otherwise tedious enforcement of the rules.

It will require a wee bit more toil, but your purpose is to generate community living comforts without generating undue expenses. With a computer in front of your face, this is not a rocket-launching task. Even without a computer, depending on the size of the complex, this is *not* a monumental assignment. If the extra $1 doesn't take care of the expenses incurred, charge $6 or $7, and keep $2 or $3. The $1 to $3 per sign that it would cost the garage-saler who picks up his own signs isn't an outrageous amount.

If the HOA doesn't want to handle this "burden," perhaps a resident who doesn't work, maybe is retired, would enjoy a little extra money, the leftover $1 to $3, and the adventure.

One gentleman solved the no-garage-sale rule in his complex by having an in-house sale.

When you concentrate on finding solutions rather than focusing on the problem, solutions will come to you. You reap what your thoughts sow. Do not plant onions if you want radishes. Plant radishes. Learn how to disperse the seeds of thought properly.

"If you keep pretending happiness long enough one morning you'll wake up and realize that you can hardly tell it from the real thing." — Arnot L. Sheppard, Jr.

More reports like this one would be refreshing

One of the first to call me was Arlene Riedmuller, president of CWCA (Columbine West Civic Association). She expressed her delight with Columbine West and her CCC single-family home. Their $10 per year dues are voluntary and they have no common area to maintain.

Arlene said, "Even though out of 1,550 homes, only 300 to 400 residents pay their dues, I am very proud to say that we have planted trees along county maintained streets that run through our subdivision and have done other landscaping upgrades. We contribute to Columbine High School's All Night Party. Board members attend meetings to give input into rebuilding the roads adjacent to our neighborhood. We are constantly seeking the best for our area.

"Last Christmas we arranged for families to hire Santa for $15 to deliver presents (supplied by the families) to their children. A hundred percent of the money collected by Santa was used to purchase a gift certificate at a grocery store. We gave it to a family in the community who was down on their luck."

Being a single-family community, their Docs do not have to contain as many restrictions as those in attached homes and condominium developments, but they could. Their slim Docs still have strength because the Columbine West Civic Association has a BOD and an ACC. Their newsletters are composed by volunteers. CWCA maintains an attractive community by politely enforcing their covenants.

CWCA's attorney advised the BOD to *be neither arbitrary nor capricious*. Arlene said, "Every community with covenants must have a goal and always strive to make certain the covenants are enforced with uniformity and not in a capricious or arbitrary manner."

Cities shouldn't be arbitrary and capricious either

BOARDROOM DISCUSSION
❖ Published by the LAW FIRM OF WINZENBURG, LEFF, PURVIS AND PAYNE, LLP ❖
• 1660 Lincoln Street, #1750 • Denver, Colorado 80264 • 303-863-1870

September 1992

COURT HOLDS GARBAGE COLLECTION POLICY UNCONSTITUTIONAL

We have reported in the past that a court in another state decided that a city cannot discriminate in providing services. A city's policy of not providing garbage removal services to a condominium Association violated state and federal due process and equal protection laws.

A New Jersey court repeated this decision. A city collected refuse for its citizens except for owners of condominium units. The Association sued the city, claiming that the garbage policy violated state and federal constitutional due process and equal protection requirements by discriminating against different classes of owners within its jurisdiction.

The court ruled that the law requires that citizens in the same situation be treated equally; and no reason existed for discriminating against the condominium owners.

RECOMMENDATION: If your Association is not receiving full benefits from any governmental unit, consider organizing a "Boston Garbage Party."

Since 1992, the New Jersey Supreme Court reversed that court decision. They ruled that it's okay for cities to discriminate against HOAs — cities *can* be arbitrary and capricious.

Now back to Columbine West. They softened the strictness of their original covenants that proclaimed matters immediately be turned over to an attorney when a resident violates a covenant. The HOA felt that was not only too expensive, but too harsh. They have established a friendly, but firm, form-letter method. The letters are reproduced with the permission of the president of CWCA.

The first letter

COLUMBINE WEST CIVIC ASSOCIATION
WE CARE

DATE _____

ADDRESS _____

_____

Dear Columbine West Resident:

The covenants for the Columbine West Subdivision were recorded in Jefferson County in 1971 and are a part of each homeowner's deed. It is therefore, by law, the obligation of each homeowner or renter to abide by the covenant provisions.

You are in violation of covenant provision(s) _____ . Please refer to the enclosed copy of your Columbine West Interpretation for an explanation of the provision(s) and the specific discrepancy.

The covenants for the Columbine West Subdivision were conceived to enhance the property values of the area and to maintain Columbine West as a high quality residential district. Noncompliance with the covenants causes property values in our neighborhood to be negatively affected. A reasonable time of 21 days (three weeks) has been established for you to correct your violation.

Should you have any questions or problems, or you feel you are in compliance with the covenants, please write to the above address. If you have recently corrected the situation, please accept our thanks.

Architectural Control Committee
Columbine West Civic Association

"Please refer to the enclosed copy of your Columbine West Interpretation for an explanation of the provision(s) . . ." pertains to a one-page, condensed version of their covenants. They are wise to enclose that. Residents have a way of misplacing their copy.

The second letter

COLUMBINE WEST CIVIC ASSOCIATION
WE CARE

LAST NOTICE

DATE _____

ADDRESS _____

_____

Dear Columbine West Resident:

You should have received a letter from the Columbine West Civic Association dated _____ requesting your cooperation in correcting a violation of covenant provision(s) _____ .

A reasonable time of three weeks (21 days) was allowed for you to correct the situation. It has been noted that the covenant violation still exists.

It should be emphasized that the covenant provisions are enforceable in a Court of Law. If the violation is not corrected in seven (7) days, the Columbine West Civic Association will be forced to take legal action.

Architectural Control Committee
Columbine West Civic Association

After the resident has complied

COLUMBINE WEST CIVIC ASSOCIATION
WE CARE

DATE _____

ADDRESS _____

_____

Dear Columbine West Resident:

The Columbine West Civic Association wishes to express thanks and gratitude to you for correcting the covenant violation that was recently noticed at your residence.

The covenants for the Columbine West Subdivision were conceived to enhance the values of the area and to maintain Columbine West as a high quality residential district.

It is a pleasure to note that you are working with your homeowners' organization to make our neighborhood a more desirable place to live.

Architectural Control Committee
Columbine West Civic Association

Hats off to Columbine West. They are a prime example of a community with a BOD who cares enough to enforce necessary rules in a civil manner. They offer beneficial activities for the good of the community and use a high degree of common sense in evaluating what is actually important. They support and propagate the advertised advantages of living in a CCC.

Arlene sent this letter to the *Rocky Mountain News* after she read Karen Abbott's article.

February 9, 1994

Rocky Mountain News
400 W. Colfax Avenue
Denver, Colorado

ATTN: Editor

How sad it is that you portray homeowner associations in such a negative light. They certainly do more than just enforce covenants, which you did point out but not strongly enough. People have a choice to live where they want and certainly can live in an area that is to their standards.

In your article you did not point out the good (besides the good of enforcing the covenants and keeping the homes at a high resale value). I am very proud to say that my association has . . . [This portion is omitted because it gives information printed previously about the great things Columbine West Civic Association has accomplished.] . . . seeking the best for our area; through our contacts with Jefferson County Zoning we stopped the housing of workers in a backyard — the homeowner was renting plots measuring six feet in length to these people; and yes, our covenants, remind neighbors that they must be in compliance to live here, as we are a covenant protected community.

Balanced journalism and not sensational headlines do a better service for the community. People have choices and you make them sound as though they do not.

Sincerely,

Arlene Riedmuller

Arlene Riedmuller
President, Columbine West Homeowners Assoc.

Arlene, if all communities with covenants ran as smoothly as yours there wouldn't be any dismal articles in the newspapers. I'm an extremely positive person who would prefer to see more good stuff reported, but I just can't imagine the following type of headline and story.

Happiness strikes again in Lucky Land Townhomes

Darlene Dimples requested permission from her HOA to install an air conditioner in her home because her doctor suggested it as a relief to her recently developed allergies.

Even though the covenants of Lucky Land Townhomes rule against air conditioners, the board unanimously agreed that from now on air conditioners would be allowed. Lucky Land will only require permission from the architectural committee for specific placement of each air conditioner.

The board legally modified the declarations to reflect their amicable decision. Residents report they feel extremely lucky to live in Lucky Land Townhomes.

Unfortunately, Arlene, there are far too many communities that are governed by those inflicted with Napoleonic syndrome. Some BODs and ACCs make Simon Legree look like Santa Claus. For that reason story after story will be reported in the media about neighborhoods who have the plight-blight.

Arlene discovered unhappiness can strike even contented communities

When I called Arlene to get her updates, she shared the following not-so-happy happening. CWCA had the "joyful" experience of sitting before a judge. They received a letter from some irritated homeowners about another neighbor who was, against the covenants, erecting a ham radio tower. The vice president of the ACC went a courtesy step further than the normal letter procedure. First she spoke to the renter/resident to explain that he was in violation of the covenants. She informed him that he must take down the partially constructed tower, before going any further, which would save him time and money. CWCA sent a letter to the owner of the property to advise her of the situation. The owner never responded.

When the 40-foot tower didn't come down, the 12 residents who had expressed their aversion to the tower agreed to defray the legal costs. CWCA moved on to court. The court ruled in favor of CWCA.

Legal costs were $2,000. CWCA collected $480: $200 from the defendant's bond money and $280 from two of the 12 financially pledged homeowners. At this writing, the remaining ten have not honored their promises. They have only contacted Arlene with new complaints. CWCA paid the remaining $1,520. Fortunately, Arlene had made certain that there was enough money in the treasury to cover all of the estimated legal fees. To recoup the funds CWCA had to cut back on scheduled projects.

The owner appealed. The appellate court upheld the decision. Down came the tower.

A *point*

The importance of the following excerpt from the two-page recorded appellate court's decision is neither that the court found in favor of CWCA nor is it CWCA's rule that is reprinted in the decision. The importance is in the second to last paragraph where the *court deemed the covenant to be* **unartfully** *(inadequately) written*. This is only one of a legion of instances of judges' admissions, via their verdicts, of vague wording in rule restrictions. It's time for new sets of friendly, clearly written covenants.

COURT, JEFFERSON COUNTY, STATE OF COLORADO
Case No. . . . .

THIS MATTER comes before the Court upon Defendants-Appellants' . . . the order below is AFFIRMED.

. . . . Plaintiff argues that Defendants' structure violates covenant § B-7, which provides:

B-7. NUISANCES. No noxious or offensive activity shall be carried on upon any lot, nor shall anything be done there from which may be or may become an annoyance or nuisance to the neighborhood. No free-standing radio or TV antennas, are installed on the roof of a dwelling, said antennas shall not exceed five feet in height or eight feet in diameter. No outside storage or inoperative vehicles or machinery of any type will be permitted. No recreational vehicles, accessories or equipment shall be stored on any lot nearer to the street than the front building line and such storage behind the front building line shall be completely screened from view by a solid fence which shall not exceed six feet in height. [Whew!]

The trial court found, in essence, that while the covenant may have been unartfully written [*please note "unartfully written"*], its intent was to prohibit antenna structures that protrude five feet above the roof of a house, whether mounted on the roof or the side of the house.

The trial court's interpretation of the covenant is not unreasonable. His findings of fact and conclusions of law are neither arbitrary nor capricious and are supported by the record . . .

Arlene said, "It is a sad commentary that we must go to these lengths to defend the value of our properties. It's not a 'win/lose' situation. Everybody loses."

Dishonorable mention and *shame* on the ten owners who shirked their *pledges of monetary aid* (a signed pledge might have been helpful) and for brazenly using the time of a caring, hard working, volunteer president of the board. Where do they gather the nerve to present new complaints? Do you suppose any one of them realizes the enormous amount of time Arlene spent to solve the situation? Would they appreciate it if they did?

Even good people will stop turning the other cheek when they are used like a dumping ground. Can't you just hear those self-centered homeowners? "I wonder where Arlene is?"

Columbine West could do a 180-degree turn to an everything-goes attitude. They are in an unincorporated area. Do you comprehend the impact? Try issuing a covenants complaint with the county zoning people and see how far you get with that one.

While I'm at it, a pox upon 77 percent of *all* the homeowners in Columbine West. Only 23 percent pay their $10 annual dues. Even my 14-year-old granddaughter could afford to pay less than 85 cents a month. With over 1,550 homes, those homeowners expect their dedicated volunteers to take care of their problems with a meager $3,000 to $4,000 a year. Don't expect a silk purse if all you offer is a sow's ear.

Step down from that soapbox and onto the next

This story illustrates how HOAs can intensify the plight by perpetrating the blight.

Responsibility demands the four-letter "W" word. Work can bring a happy ending.

Martha "Marty" Walker lives in a townhome complex in Aurora, Colorado. Martha made a request to the president of the HOA that she be allowed, for health reasons, to place an air conditioning compressor just outside her patio on common area.

Surveying the area she counted 14 other homes that had done just that. After not hearing back from the board she proceeded with her plan.

The next thing she knew she was getting sued.

Martha said the board was allowing use of the common area for end units only and treated the middle units with a different set of rules. [*Sounds like another instance of inconsistency to me.*]

Stated in the annual meeting report that was sent to all residents: "We currently have one legal matter — a homeowner has placed an air conditioner compressor in the common area in front of her home. As this is a legal matter, our attorney has advised that we should not discuss it openly. When matters of this nature are presented it will usually take a year to resolve."

Well, Martha fired a letter right back, in which she confirmed she not only had requested permission, she had submitted a picture of the unit at the office of the HOA on April 10, 1993.

She went further to say, "I, too, plan to seek costs and punitive damages for any action taken by the Association due to the board's inconsistency toward all property owners.

"If this issue is to be litigated, I will request approved documentation of all of those who have installed these compressors without threat of legal action of the board."

Martha said, "The HOA is harsh, demanding, Gestapo-like, and doesn't even try to get along with people. Besides that, they are arrogant, rude, and over-authoritative."

On page 2, Article 1, Definitions, Martha found her answer.

(C) *"COMMON PROPERTIES" SHALL MEAN ALL REAL PROPERTY OWNED BY THE ASSOCIATION FOR THE COMMON USE AND ENJOYMENT OF THE OWNERS.*

They did end up in court. I'm happy to report that Martha is keeping a cool head with her air conditioner. The accompanying compressor remains happily on the common area. The HOA is now putting shrubs around *all* the installed compressors.

BODs and ACCs, be *neither arbitrary* nor *capricious!*

"Standing in the middle of the road is very dangerous; you get knocked down by the traffic from both sides." — Margaret Thatcher

Marty distributes a newsletter to the homeowners in her community. Here's part of sample letter.

S.U.N. 1994
Speak Up Now!
Newsletter

December   Vol 12

We want to thank our readers for their wonderful support throughout this year. It has been a very enlightening year.

What makes our experiences so great is the fact that, "We have so much in common." We will continue to share with you comments and concerns of our neighbors, families, friends, and even those who disagree.

Neighbor to neighbor, we can make the difference. Communicate, communicate, communicate. Neither "correctness nor rightness" is the issue.

That is much more appealing to me than the announcement of *COVENANT OF THE MONTH.* Marty uses the newsletter as a method to inform all residents exactly what the BOD is and isn't doing. Marty said, "If you stick to the facts you won't get in trouble and an enlightened community will emerge to help make needed changes."

It worked. They now have a new BOD with a caring attitude. Marty said, "Now it's wonderful. It's as though I had moved to a different development. Believe me, getting involved to make needed changes is gratifying and a lot easier than moving."

Hang in there, Marty. Keep the peace and your pace. Don't let your complex slip back.

Einstein's three rules of work

1) Out of clutter find simplicity.
2) From discord make harmony.
3) In the middle of difficulty lies opportunity.

Homeowners' involvement produces another happy ending

Wilnetta Fanning lives in a townhome complex in Colorado Springs.
Wilnetta said, "The board of directors is comprised of geriatric-minded members who would prefer it if the complex was for adults only. So they removed the basketball net. Then they closed the pool, using the excuse that there were no funds available for repair. Finally, they consented to allow a

volunteer committee to get bids to repair the pool and then, proceeded to make it impossible for contractors to have access to the equipment room — a room necessary for the contractors to view in order to make their bids.

"Generally, they do everything they can to make it miserable for the children and not particularly pleasant for the adults.

• "One man got a trespassing charge because he walked across a neighbor's driveway to get his mail.

• "Another resident was asked to remove items from the yard. The items were bikes that were there during play hours.

• "My husband was in the process of changing the water pump on his car in his driveway which took three days because of his work schedule. He was told to stop the work immediately, which he did, or there would be a fine. He received the fine anyway — eight months later!

• "An elderly lady in the complex was sent a notice that her backyard was a disaster area. The disaster: she raises tomatoes in the summer. All units have six-foot fences around the backyards.

• "One resident's grandson was hit by a car, after being told by the president of the board to go ride his bike in the street.

• "The board takes offense to children using the common area. Four children were raking leaves and playing in large boxes and were told to go home.

"The common area belongs to the homeowner association. As we are homeowners, the common area belongs to us and to our children. As long as they are not damaging anything, what is wrong with children playing?

"They deprive the children of normal and healthy activities. The overly strict interpretation and enforcement of the rules and the board's rude behavior are forcing the children into a rebellious, angry, and unhealthy state of mind. It's discrimination and harassment. What about the fair housing laws?"

That was Wilnetta's story when she called in February 1994 and asked me to attend a meeting of the homeowners and renters who were organizing to civilize their community. Yes, I said renters. Don't be surprised. Many times, renters demonstrate more concern than apathetic, ride-the-waves homeowners.

Common, considerate goals were the subject of the open meeting. Two of the unfriendly board members attended, but only stayed for a short time. It appeared their attention span was too limited to focus on common and considerate goals.

What about the fair housing laws?

BOARDROOM DISCUSSION
❖ Published by the LAW FIRM OF WINZENBURG, LEFF, PURVIS AND PAYNE, LLP ❖
• 1660 Lincoln Street, #1750 • Denver, Colorado 80264 • 303-863-1870

<u>SOME FHA VIOLATIONS</u>   April 1995

"From 6:00 p.m. to 9:00 p.m. — ADULTS ONLY swim time."

"Kids must play only at the playground."

"Kids in diapers are not allowed in the pool."

Wilnetta's complex now has an entirely new BOD and everything is going swimmingly. The children are no longer treated as insignificant beings in waiting to become adults.

Wilnetta's and her neighbors' happy outcome is entirely attributed to their getting involved and organizing their efforts to better their community.

Getting involved definitely pays off. It's well worth stealing a few hours from more entertaining activities to stabilize and balance a comfortable lifestyle.

When adversity strikes, don't draw back. The misfortune may be your opportunity to become a stronger and happier person. Words to remember: All sunshine makes a desert.

The stories continue ...

Sunday, July 16, 1995
Reprinted with permission of *The Denver Post*

ANN SCHRADER

Hung up
Covenants can be all wet

The house and price were attractive. Ditto the neighborhood and the people who lived there.

When it came time to sign the bottom line, little concern was given to the rules that go with the suburban dream.

Sure, copies of the Design Standards and the Declaration of Covenants, Conditions and Restrictions were handed over. It wasn't until later — when the fence needed to go up and the landscaping was crying to be done — that the true nature of what governs use of your property sank in.

There are the covenants. That's another word for "whatever you want to do must be *against* the rules."

People used to demonstrate in the streets against the rules. Now they acquiesce, sometimes with a few grumbles, but they say yes.

An estimated one out of ten people in the United States now lives in a community with covenants. Most of these rules are intended to defend property values. Usually, they aim to ensure that there are no houses with wheels and no vehicles without wheels.

There are the rules about the maximum number of domesticated animals, antennas, bizarre color schemes and "noxious and unreasonably offensive" sounds or odors "emitted from any property within the community area."

But there are some that border on the absurd. No flagpoles, no open garage doors "when not in immediate use," no *swamp coolers* on the roof, no tree houses, no basketball backboards that don't match the original paint scheme.

Our family recently moved to a suburban covenant-controlled community. Within a month, there was a run-in with the Design Review Committee over a proposed fence. The committee, which did a drive-by design check, wouldn't even listen to reasons supporting a waiver for the fence.

Friends implored us to move back into Denver. "You can do anything in Denver. Sure, the schools aren't great, but it's a wide-open town. They let you do anything," one woman cajoled a friend who lives in a covenant-controlled community. She supports having some common rules. But she also likes to hang her sheets outside.

"Clotheslines or hangers — not allowed" states the 15-page Design Standards document.

Once a week, for no longer than an hour or two, she wants to hang her sheets on the line to dry in the sun. "I love the way sheets hung outdoors smell," she says. "It makes the whole house smell like sunshine."

It's also a way to meet neighbors, and a way for the neighbors to learn a little about her without being conspicuously nosy. Just check out those designer sheets!

Hanging sheets outside also would *save* energy. Environmentalists like to reduce energy consumption. But not the covenants.

So she has devised a plan. A clothesline stuck in cement would be a permanent blight, she acknowledges. So with a next-door neighbor or two saying they certainly don't mind, she's installing a retractable clothesline.

"It's my stealth clothesline," she says. She will sneak out early, zip out the line and drape her sheets in the most private corner of her yard. She may get caught, and the Design Review Committee may get rough with her, but she doesn't mind. She's just boggled that life has come to this.

The only other option is to get 75 percent of the other homeowners to change the Design Standards and allow clotheslines. Ever try to get 75 percent of any group to agree on anything?

Ann Schrader is a Denver Post staff writer

"An estimated one out of ten people in the United States now lives in a community with covenants." That means one out of ten people run the chance of discovering they moved themselves into a very uncomfortable living environment. As more and more such communities are built, that figure grows daily by leaps and bounds and will soon double.

Up pops the old "No clotheslines" rule again. Way before I moved to my townhome one resident was allowed to use a retractable clothesline. So we modified our Regs to make retractable clotheslines legal for all. There is a stipulation that clothes are to be removed within a reasonable drying time and the clothesline to be immediately retracted. We have only a few who take advantage of that, but it makes those few very happy when they smell the freshness of their air-dried clothes.

You tell me. Are clothes hanging on the line for a few hours a threat to lives or property values? Can you envision the "appalling" sight if *all* of the homes had clothes drying at the same time? If that scene turns you off, it may be time for you to acquire a real life.

A *point of law*

Two attorneys gave their opinions about bending the clothesline rule. The first attorney said it would be unlikely to cause a legal problem because the intent of bending would be for the benefit of all homeowners. The second attorney said restrictions in the Decs can only be embellished, never diminished and which part of "no" in "no clotheslines" didn't we understand? Who knows how a judge would rule? Caveat: Modify or bend rules at your own risk or with the assistance of a good attorney.

For that very reason, I plead with the developers and the legal profession to create less petty and vise-like rules in the Decs with more latitude for living.

Many covenants *or* enforcers don't allow basketball backboards no matter *what color* they're painted. The restrictions in our townhome complex do not specifically address the installation of basketball backboards, but a previous BOD (and it wasn't The Clan) denied such an appendage for one resident. Reason given: The resident won't keep it in neat and tidy order. We will now allow basketball backboards and nets on the garage. The stipulation is that they *must* be kept in neat and tidy order. Wasn't that a simple solution?

The list of absurd rules is interminable. Let your mind run wild. If you can think of it, some attorneys have already formed a rule to restrict it. I adore Ann's statement,

"Covenants, that's another word for whatever you want to do must be against the rules."

Many BODs and ACCs put everything from a birdhouse or a hanging plant on a par with knocking the front wall out and inserting a dog run. They categorically deny homeowners' requests for anything and everything.

The mere installation of innocent sounding security or storm doors gave birth to havoc!

A real struggle to reach a happy ending

Betty Procter lives in Pleasant Meadows, a small complex in Lakewood, Colorado, where the majority of residents wanted to install security, storm, or screen doors.

Many of the residents are single women. They wanted the added feeling of safety by installing security doors.

Due to an interpretation of a restriction in the Documents by an attorney/board member, the complex was required to obtain a majority vote from the mortgage companies in order to set this into place. [A copy of the form they used to obtain that majority vote is on the next page.]

Betty offered the possibility that there was more than a slight chance the attorney board member, who was opposed to the project and interpreted the Decs, was serving his own personal agenda.

The attorney said, "No modification to the exteriors can be performed without approval by 75 percent of both homeowners *AND* the mortgage companies that hold mortgages on the units. That means we can't do this without first obtaining such approval." He knew, quite well that getting an affirmative vote from 75 percent of mortgage companies would be close to an impossible task.

The attorney/board member said his interpretation was, without doubt, correct. His personal opposition stemmed from his desire to keep everything uniform. [I know that complex and not only buildings, but unit styles in each building vary.] He felt, if doors were to be installed, the HOA should install the same type of door on ALL units, knowing that would negate the project because the HOA couldn't afford the expense. The alternative of the homeowners opting to do it themselves, he said, meant that some would and some would not. That obviously terrified him. [He must be a very boring, regimented person.]

Another interpretation of the Decs would very likely have revealed the mortgage companies' votes of approval to be absolutely unnecessary for security doors. Betty didn't pursue that possibility. She and another homeowner formed a determined committee of two. They started the necessary process to accomplish "Operation Doors."

Mortgage companies don't really care one way or the other about security, storm, or screen doors. With or without such doors, there would be no momentous impact on property values. Security for their loans would not be affected. The triviality of the subject placed "Operation Doors" low on the lenders' priority lists.

Mortgage company approvals did not quickly pour back. That necessitated a multitude of phone calls to the lenders requesting that they please reply.

Betty said, "As we started receiving approval letters back, the attorney/board member questioned the titles and validity of the signatures on the letters!"

Another fire-breathing dragon had just been thrown onto the committee's path.

The attorney/board member was no less determined to block "Operation Doors" than the committee was to follow it through to fruition.

The committee had come close to accomplishing the impossible once. Betty said, "So, we just started all over again with a more definitive request letter." The committee produced an official form to send to the mortgage companies. You can bet it wasn't with the help of the attorney/board member. They duplicated their previous dedicated efforts with determination and follow-up phone calls to inspire the mortgage companies to reply.

**AMENDMENTS TO DECLARATION OF COVENANTS,
CONDITIONS, RESTRICTIONS AND EASEMENTS
FOR PLEASANT MEADOWS TOWNHOMES**

Know ALL MEN BY THESE PRESENTED:

WHEREAS, there was executed and recorded on June 24, 1982, under Reception No. 55500055 in the records of the Clerk and Recorder of Jefferson County, Colorado, a Declaration of Covenants, Conditions, Restrictions and Easements for PLEASANT MEADOWS TOWNHOMES: AND,

WHEREAS, in accordance with amendment provisions set forth in said Declaration's paragraph 25, approval of at least 75% of owners and 75% of mortgagors is required for any amendment, the undersigned desires to amend said Declarations to change one of the provisions thereof as hereinafter set forth.

Now, therefore, the undersigned do hereby make the following changes and amendments to said Declaration, to wit:

Paragraph 9 (a) on page 6 is hereby amended by the addition of the following:

Each homeowner will have the option of installing a security storm door, upon approval by the board of its design for consistency of design throughout the complex. The expense of installation and maintenance of such doors will be the responsibility of each homeowner.

The instrument is hereby executed by the undersigned with an effective date of _____, 19 ____

_____
(Name)

**THE FOLLOWING IS THE AUTHORIZED SIGNATURE
FROM THE OWNER'S MORTGAGE COMPANY**

_____
(PRINT name, address, and phone number of your lender here)
LOAN NUMBER _____

_____
(PRINT name and position of signature for said Mortgage Company)

_____
AUTHORIZED SIGNATURE FOR SAID MORTGAGE COMPANY
DATE _____
RETURN TO
PLEASANT MEADOWS TOWNHOMES
(Address and Phone Number)

"We did get the required 75 percent approval. Many of us now have the doors we wanted so much," said a smiling Betty.

The exact required percentage of lenders' votes fluctuates from complex to complex and restriction to restriction. Check your Decs.

A sad commentary compounds an insult: Lenders' interest and cooperation levels are extremely low when their votes are needed to modify rules to afford homeowners a more civilized lifestyle. It doesn't matter that the modification would not cause property values to diminish. Actually it is the lender's *lack of cooperation* that threatens to *cause property values to decrease.* Pride of ownership is the main ingredient needed to maintain property values. Homeowners' lose that precious ingredient when they are treated unfairly.

Along with other paperwork on your loan, lenders have the set of recorded restrictions in their file. Their making a decision to give their approval to modify a restriction that is tucked neatly in their file offers absolutely *no benefit to the lender.* Status quo rationalization has affected their minds. I can hear all of them, with right hands raised, voicing the first pledge of the day, "I pledge to honor the status quo, no action policy."

So YEA for you, Betty, and the other member of your committee of two! Another victory for the good guys. (Another of Betty's stories, *The HOA doesn't always win, even when it should,* is in chapter 10.)

Lenders' approval for some specific matters in the Decs is necessary because lenders must have control over *significant* changes that could lessen the value of the properties that secure their loans. *Some significant* changes to one unit could have an impact on the values in the entire complex. That is why they insist on a majority vote of the lenders. The last I checked 51 percent *is* a majority. Anything over 51 percent is just mean.

Life would be easier for CCC inhabitants if developers and attorneys would limit the lender approval requirements exclusively to issues consequential to property values. This would easily be accomplished if only significant rules and restrictions were in the Decs in the first place. Embellishment, deletion, and modification of other rules and restrictions should only require the agreement of the majority of homeowners.

I had a mortgage on a single-family home for over 20 years. My deed of trust established that the property was to conform to local codes and zoning rules and that the property was to be maintained in such repair as not to lessen the value of the property. Lender permission wasn't a requirement when I modified my home by installing metal siding above the brick, attaching ventilation fans on the roof, adding two redwood decks (one covered, one not), and enlarging the driveway. The legal society has granted lenders a vested interest in petty issues on CCC properties. That seems to verge on discriminatory practices against covenants-controlled properties.

Lenders need cooperation, too

Lenders reported a lack of cooperation by many BODs and management companies to provide pertinent information such as the financial status of the HOA, the ratio of owner-occupied to non-owner-occupied homes, and so on.

Lenders are obligated to obtain specific data before they are allowed to fund a loan to purchase or to refinance. Not to supply those items is unacceptable inattention to details.

BODs and their representatives need to support homeowners' needs.

• If a homeowner is selling his property, the buyer cannot purchase the property until his lender receives all the pertinent information.

• If a homeowner is planning to refinance, the lender cannot accommodate the homeowner without the needed data.

Stories trickle in on a worst case scenario

Carl Alessi ferreted out some of the bad guys; there's an abundance of them implicated in this nefarious, tangled mess. Cases of theft, fraud, felony, and a federal investigation unravel in the five following articles that extend through the end of October, 1996.

Wednesday, February 21, 1996
Reprinted with permission of *The Castle Rock Chronicle* and K.T. Kelly

Residents look for new management

By K.T. Kelly

The Meadows Homeowner Association has terminated the contract with its management company in the wake of alleged financial wrongdoing by a former association board president.

Carl Alessi, board president of the association, said, "Hammersmith Management Company was served notice of the termination last week after the board determined it would be in the residents' best interest to seek a new management company."

Alessi said, "The contract, worth about $40,000 a year, ends March 16. The board plans to take bids from other management companies within the next week. We are cleaning house!"

Hammersmith Management had handled the association's affairs since mid-1993. It was within the past two years that former Association Board President, Bruce Peterson, a former employee of Meadows developer Yale Investments, allegedly made "questionable disbursements" of more than $49,000 to two companies Peterson owned while heading the board.

Peterson was arrested and charged with felony theft earlier this month after an investigation by the Castle Rock Police Department and Arapahoe County District Attorney's Office. He is scheduled for a preliminary court hearing April 8. Alessi is scheduled to testify against him.

"In addition to the $49,000, police also are investigating a disbursement of $6,500 allegedly taken out of homeowner funds to pay for a sprinkler system at the Littleton home of Peterson's parents. The landscaping company which performed the service for Peterson changed its name to Apex Landscaping from Wyland & Bugas," Alessi said.

Alessi also discovered a disbursement of about $3,000 for "Christmas lights" in the Meadows in 1994.

"That's enough money to light up the entire capitol building," Alessi said. "I wanted actual invoices to support all of this."

Alessi, the first Meadows resident to sit on the homeowners board, testified February 7 in favor of state legislation preventing developers who control the majority of homeowner boards from entering into contracts with the board which may financially benefit the developer unless 67 percent of the homeowners approve it.

Sponsored by Senators Doug Linkhart, D-Denver, and Mike Kaufman, R-Arapahoe County, the bill was passed by the Colorado Senate earlier this month.

"It's great that these two senators from different parties united and worked together for the benefit of the people," Alessi said.

Wednesday, February 28, 1996
Reprinted with permission of the *Rocky Mountain News*

Developer takes homeowner off board
Removal causes uproar at meeting of residents of Castle Rock subdivision

By Shelley Gonzales
Rocky Mountain News Staff Writer

CASTLE ROCK — Gary Vose, developer of The Meadows subdivision in north Castle Rock, has ousted the first homeowner representative on the community association's board.

Carl Alessi received notice that he is no longer on the board in a letter from Vose delivered to him at the beginning of Monday night's meeting.

Alessi had questioned expenditures made under the leadership of the former board, which consisted solely of Vose employees. The board oversees expenditure of fees paid by property owners in the subdivision.

The action caused an uproar among the dozens of Meadows residents attending the meeting.

"I don't think I've ever been so mad," said Caron Waldron, a two-year resident who sits on the covenant committee. "I mean this is America. This is not right.

"I think he's [Carl Alessi] asked too many questions and ruffled too many feathers. But to me, he was just asking those questions for the rest of us, and now everything is going to get swept under the carpet."

Alessi was appointed by the developer to the board in December, replacing Bruce B. Peterson, who is accused of pocketing homeowner association's fees by funneling them into two companies he owned.

Peterson was a vice president at Yale Investments, Vose's company in charge of The Meadows. He has been charged with felony theft in Arapahoe County District Court.

Since he was named to the board, Alessi has publicly cited questionable payments ordered by Peterson since 1993, when Vose bought the subdivision.

Last week, the Meadows' management company went to court, asking a judge to order Alessi to stop talking to reporters. That request by Hammersmith Management, will be heard in Douglas County District Court this morning.

Hammersmith also is suing Alessi for libel and slander. The company was fired by the Meadows board last week.

At Monday night's meeting, Yale employee Angela Olthoff, a member of the board, cited the lawsuit against Alessi as she announced the appointment of his replacement. "Mr. Alessi has attracted a lot of attention to the association," she said.

David Garner, named to replace Alessi on the board, said he didn't learn of his appointment until Sunday afternoon. He said he had interviewed with Yale about serving either as an additional homeowner representative on the board or a member of the finance committee.

"Mr. Alessi has attracted a lot of attention to the association." Well, excuse me. Mr. Alessi's "crime" is exposing the bones in the closets. Some people just hate it when roguish deeds are unmasked. Homeowners better take over where Alessi ended when the developer chopped him off at the knees.

Have you ever noticed the strange effect money has on greedy people? The whole jumbled mess almost parallels incest or *Murder She Wrote*. Jessica Fletcher could flush out all of the real culprits.

The plot sickens and continues

Tuesday, April 2, 1996
Reprinted with permission of *The Castle Rock Chronicle* and K.T. Kelly

OUT OF TIME
Stolen Rolex marks change in Meadows

By K.T. Kelly

Recent revelations about a past theft conviction of John Edward Hammersmith, the owner of The Meadows' former management company, make Meadows residents even more relieved they have a new company overseeing community affairs.

Such was the opinion of former Meadows Community Association Board President Carl Alessi Monday.

"It shows a problem with integrity when someone is convicted of theft," Alessi said. "The homeowners give their complete support to the new management company, Choice Management. I think Hammersmith Management Company was clearly a part of the mismanagement which occurred in The Meadows recently. Mistakes were made."

According to Arapahoe County Court records, Hammersmith was charged with felony theft in November of 1985 for allegedly stealing and selling a Rolex watch worth $2,675 while managing a Zales Corporation jewelry store in Littleton.

In a plea bargain arrangement, Hammersmith plead guilty to a lesser charge of misdemeanor theft and was ordered to pay $5,000 in restitution and serve three months of unsupervised probation.

Alessi — who recently was removed from The Meadows board by developer Yale Investments after making waves over past financial records — said he finds it interesting Hammersmith recently dropped his efforts to obtain an injunction against Alessi for statements made to local newspapers.

"I'm sure information about Hammersmith would have come out in a trial scenario," Alessi said.

Tuesday, October 29, 1996
Reprinted with permission of the *Rocky Mountain News*

Audit: Homeowners' fees were misused

Association at Meadows considers settling for less than full payment; deal would clear way for ownership transfer

By Shelley Gonzales
Rocky Mountain News Staff Writer

CASTLE ROCK — A partial audit shows that The Meadows developer improperly used tens of thousands of dollars in homeowners' fees.

Homeowners are considering settling for less than full payment from developer Yale Investments, which is in the process of divesting itself of ownership of the subdivision in northern Castle Rock.

"Sometimes you've got to fish or cut bait," said Porter Barrows, a member of the finance committee reviewing the documents. "Of course, it depends on what level of reimbursement Yale (Investments) is willing to give, but the happy bottom line is that Yale is gone forever."

The homeowner association's board will meet at 9 a. m. today at New Hope Presbyterian Church, in The Meadows, to discuss the settlement agreement. Dave

Garner, the homeowner on the developer-controlled association board, estimated the settlement figure at $28,000 to $29,000, with $20,000 more set aside in an escrow account for possible future claims.

A resolution of the matter would give Gary Vose and his Yale Investments the green light to settle a civil lawsuit that would transfer ownership of the subdivision and a ritzy housing development in Summit County to the Hawaii insurance commissioner.

The Lakewood accounting firm Bretzlauf & Husman conducted the partial audit, and the draft was given to finance committee members Saturday.

Ned Husman acknowledged that the review was "very limited" and encompassed only areas and dates directed by the community association board. Two of the three members of the board are Yale Investments employees.

Among its findings: Lavish Fourth of the July parties, which included sky divers and hot air balloons, appear to be "developer and builder promotions, rather than events for the specific and exclusive benefit of homeowners." The cost to homeowners: $14,000.

Homeowners fees also improperly paid for $4,600 worth of repair to monuments at the subdivision's entrances and for nearly $800 worth of directory signs, the audit says.

The community association, which paid $16,000 for the audit and attorney's fees, wants the developer to split those costs.

Vose spokesman Bill Kostka said Yale has made no decision on the escrow request.

The Hawaii insurance commissioner, as liquidator of the Investors Equity Life Insurance Co. of Hawaii, had accused Vose of racketeering, fraud and other criminal conduct in buying The Meadows. Vose who acknowledged late last year that he was the target of a federal investigation, bought IEL in 1991.

Vose's Yale Investments used IEL assets to buy The Meadows for $23.3 million from the Resolution Trust Corp. in March 1993 after the Lincoln Savings and Loan failure.

The Hawaii insurance commissioner at the time, Lawrence Reifurth, alleged in court documents that the purchase was "part of a scheme to convert IEL's cash assets into speculative and overvalued bonds and real estate and to divert IEL's assets to (Vose's) own use and benefit."

In doing so, IEL's financial health faltered to the point that it went broke, Reifurth wrote.

In 1994, Reifurth was granted a petition to seize and rehabilitate IEL. As the state-appointed liquidator, he filed suit in Douglas County asking to be granted Yale Investments' undeveloped Colorado properties, The Meadows and Summit County's Eagles Nest to recoup the insurance losses.

The transfer of property did not close last week as expected.

Shelley Gonzales shared some of the missing pieces to this untidy puzzle. The saga began with the Charles Keating venture when Lincoln Savings and Loan was in the avalanche of S & L failures. Gary Vose owned an insurance company in Hawaii when he purchased The Meadows and The Eagles Nest for pennies on the dollar from Resolution Trust Corporation. When Vose's insurance company went bankrupt, the Hawaii insurance commissioner allegedly accused him of illegally using the insurance company's money for his own benefit. The commissioner filed a *lis pendens* on The Meadows and The Eagles Nest to halt Vose.

Before hiring a management company, it wouldn't hurt to check with the county courts to determine whether the representative you're about to put your trust in has a clean public record of trustworthiness.

Criminal Docket Number C-86CR119, Arapahoe County, Colorado states that on July 30, 1986, John Hammersmith pled guilty and was convicted of theft. That was prior to his forming Hammersmith Management Company.

The last of the five articles

Tuesday, October 30, 1996
Reprinted with permission of the *Rocky Mountain News*

Meadows settlement reached

CASTLE ROCK — The Meadows developer Tuesday agreed to pay the community association $14,000 in exchange for releasing him from liability at the beleaguered northern Castle Rock subdivision.

The settlement clears the path for Gary Vose and his Yale Investment company to settle another lawsuit in which ownership of The Meadows and a Summit County development will be turned over to the Hawaii insurance commissioner.

The homeowners, who had sought more than $48,000, said they were willing to accept the settlement so they could move forward with a new developer.

The settlement didn't even cover the $16,000 The Meadows paid in legal fees and the cost of the partial audit! Without putting my calculator to it, that whole hodgepodge had to cost The Meadows well over $100,000! Do you wonder how much more money would have slid under the door if Carl Alessi hadn't stepped in when he did — at the time when *"Mr. Alessi attracted a lot of attention to the association"?*

Homeowners in The Meadows were devastated by overt criminal actions. Homeowners who are harassed by a contemptible HOA, trying to force pride of ownership down their chimneys, feel nonetheless devastated. They feel as though a felony had just been committed on them. Pride of ownership is tough to hang onto at that point.

▶ *PRIDE OF OWNERSHIP CANNOT BE LEGISLATED*

I've lost count of how many verses I've sung of this song. I have a feeling I'm just warming up.

Pride is an attitude not an act. Acts are the *result* of an attitude. Try legislating an attitude or anyone's pride about anything. The next time you see someone crying (crying is the act), mandate that they stop crying and immediately get happy. Don't hold your breath too long. You'll accomplish that one when turtles sprout wings and fly!

Covenants are not, and never will be, the savior of property values. Pride of ownership is. When residents respect their community, property values maintain and climb.

When a complex becomes a hard-hat zone, homeowners often rent their homes and move to more pleasant surroundings. Those who need to sell before they can afford to move often have problems caused by the community being laced with too many rental units.

Lenders will not finance, except with higher than normal rates, in communities with a high percentage of rental units. As one thing leads to another, property values of the entire complex spiral downward.

One of the reasons property values maintain and climb in our community is we encourage a degree of individuality to prevent that plastic, cookie-cutter look. There aren't two homes with the same plantings. Rather than say "no" to everything just because we have the *power* to do so, we approve projects that enhance homes and the entire complex.

I received unanimous approval from our architectural committee, the other two board members, and my immediate neighbors to add a study off the master bedroom and over the garage. This addition will be a lot more imposing than a birdhouse.

The reason this was approved was because the project will enhance my home and the community and, in my location, it won't block anyone's view or sunshine. My position as president had no effect on the outcome when the ACC and the BOD voted on my addition. I only have one vote. I don't pull any special weight. Whatever I come up with had better make common sense or I'm outvoted. That's exactly as it should be.

Quite fortunately, we needed no lender approval. We were not modifying any rule or regulation. We were using the authority of an existing regulation for the BOD and the ACC to grant or deny permission.

The result of our HOA not taking a controller's stance is that we have a very warm and inviting subdivision. We're always getting delightful comments about the welcoming and homey feeling of our community from people who visit our complex.

Know that allowing individuality is not synonymous with subscribing to trashing the community or deferring and ignoring maintenance. We constantly keep on top of needed maintenance and repairs to assure the continuing attractiveness of the complex and the ongoing rise of pride of ownership and property values.

This portion of one of our newsletters illustrates a friendly overtone to our residents.

Pleasant Valley Homeowner Association
A Covenants-protected Community
Newsletter April, 1997

Congratulations to everyone for your display of pride of ownership! Your caring is responsible for our being considered a uniquely beautiful and caring community. Those who come into our complex, for the first time, comment about the matchless warmth of Pleasant Valley.

Thank you!

Have a great summer and a fantastic 1997 !!!

• **THE ANNUAL MEETING** (Tuesday, March 11th) Each year one . . .

CHAPTER 5

So What's New? Isn't Life About Taking Responsibility?

Not all HOA woes come from hostile BODs. Homeowners have responsibility, too. Responsibility means the ability to respond. If you don't accept the responsibility for all of life's occurrences, you are doomed to assume the role of a victim. You'll be like an empty bottle set afloat upon the ocean to be pushed around by the waves of life forever.

Learn to direct your route and swim in formation. Team up with your neighbors. Respect their needs and value their rights to enjoy a comfortable living style. Take the responsibility to get involved in your community.

Respect the opinions of those who have viewpoints different from yours. Either one's standpoint may be right, wrong, or there may be a position in the middle that could be acceptable to all.

❯ GET INVOLVED!

• **GO TO THE MEETINGS.** Participate in perpetuating or effecting a radiant condition for your subdivision.

• **ACCEPT RESPONSIBILITY FOR YOUR ACTIONS.** You and the BOD both have the responsibility of maintaining your complex and pleasant surroundings for *all* residents. Even the most considerate BOD cannot accomplish that single-handedly. Remember, the BOD wasn't elected to Mission Impossible Construction and Maintenance Company.

If you're called by, or receive a letter from, the HOA or management company citing an infraction, don't behave as though you had just been ambushed. Take a deep breath, reflect on the specific issue, do what you need to do to correct the violation, and move on with your life. If you believe the citation to be frivolous or unjust, request a meeting with the HOA to present your side. *Never* withhold your dues to use as a hammer over the BOD's head. That invites a lien on your property and will weaken your case if you go to court.

The usual chain of events: The resident doesn't deliberately breach a rule or regulation. It's an innocent oversight. He is embarrassed when the misdemeanor is brought to his attention. Too often, the reaction to any embarrassment is quickly to identify someone else to blame. The resident doesn't have to look too far. The BOD, the ACC, and the management company are standing in line eagerly awaiting to see who will be awarded the celebrated "crown of blame."

"Psychiatry enables us to correct our faults by confessing our parents' shortcomings."

— Lawrence J. Peter

An HOA *doesn't* enable us to correct our faults by confessing another's shortcomings.

Residents prefer never to receive that phone call or letter. The BOD of Compassionate Townhomes prefers never to find it necessary to make one infraction phone call or to send one violation letter. The BOD would opt for every resident to be aware enough that no resident would ever transgress. There would be fewer issues that would become problems.

● **COOPERATE** with the BOD or management company when they make requests such as asking for the name and address of your mortgage company, your current phone number(s), or permission to publish your home phone number in the community directory. **RESPOND.**

Don't just sit back and expect your best interests to be taken care of by "George or Sally board members" without your taking at least a modicum of personal interest and responsibility. Neither George nor Sally volunteered to be the homeowners' secretary, mother, father, nor baby-sitter. They aren't in place as a whipping post either just waiting for a resident to hit them with complaints about a neighbor — complaints that homeowners should handle themselves.

Board members are not community flunkies

> Ron was president of Pleasant Valley Townhomes HOA. Ann, a homeowner, called him complaining that she had called the snow removal service to plow her driveway that day and they didn't do it. Snow removal from driveways is not included in the HOA fee. It's the homeowners' personal responsibility to contract with a company of their choice and pay for that service.
>
> Ron took the position of the neighborhood keeper. He called the company and learned that Ann had called too late. The crew had already left by the time she left a message on their recorder. They didn't know she wanted her driveway cleared.
>
> He shoveled Ann's driveway!

Board members are not a magic wand to *fix it all*. Ron volunteered as a personal secretary and maintenance man. Those positions are not in a board member's job description. Chances are that Ann still wasn't happy. By his claiming her responsibility as his, he set himself up to become a "culprit" board member — guilty by association of not getting Ann's job done right.

A *preferable scenario*

Ron could have simply said, "Ann, the best way to resolve this is for *you* to call the snow removal company and find out what happened." Feeling neighborly, Ron could have offered his services by saying, "Ann, if there's any problem, as a neighbor, not as president, I'll gladly come shovel your driveway to ease your predicament." That would have qualified him for the designation as a good neighbor rather than as a flunky president.

Ron, an extremely caring person, resigned as president after only six months. He created much of his own stress. He compounded situations by permitting himself to be browbeaten.

After I became president, Ann tried a similar scenario with me. She informed me that the trash company hadn't picked up her trash that day. Understanding that I had not volunteered as a community secretary, I said, "I've had that happen to me. If you call the trash company they'll send a truck out to pick up your trash today."

It has been said that 20 percent of a sales force generates 80 percent of the total sales. It's called the 80/20 rule and it applies to all walks of life. It runs the whole gamut of professions: painters, doctors, and candlestick makers. If you don't know the person you're hiring you run only a 20 percent chance of finding one who is highly skilled and caring. Too often here is how that rule works in communities: 20 percent of the residents accomplish the tasks, 80 percent coast and complain. Board members and management companies have the same 80/20 ratio regarding their abilities and attitudes, too. Hopefully, the luck of the draw will give you a BOD and a management company that are in the 20 percent group.

Be a homeowner in the 20 percent group. Support your community. Keep your property and your neighborhood tidy and in good repair. If you're prudent with your responsibilities, you'll never get a call or a letter that points out an oversight. If you are remiss and are cited for a blunder, you don't merit the liberty to complain about the BOD. Ideally, you'll apologize for your mistake and express your regrets of making the citation necessary. Good BODs and management companies derive absolutely no pleasure from issuing mandates.

If, however, you receive an undeserved "you're negligent" letter, call the letter-senders and inform them they have been negligent in their duty to check the validity of the facts before placing blame and taking action.

If you and your HOA seem to be at an impasse, request a meeting with them. The primary goal of a good BOD is to protect a pleasant lifestyle for the residents. GET INVOLVED. Help your BOD attain that goal.

❯ IT'S ABOUT HOA FEES

Too often the attitude of living in a community with an HOA is that the HOA is supposed to take care of everything with the HOA fees. I've heard residents make such statements such as "What? Pull that weed?" "Pound a couple of nails in that fence?" "Pick up that piece of paper?" "Well, get real. That's why I pay an association fee. That's the HOA's responsibility. Why should I perform a task that I've already paid to have done?"

That thought process makes about as much sense as leaving the motor running because you have a full tank of gas or opening your windows and turning your heat up because your utilities are included in your monthly HOA fee. So why should you care? You will care when you run out of gas or when your HOA fee climbs. Will you take any responsibility for the fee escalating or will you just curse the BOD?

HOA fees seldom cover everything

The HOA fees shouldn't cover every teensy, nit-picky thing. Take time to know what is and what is not covered in your fee.

Statements like, "Well, I don't see why I have to pay for *that*. The HOA should pay for *that*." *That* sounds as though the homeowner thinks the HOA is a separate entity. It isn't. HOAs don't get their money from government grants or Santa Claus, like manna from heaven.

The HOA collects its money from your pocket and the pockets of all the other homeowners. Remember HOA stands for Homeowner Association. You are an Owner within and a member of the Association. It should be *Homeowners'* Association.

The HOA has monthly commitments for such items as *your* lawn care, *your* water and sewer, *your* insurance, *your* trash removal, and *your* community's maintenance and improvements. Then there are always unexpected obligations that pop up.

Reaping all those *"benefits"* that you so richly deserve by virtue of paying your HOA dues can be expensive. Everything is paid for with *your* funds. When the HOA adds *"it"* (whatever *"it"* is) to their list of financial obligations, you run the risk of your fees being raised or causing a special assessment because the HOA paid for *"it."* Get it?

Same song, second verse. When HOA funds get anemic, the BOD has to take more of your money. Take responsibility to help conserve your HOA's bankroll. That bankroll contains your greenbacks. Perform some community chores instead of expecting the HOA to pay for *all* the deeds to be done.

The majority of homeowners in our complex voted to have the homeowners retain the responsibility for some of the exterior maintenance such as fences, driveways, gutters, trees, shrubs, flowers, and weeding on each homeowner's property.

Our dues are $90 a month. Approximately $65 per unit pays our monthly obligations. The remaining funds go into the reserve. We do not raise fees unless we see reserves are waning to a level that would not allow anticipated projects such as painting and street repairs to be completed. Another instance would be if our monthly bills are increasing to the point that we're eating into the amount that should be going toward reserves.

We have no amenities other than a small amount of common area. Our HOA fees pay for water (inside and outside), building insurance, trash removal, mowing front lawns, exterior painting, roof repair, street repair (we have private streets), street snow removal, electricity for street lights, management company fees, and maintenance of the common areas.

‣ SPEAKING OF MONEY

Judy Weinstein, a resident in an exquisite condo unit and owner of several other CCC homes in Colorado, said "Residents don't understand they have to become a part of it. They think they're living in vacation land. We had to build a reserve fund. Many homeowners don't even know what a reserve fund is. Most of the residents talk about the HOA funds as if they were someone else's money. They don't realize it's their money!"

Avoid any incidents of *disappearing dollars*. Make sure the HOA's money is being handled by a responsible, bonded individual or company. If you feel something is askew with the finances, make arrangements to examine the books and look at current bank statements. If you have 100 homes in your community, then one 100th of that money is yours. You put it there. Take the responsibility to keep a discerning eye on it.

BOARDROOM DISCUSSION
❖ Published by the LAW FIRM OF WINZENBURG, LEFF, PURVIS AND PAYNE, LLP ❖
• 1660 Lincoln Street, #1750 • Denver, Colorado 80264 • 303-863-1870

Reprinted with the permission of *Common Ground* ©*1991* Community Associations Institute

April 1995

EMBEZZLEMENT

A RECENT ARTICLE IN *Common Ground*, discussing a California Association embezzlement, reminds us that all Associations must keep in mind that temptation can be too much for an occasional treasurer or bookkeeper who deals with money.

<u>Legal Tip</u>: *Boards have a duty to institute procedures to prevent embezzlement.*
For more information on *checks and balances*, call Kami at 303-863-1870.

Trust in God, but keep rowing to shore. It would behoove you to make certain proper procedures are solidly set into place. Ascertain that there is sufficient money in reserve for upcoming painting and other known and unexpected needed repairs and maintenance. Check to see that money is added every month to maintain a reserve fund large enough, hopefully, to negate the necessity of special assessments being levied.

It's wiser to raise monthly dues to build reserves. Paying a little more each month is less financially brain damaging than coming up with $500, $1,000, or more in one chunk for a special assessment.

Far too frequently, **DEFERRED maintenance** (negligence) is chosen when reserves are thin or nonexistent. That practice *never* solves money problems. It compounds them. When there is absolutely no choice other than to make needed repairs, it costs considerably more for extensive work than it would have cost with timely, preventive maintenance. Ten dollars of prevention could avoid a thousand dollars of cure.

With 51 homes in 14 buildings, we practice a rotation plan of painting one-fourth of the homes each year. After a couple rotations have been completed, we may possibly have a year or two before we have to start the next painting rotation. That will help our reserves grow.

Another complex (between 250 and 300 homes in some 70 to 75 buildings) has approximately half the dollar amount in reserves as we do! Those homes are larger and in a higher price range than ours. Their BOD's solution to strengthen their reserve fund was to *suspend painting the five buildings that had been scheduled for the rotation painting until the following year.* Do you see the blunder in that scenario? If they painted five buildings a year it will take 14 years to complete one painting rotation. Talk about property values dropping. Some buildings are likely to be falling on the ground by then. In those 14 years other disasters are bound to occur that will need immediate attention and preempt the painting again. The reserve fund is destined to be chronically anemic. Deferred maintenance will increase the length of time required to complete the painting. All the while the BOD and the ACC will make their "Solomon" decisions that could put the HOA into bankruptcy. Can't you just hear them? "Oops, sorry homeowners, guess we goofed. You'll just have to pay a mammoth special assessment or sell, if you can. We'll keep trying to work things out." Remember the 80/20 rule? I would say that BOD is definitely in the weak 80 percent group. Homeowners had better look for a new BOD in the 20 percent group.

An elderly gentleman in that same community called me the Wednesday before Thanksgiving to share an incident. He received a call from a friend in the community who needed help. He told me that he had one slippery time walking to his friend's home. The sidewalks were covered with ice and snow. The maintenance man told him the association was building their capital reserve fund so they weren't going to spend money to remove the ice and snow.

That incident resembles saving money by not getting needed repairs made on the brakes of your car. Imagine how much their funds could be depleted if someone fell and injured himself.

That BOD seems to get worse and worse. Each stupid idea they come up with outshines the last stupid idea. Those residents should quickly replace that simulated BOD with authentic humans who comprehend that two and two don't make six.

Read the projected budgets and the statements of actual expenditures

Make certain the HOA's money is being spent only on essential items. Register a complaint if you notice something like the board members' buying fake owls, at $125 to $300 a pop, only for their own homes to deter noisy woodpeckers tapping on their chimneys. That is inconsistent and capricious spending. You may think that is a ridiculous illustration. It actually happened in my complex with a previous BOD.

Volunteer isn't a four-letter, obscene word

Call the BOD. Tell them you would like to help. Ask what committees you could serve on or what duties you could perform. When you call to make this gesture, unquestionably you'll hear a thud and then no sounds at all. Just wait a few minutes until that board member wakes up from the fainting spell.

A happy community that uses homeowners dollars wisely . . .

Judy Lopez, president of Columbine Knolls for 17 years, evaluated the covenants and, with the help of an attorney, modified the Rules & Regs and drew up a policy plan. Columbine Knolls, with dues of only $15 a year, now . . .
- enforces covenants with common sense to solve important problems,
- issues a community directory,
- has an annual cleanup day,
- has an annual beautification day,
- has an Easter egg hunt,
- has an annual community garage sale, and
- keeps the entrances of the community maintained.

Judy attributes the mailing piece (reprinted on the next page) as a big reason that 50 percent of the homeowners pay Columbine Knolls' voluntary dues. They include a self-addressed envelope. The form is printed in soft blue ink (a grayed blue). It's a very attractive, non-threatening mailing piece.

Columbine Knolls Homeowner Association
P.O. Box 620095 Littleton, CO 80162

Dear Resident: **December**

It's time to join or renew your membership in the Columbine Knolls Homeowner Association. The annual dues are still only **$15** for the entire family!

The following programs and activities are supported by your annual dues: volunteer CKHA Board, support of protective covenants, representatives at Jeffco hearings and COHOPE, major entrances and perimeter maintenance, Annual Clean-Up Day, Annual Garage Sale Days, Children's Easter Egg Hunt and Halloween Party, and the annual membership directory.

Please send in your **$15** membership dues today!

□ YES Count me in!! I/we are interested in helping out with the following activities this coming year.

	Check		Check
Easter Egg Hunt		Serve on CKHA Board	
Annual Clean-Up Day		Attend Jeffco Hearings	
Annual Garage Sale Days		Membership Directory	
Halloween Party		Beautification Projects	

Your SUPPORT is essential to our neighborhood's high standards!

Please print the following information **EXACTLY** as you wish it to appear in the annual directory and return with your **$15** membership dues by January 15th.

_____

Name(s)

_____   _____

Street Address   Phone

It's philosophical time again.

If you don't get involved with life, life will involve you.

"We must learn to live together as brothers or perish together as fools."
— Martin Luther King, Jr., speech in St. Louis, March 22, 1964

We must learn to live together as neighbors or suffer together as fools.

Required Reading Isn't Enough

❯ *REQUIRED READING — THE DOCUMENTS*

"I wonder what the true meanings of the Docs really are." That thought hardly seems important enough to keep one awake at night. I've never found a better cure for insomnia than reading Docs. However, it *is* necessary to know what rules are specifically addressed.

It is *no less* necessary to feel the pulse of those in charge. Learn *everything* possible about the enforcers of the rules.

It's conceivable that the Docs are civilized and friendly. It's also conceivable that those in charge of enforcement are not. Whether you're an intended newcomer or you planted your roots there years ago, knowing the profile of who's in charge of enforcing the rules of the community is of utmost importance.

❯ *KNOW WHO'S IN CHARGE — THE ENFORCERS*

- **It's likely that the enforcers are the board of directors.**
  - Who are they?
  - What expertise do they have?
  - Are they concerned with the happiness and good for the majority of homeowners?
  - Do they have private agendas that may supersede and set aside decisions that would promote a contented, neighborly community?
  - Are decisions made by a majority vote of the BOD or do only one or two members make unilateral and arbitrary decisions?
  - What is their tolerance level? Are they sue-happy or do they mediate with residents?
  - Do they make benevolent or belligerent interpretations of the rules?
  - Do they creatively fabricate rules? Do they spend their recreational time embellishing the Decs by adding more and more antagonistic rules to the Regs?
  - Do they understand and follow all procedures correctly?
  - Or, do they take action without following the proper procedures specified in the Docs and by law?
  - How long does each member serve?
- **What if the enforcers are the architectural control committee?**
  - The above questions apply equally as well to the architectural committee.

- Usually the ACC is appointed by the BOD.
- If the ACC is hostile, the ACC can be un-appointed by the BOD.
- If the BOD refuses to un-appoint a hostile ACC, remove the BOD (***How to organize your coup d'état*** is coming up later in this chapter). Then appoint a new ACC.

- **What if the enforcers are the management company?**
  - That happens, but it is not acceptable. (More in chapter 7, ***Indeed, what is in a name?***)

Walt Bateman, a homeowner in California, made certain the enforcers were following the proper procedures. He shared this, "After serving on a small BOD for a couple of years in a small association, I decided to see if the meetings were conducted properly and if the governing documents were being followed appropriately.

"I made a table consisting of five columns. I put the topics in the first column, with one row for each topic. The next three columns were for each of the governing documents — the Articles, By-laws, and CC&R's. I put my comments and questions in the fifth column. Most topics were only mentioned in one document. Occasionally a topic was mentioned in two — usually the CC&R's and By-laws.

"A time consuming process, but a useful strategy to make sure the BOD is following correct procedures. It is very helpful at BOD meetings when no one really knows the answer. I achieved my real purpose. I am now able to challenge the methods of doing business with these immediate, verbatim readings of what our governing documents actually say about various topics rather than someone's vague recollection of what they think it is supposed to be.

"All I have to do is look up the topic heading in the first column and read across the row to see what is stated in each document about that topic. I recommend this to all boards, but maybe hire someone to do it." A consideration might be to put the page number of the document in the column rather than reprinting what each document states.

"It turned out that our method of doing business was quite different from what is stated in our documents. So different that, after 25 years of existence, we are now voting on amendments to change our documents to bring them into line with what the members have been doing and want to do."

▶ *IF YOU'RE CONSIDERING A MOVE TO A COVENANTS-CONTROLLED "DREAMLAND"* . . .

- Is the complex in good repair with no apparent deferred maintenance?
- Do homeowners have the opportunity to speak at regular board meetings? If so, must they first get on the agenda?
- Check the thickness of the Docs, the entire set of governing papers. Review the contents as soon as possible.

If the document that runs with the property forever as recorded restrictions on the deed is particularly unfriendly, check for the modification provision. Remember the Decs can only be modified within the provisions set forth in the Decs. 'Tis a bit of a vicious circle — a vicious circle that demands your most prudent scrutiny. (A sample modification provision is on page 86.)

There's a 3,000-unit complex in Denver, built in the 1960s and 1970s, with absolutely *no provision* for ever modifying one rule. Jim Winzenburg, the attorney, told me the only hope for that complex to ever modernize their Decs would be to get practically all the lenders and homeowners to vote for specific changes. The apathetic, status-quo syndrome would preclude such a major event.

• If the Docs appear satisfactory, take the next steps:

• Attend a homeowners' meeting, if at all possible. The atmosphere of a meeting can be notably revealing. Meetings can be anywhere from well attended to virtually un-attended. They can be from congenial, to screaming, to no one speaks except the enforcers.

• Even if you attend a meeting, take time to knock on some doors. Ask residents how they feel about the community and the operation of their association. If they had it to do over, would they buy a home there? Would they make a recommendation to their very best, bosom-buddy-friend to buy a home there? Ask about the enforcers. Ask the questions listed on page 83. Also ask the questions in chapter 2, *The Dream Comes True*.

At some point in your interviews it would be wise to ask homeowners if they, their spouse, or a friend happens to be on the board. If they have less than an arm's length association with the board, their opinions might be slightly tainted. Though that likelihood is present, that isn't sandblasted in marble. This is in marble: a ballistic board member will never disclose the hostilities of the community. They will give a false proverbial "snug as a bug in a rug" report.

Sometimes the "Don Quixotes" of the BOD are consistently outvoted by a clan of "Little Napoleons." "Don Quixotes" try to encourage decisions that will better the community. Many times they tilt their swords at overpowering windmills. If it's one of the "Little Napoleons" you're speaking with, rather than a "Don Quixote," it's guaranteed you'll receive a counterfeit picture of the community's comfort level.

• As you look around the complex, there are usually obvious clues even before you start your polling process. Does the community have a welcoming feeling? Is there some individuality allowed or, does it look as if someone had just taken a cookie cutter and stamped everything out to resemble a consistent barracks motif? Is everything painted the same dull, depressing shade of brown or maybe gray, or . . . ? Are there only rocks or three evergreen bushes and five white petunias placed precisely in the same design in front of every home? Is not one home sporting six or seven white petunias, one purple petunia, let alone a yellow marigold, or . . . a rose bush? I apologize for that. I didn't intend to refer to anything as obscene as a non-conforming rose bush.

Personally, I wouldn't spend my time even polling *one* resident in that type of community. That's my preference. Perhaps you prefer knowing how many white petunias will be on the spring scene, *knowing* exactly what to expect and when to expect it. Maybe you would feel threatened in a community where some individuality is accepted. That's fine. Match the community to your preferences. If you get the right answers when you poll the residents and if the home is in your price range, buy it. If you're a "five-white-petunia person" please don't locate in an "open to a rose bush community." You'll either be miserable or you'll get on the board and make everyone else miserable.

Look for the provision to modify the Decs

Article XI gives the requirements for first mortgagees' approval for modification of the

Decs. Article XII is the general provisions for modification. These are taken from a set of Decs that are much friendlier than most. You'll see what I mean when you read the modification provision in the Decs of . . . let's just name them Carolina Condos in chapter 11.

Article XI is printed in total to give you the *option* of reading the entire set of "interesting" regulations. Only the portion of Article XII that is relevant to modification is reproduced. Unless you enjoy pain, only read the ***bold, italicized sentences*** of both articles. My comments are in [ ] brackets.

ARTICLE XI
FIRST MORTGAGEES

Section 1. <u>Member and First Mortgagee Approval</u>. ***Subject to Article XII, Section 7 (b) of this Declaration, but notwithstanding any other provisions of this Declaration to the contrary, the Association shall not:*** [That is a C.Y.A. (cover your anatomy) phrase in case the attorney pulled a restriction off the "rack" that might be contrary and might not work.]

(a) ***unless it has obtained the prior written consent of at least sixty-seven percent (67%) of each class of Members and sixty-seven percent (67%) of First Mortgagees (based upon one vote for each First Mortgage owned):***

(1) by act or omission, change, waive, or abandon any scheme of architectural control, or enforcement thereon or Common Area;

(2) fail to maintain full current replacement cost fire and extended insurance coverage on the Common area;

(3) use hazard insurance proceeds for Common Area property losses for purposes other than to repair, replace, or reconstruct such property;

(4) by act or omission, seek to abandon, partition, subdivide, encumber, sell, or transfer any common property owned, directly or indirectly, by the Association for the benefit of the Owners (excluding the granting of permits, licenses and easements for public utilities, roads, or other purposes reasonably necessary or useful for the proper maintenance or operation of the Properties or the Association);

(5) change the method of determining the obligations, assessments, dues, or other charges which may be levied against an Owner; or

(6) terminate the legal status or the Properties as a planned unit development, provided that this section (6) shall not apply to amendments to this Declaration, the Articles of Incorporation, or Bylaws of the Association made as a result of destruction, damage or condemnation of the Properties or improvements thereon; provided, however, that any distribution made as a result of said termination shall be accomplished on a reasonable and equitable basis. [Is that legalese at its finest, or what?]

(b) ***unless it has obtained the prior written consent of at least sixty-seven percent (67%) of each class of Members, and fifty-one percent (51%) of the First Mortgagees (based upon one vote for each First Mortgage owned), add or amend any material provisions of this Declaration, the Articles of Incorporation or Bylaws of the Association*** which establish, provide for, govern or regulate any of the following, provided that such additions or amendments shall not be considered material if they are for the purpose of correcting technical errors or for clarification only:

(1) voting rights;

(2) assessments, assessment liens or subordination of such liens;

(3) reserves for maintenance, repair, and replacement of those

elements of the Common Area which must be maintained, repaired or replaced on a periodic basis;

(4) responsibility for maintenance and repair of any portion of the Properties;

(5) rights to use of the Common Area;

(6) boundaries of any Lot;

(7) convertibility of Lots into Common Area or of Common Area into Lots;

(8) expansion or contraction of the Properties or the addition, annexation or withdrawal of property to or from the Properties;

(9) insurance, including but not limited to fidelity bonds;

(10) leasing of Lots or dwellings constructed thereon;

(11) imposition of any restriction on the right of any Owner to sell or transfer his Lot;

(12) any decision by the Association to assume self-management of the Association, when professional management has previously been a guarantor of a First Mortgage;

(13) any restoration or repair of the Properties after a partial condemnation or damage due to an insurable hazard, other than substantially in accordance with this Declaration, the Articles of Incorporation and Bylaws of the Association;

(14) any action to terminate the legal status of the Properties after substantial destruction or condemnation; or

(15) *any provisions which are for the express benefit of First Mortgagees, or insurers or guarantors of First Mortgages.* [That's a wide open, undefined statement. Would it include the need of their approval to modify the no-clotheslines rule?]

ARTICLE XII
GENERAL PROVISIONS

Section 7. Duration, Revocation, and Amendment.

(a) *Each and every provision of this Declaration shall run with and bind the land for a term of twenty (20) years from the date of recording of this Declaration, after which time this Declaration shall be automatically extended for successive periods of ten (10) years each.*

Except as provided in Article XI hereof, this Declaration may be amended during the first twenty (20) year period, and during subsequent extensions thereof, *by any instrument approved in writing by not less than fifty-one percent (51%) of the Members of each class [while the developer is still building he is one class, usually class B, and the homeowners are another class, usually class A].* Such amendment shall be effective when duly recorded in the County of Jefferson, Colorado.

(b) Notwithstanding anything to the contrary contained in this Declaration: [There's the C.Y.A. again.]

(c) To be effective, all amendments to or revocation or termination of this Declaration must be recorded in the office of the Clerk and Recorder of the County of Jefferson, Colorado, and must contain evidence of the required approval thereof.

(d) *One method of satisfying the requirements of Subsection (c) of this Section 7 shall be the recordation of a Certificate of the Secretary of the Association certifying that Owners recording the requisite percentage of the Lots, and that the requisite percentage of First Mortgagees, if any, have given notarized written consent to the Amendment. The Secretary must*

As previously stated, those provisions for modification are much friendlier than most. Some Decs stipulate that there can be *no* modifications for a specified period of time, as long as 20 years. There is usually only a brief window of time for any modifications to be made. After that, a time period starts ticking again. One complex with a 20-year stipulation has to have an affirmative vote of 90 percent of their 1,500 homeowners to affect any changes. Then successive ten-year periods are set into place. The unrealistic 90 percent negates updating any of the rules that are recorded as restrictions on the properties.

Are we having fun yet? Reading Docs is not my idea of a cheerful way to spend a day. My reaction usually is, what on earth did I just read? When the wording is unclear, as it usually is, and the subject is critical, it's frequently essential to get an opinion from an attorney. Depending on which attorney you hire, the interpretation will vary both in exact meaning and in clarity.

A few years ago I went to a high powered real estate attorney with a personal real estate question. I knew less when I left his office than when I entered it.

Understanding pat-head, rub-stomach Docs can be an exercise in futility. Have a merry time reading them. Then check out the disposition of the border patrol.

If the community is brand new the border patrol is probably on temporary duty. The developer/builder will probably be in charge. You won't know *who* will be "on board" and their disposition until after the developer's tour of duty ceases.

Ancient Chinese proverb: "Prediction is very difficult, especially when it concerns the future."

If the new development's Docs are expansive with a preponderance of antiquated rules, smile and relay to the builder you'll consider buying one of his homes when he changes the Docs to allow a congenial lifestyle that corresponds with today's world. You might also suggest he offer a svelte set of Docs that doesn't necessitate a panel of attorneys to decipher. And, "Oh yes, Mr. Builder, make certain there are only vital restrictions in the Decs with sufficient latitude for homeowners to modify the rules. As the world changes, homeowners like to participate."

Thoroughly investigate before you buy

Nolan Winsett, a retired real estate broker and appraiser, said, "There's a scourge sweeping the Denver metroplex. It's homeowner associations." Nolan and his wife, Linda, live in a large townhome community in Denver (over 200 homes on 20 acres, plus another 700 homes on 75 acres butting against an interstate highway).

Nolan said, "When the developer started building the complex in 1965, the property was in Aurora [a city adjacent to Denver]. Aurora insisted the water system be installed to code.

"So the developer annexed the land to Denver. Denver proceeded to look the other direction as the developer connected less expensive, 'creative' plumbing fixtures." Nolan said, "There's a variance of pipes anywhere from four to eight inches. The residents have been constantly plagued with leaking and breaking pipes. Denver allowed the substandard materials and now they maintain a hands-off position.

"There's a plethora of 'professional' management companies. Many who surfaced in the late 1980s have filed bankruptcy, after absconding with millions of dollars of the homeowners' money, leaving the associations high and dry. The most dangerous, however, is the association run by the homeowners themselves. A design that can divide, polarize, and destroy the very core of community harmony in condominium, townhouse, patio homes, cluster homes, and single-family homes.

"It's no secret that there are homeowner associations that deny homeowners the right to fly the American flag, put silk flowers on their windowsills, have tiny Lucite Christmas light holders on the outside of their home, or even hold garage sales. Others have forced homeowners to

- cut down their trees over a certain height and
- pay unreasonable costs per page to obtain copies of financial statements, audits, minutes, or other financial data the homeowner has a right to by virtue of homeownership and payment of all fees and dues to the association."

Nolan said, "My knowledge of the genocide of mature trees is firsthand. We were in a dark era of being overpowered by an imperialistic board, diametrically opposed to the homeowners' wishes. In a witless explosion of the board's power they chopped approximately 40 beautiful maple, locust, and evergreen trees to the ground. They went through our community like a plague. To add insult to the injury, they sneered and laughed at the homeowners as they proceeded to destroy the ecology of our complex, at the cost of neighborhood harmony. We look like a barren wasteland. Four of the five perpetrators of the crime have now moved and we are in the process of replanting about 20 trees at a cost of around $7,000. I probably won't live long enough to see them to the maturity of those that were destroyed.

"Reasons for being on the board of directors of an association can be classified as follows:

- *Greedy, self-serving glory seekers* — they take the opportunity to institute rules to satisfy their own desires with no concern for the community as a whole, along with nepotism;
- *Power-hungry egomaniacs* — they are characterized by imperialistic designs and the establishment of minor fiefdoms with homeowners acting as serfs;
- *The honest-to-God individual who wants to serve the community* — he is pure of heart, a peacemaker who wants to accomplish goals to benefit the association of owners.

"Needless to say, there are more of the first two than of the last.

"In financial terms, homeowner associations have access to multi-million-dollar budgets to maintain their imperial kingdoms. Is there any control over this money? Not always, as many homeowners in one association found out when the maintenance manager purchased a competing development's property for cash. No charges of embezzlement were ever filed because of possible bad publicity. [Vanity is a foolish reason for allowing such a travesty of justice. A good embarrassment can be very cleansing.]

"Is there any control over the board of directors of a homeowner association? No. The board of directors can use the homeowners' money to hire large law firms to represent the board. This ties homeowners up in knots, while raping their wallets. There are no county or state offices that protect a homeowner from abuses by the pretenders to the throne (the board of directors) of homeowner associations and there is no protection from the ill-treatment by corrupt architectural committees or greedy management companies.

"What about the democratic icons of the election or recall movements? The board of directors or management company who controls the proxy votes of uninvolved homeowners and absentee landlords controls the outcome. Most homeowners in a complex are either retired and easily intimidated or they work full time and do not have the strength to put up with a homeowners' meeting. Most homeowner associations' elections would put Tammany Hall to shame. Those who do stand up for their rights as homeowners may be subjected to ridicule, vandalism, terrorism, and are often labeled as troublemakers.

"So where does this leave the owner of a home involved with a homeowner association? *Out in the cold looking in!* The owner can move if he or she has the money and the association approves of the sale [some associations still cling to archaic "First Right of Refusal" on sales], hire a good lawyer to defend his or her rights, or put up with ignorant, greedy, imperialistic egomaniacs. Too often residents merely join the crowd of thousands of dissatisfied homeowners and do nothing [a double brand of shame]. It is sad but true that when a development has a reputation of tyranny, property values plummet.

"One important reason a board of directors fails is that the board is in the strait jacket of "Robert's Rules of Order." If boards would untie their hands and engage 'Complex Rules of Common Sense and Caring,' there would be a new, refreshing reputation about communities controlled by covenants. That would be the beginning of truly desirable neighborhoods in which to live.

"The moral of the story is: Don't buy a home in *any* community controlled by covenants unless you have thoroughly investigated the property, accepted the conditions of living in such a development, are comfortable with those in charge of enforcing the conditions and handling the finances, and understand that the board can change."

Take heed where your future may be shoving you. Complex issues are hardly a stroll through an amusement park. Do make certain you are comfortable with those in charge of enforcing the conditions and handling the finances. Too often problems arise because the BOD is experimenting with fuzzy logic.

Be careful of complexes that were built pre-1980s.

Nolan Winsett said, "From experience, I know older units have a lot of things that can keep you awake at night."

Nolan's suggested list of precautions:

• Energy efficiency was not an issue and building codes have changed since then. Insulation is unlikely to be sufficient and the windows will probably be single pane, with casements of aluminum or steel. All this is energy-expensive. Call the utilities company. They will give you the amount of recent (12 months) gas and electric bills for that unit.

• Replacing windows to efficient double pane will require retrofitting. Don't rush. Take your time. Investigate several window companies. Take six months to explore the window industry. Be certain you have located the best windows and a company that will perform well at retrofitting.

• If you have a crawl space, it should be insulated to keep your floors warm and reduce further loss of heat.

- Wiring may be aluminum (a fire hazard) and there may be an insufficient number of electrical outlets. [Nolan added 40 electrical outlets to his 1965 townhome just to accommodate normal needs.]
- Plumbing could be questionable. It could be corroded and it could be lead (a health hazard).
- The dryer vent could be stuffed with lint (a fire hazard).
- Attic and home ventilation may be inadequate or nonexistent (a comfort irritant).
- When ancient vent fans need replacement, drywall work is normally required because fans are smaller now.
- There may be an inadequate or nonexistent fire wall between the units in the attic (a huge fire hazard).
- The foundation should be tarred below ground level to make it waterproof.
- If the sprinkler systems do not have the proper prevention for back-flow, residents are in jeopardy of drinking contaminated water.

Nolan's list of precautions came from his being in real estate, being an appraiser, and his experience of living in an older CCC. Newer homes should have a thorough professional inspection too. Don't hire your friend in construction or Uncle Joe. This is no time to scrimp on cost. The difference in price between a so-so and a good inspection is about $100.

- Even if the inspector was referred to you by a qualified person, ask the inspector
  - What components do you inspect?
  - How long have you been in the business?
  - What type of written report do you give?

The inspector should give a comprehensive, customized report of ten or more pages. A little one or two-page check list is not sufficient. It's preferable to hire an inspector who is licensed, is a member of ASHI (American Society of Home Inspectors), and who has Errors and Omissions insurance.

- A good inspector spends one to two hours or more and checks, among other things
  - every appliance that is included in the purchase of the home,
  - the water heater,
  - the furnace,
  - the insulation,
  - the electrical box,
  - every electrical outlet,
  - the plumbing, and
  - the stability of the walls behind the bathtub, shower, etc.

- If you suspect possible structural problems, hire a structural engineer. Ask him if he also inspects all the other important aspects. Some structural engineers do and some don't. Be prepared. Don't scramble around at the last minute. Find a good inspector *before you find the home you want to buy*. Ask your real estate agent for a list of qualified inspectors.

Further words of caution

Matthew Gargan and his wife bought a condo close to Glenwood Springs, Colorado as a getaway place in the mountains. Of the 14 units, 11 were owner-occupied.

They spent a considerable amount of time and money updating and remodeling their condo.

Before Matthew purchased he thought he had thoroughly investigated every detail with his methodical check-it-out list. Then the proverbial "stuff" kissed the fan. *The complex was not legally registered with the state. The registration had been filed, but the developer had taken a name that was already used! When he discovered that he couldn't use the name he just stopped the filing!* The nonprofit corporate standing was not established.

The manager kept the *un-audited books* and it was discovered that checks, signed by the manager, were written to the manager's wife!

The number of owner-occupied units dwindled to three. Those who wanted to sell were duty bound to disclose to buyers the lack of legal registration with the state. That and the high percentage of rental units made the condos virtually un-salable.

Eventually, the plight did get straightened out. The complex is now in good standing with the state. The area experienced a burst of growth and Matthew and his wife were later able to sell their little getaway place in the mountains. Nine of the homes are now owner-occupied.

Matthew suggests, "Before buying go one step beyond the normal check-it-out list and contact the Secretary of State to make certain the association is in good standing."

The cliché, "Look before you leap," is very appropriate when purchasing a home in a CCC. So, do investigate, investigate, and investigate before you buy.

▶ *IF YOU HAPPEN TO GET ROMANCED INTO A SUB-HAPPY COMMUNITY . . .*

. . . and your backbone is straight up at a full 90 degrees, you have five choices:

1) Bite your tongue.

2) Grit your teeth.

3) Cry in your pillow.

4) Move. (Keep the motor running and make a dash for the border.)

5) Consider a remove-the-"Hitlers"-from-the-board coup d'état.

As homeowners get beaten down and bludgeoned by a Gestapo-like association, without fail, adversity and screaming matches prevail at association meetings. Attendance either dwindles, to avoid the unpleasant screaming or attendance increases, as residents come out in swarms to make sure their screams of pain are heard.

The "Gestapo" wants attendance to dwindle. They plan to diminish and conquer. If you allow yourself to be intimidated into staying away from the meetings to avoid the unpleasantness, you will be instrumental in strengthening the dictatorship.

Support your neighbor if he has a legitimate HOA dilemma. Especially support him if enforcement of the rules is performed in an arbitrary and capricious fashion. If intimidation causes you to acquiesce, if you turn your back on your neighbor out of fear of reprisal from the enforcers, you place your entire community in jeopardy of acquiring a rotten reputation. Guess what that does to property values.

If you or a neighbor is unhappy with heavy-handed enforcement and arbitrary interpretations of the rules, it is more than likely that the majority of residents is equally unhappy. Usually, each discontented resident feels like the Lone Ranger. But, when a tally is taken, invariably it is discovered that the bulk of the residents has been putting up with pure misery for the likes of a *small* minority. There's a gigantic flaw in that picture. Get ready. Get set. *Go for it!* Be a great spirit and remove the mediocre enforcers.

"Great spirits have always encountered violent opposition from mediocre minds."
— Albert Einstein

▶ *HOW TO ORGANIZE YOUR COUP D'ÉTAT*

Once you've decided that a coup d'état of the board is your CCC's best route, carefully make your plans and follow through with them. This is no time for shortcuts. If it's the ACC that is causing the pain, you'll still have to remove the board and then appoint a new ACC.

- **Take a poll.** Determine if your misery is shared by the majority.
  - Keep track of each resident's attitude level. Place an appropriate mark by the name of each homeowner. For those who are. . .

    . . . all for the project — a large star (an asterisk),

    . . . not committed one way or the other to the project — a question mark, and

    . . . adamantly opposed to the project — a large X.

    The appropriate marks create an attitude list that will be of value later in the coup and can prove helpful in subsequent situations.
  - Organize the bulk of homeowners whose woes invade too many of their waking hours. Come to a decision as to who in your community would be appropriate and willing to be scooted into the positions about to be vacated and proceed as follows:
  - *If your community is large,* the polling process will require a committee. Assign a specific number of homeowners to each committee member. Give them a list of names, addresses, and phone numbers. You can get the list of owners and their addresses from public records. Pre-mark each list with Xs by those homeowners you know are antagonistic to the cause. You do not want any of the current BOD that you plan to remove or any of their apparent allies to be accidentally contacted.

    IMPORTANT: To be effective, polling must be done by personal contact. If at all possible, even absentee owners should be called. Follow up by mailing information to them. Each committee member is to introduce himself, tell where he lives, and offer some friendly, but brief, chit-chat. You don't want anyone to be guilty of leading the "witnesses." So the very next words out of the pollster's mouth must be, "How do you feel about the way the BOD is handling our HOA affairs?"
  - Go for it if the resident makes assertions similar to, "Like road kill." or, "I would like to punch them in the mouth every time I get one of their hostile newsletters. They've taken over our housing development like Grant took Richmond." Mark a star and tell him you'll contact him when the petition is ready and that you will bring a proxy with you for him to sign at the same time you bring the petition.
  - If the homeowner appears to be on the legendary fence put a question mark by his name and move on. If he seemed real iffy you might put two question marks by his name.
  - Mark an X if the homeowner's answer sounds anything like, "I think it's marvelous and getting better all the time. I loved the announcement in the last newsletter to keep the kids off the grass." Nod your head, smile, and hightail it to the next door.

- **Determine what your Docs state are the proper procedures.** Then ascertain the number of petition signatures required for the purpose of removing unsatisfactory members from the board. If you don't feel confident in deciphering the Docs, see a *good* attorney, one in the top 20 percent group.

  - Don't stop the polling process when the stars total the number of needed signatures. No matter what their professed miseries were, not all will sign the petition.

  - When you're in the process of getting the actual petition signed, go to the stars first. If you're short of the required number of signatures, then approach the one-question mark homeowners. At that time you can gently explain to them that there are homeowners (give them the exact number of the stars you have) who want to elect more considerate members to the board because they are truly up to their earlobes in misery. It's okay to give a couple of condensed, mirthless circumstances. Do not mention names. Even if they don't voluntarily become a star say, "Would you be willing to sign our petition?"

  If the answer is no:

  - Say, "Would you mind telling me what you *like* about how our complex is being governed?" You might even learn some good stuff of which you were unaware.

  - With a pleasant, genuine smile on your face, be quiet. ***Do not say one word! Let them speak first.*** Quiet time can be unnerving. Tough it out. Bite your tongue, if necessary. The normal tendency is to break the silence by speaking. Don't.

    Consolation: Not particularly wanting to talk, the resident is equally as nervous as you are. Let the resident break the silence with his feedback.

  - Sincerely listen to the resident's comments. If he is unmistakably unwilling to sign the petition, just say, "It sounds like you're not having the same problems as the rest of us. That's great. Thank you."

- **When you create the petition** you may want to have an attorney in the 20 percent group draft it.

  - If there is a regularly scheduled meeting that fits your time frame, circulate a petition to add two items to the agenda: the removal of old board members and the election of new members.

  - If no regular meeting is in near sight, circulate a petition that also calls for a special meeting for the singular and specific purpose of removing board members. Don't confuse and weaken your primary issue by throwing other topics into the meeting.

  - Present the signed petition to the proper board member by certified mail.

An added benefit: Once a coup has been successfully executed, until many years pass, narrow-minded homeowners are less likely to compete for a position on the BOD. That type is so intimidated by the possibility of the embarrassment of being removed from the office.

Sample of the petition we used

To the Secretary of
  PLEASANT VALLEY HOMEOWNER ASSOCIATION, INC.
  A Colorado Corporation

The undersigned, constituting at least one-fourth of the voting members, call a special meeting of the Members of the Corporation to be held on _____ 1990, at ___ o'clock at _____ Arvada, Colorado to consider and take appropriate action with respect to the following matters:

A. Removal of all current directors from the board.

B. Amendment of Article IV, Section 3 of the Bylaws to provide that, in the event that there are no remaining directors, successor directors shall be selected by a majority vote of the Members present, in person or by proxy, at a meeting at which a quorum is present.

C. Amendment of Article V, Section 1 of the Bylaws to provide that nominations from the floor may be made at the annual meeting or special meeting of the Members.

Election of successor directors.

You are directed to either give or cause to be given in accordance with applicable law written notice of the place, day, hour and purpose of the meeting to each Member entitled to vote at the meeting.

Name of Member	Address	Date
_____	_____	_____
_____	_____	_____
_____	_____	_____

- **Design a proxy** specifically for the singular purpose of removing the offending board members and voting for replacements. (A sample proxy is in chapter 7, ***Important step***.)

  - Accomplish two tasks with one visit. As each homeowner signs the petition, *get a proxy signed at the same time.* **_Insist_** *that each resident sign a proxy!*

  - Explain to the homeowners that the signed proxy will be used at the meeting to put reasonableness back into the complex by unseating the trouble makers. Have a list of the names of the organizers of the coup and tell each homeowner to choose which one on that list they prefer to assign their proxy vote.

  - Count the votes you know you'll get from those who are *totally committed* to attend the meeting, the organizers. Get a sufficient number of signed proxies "in your pocket." The total must be *more* than the votes required in your Docs to get the mission accomplished. You may lose some votes. The other side may influence some residents.

▶ *DON'T LEAVE WITHOUT A SIGNED PROXY!*

Some homeowners, adamant about their displeasure with the BOD, will tell you that they will not rest comfortably until the troublemakers are replaced with peacemakers. Those same homeowners will carefully explain that they'll *certainly* attend the meeting and so there's no need for them to sign a proxy. Clarify that their signed proxy is just an assurance there will be an adequate number of votes to accomplish the desired objective. If they *do* attend, their presence at the meeting will override their proxy. Their proxy will be given back to them at the meeting prior to the voting process. They can still personally vote.

You must get the signed proxy! Good intentions too often get replaced with good excuses: "Really? There weren't enough votes to get the job done? Are you serious? My vote would have prevented that? I'm really sorry. I had every intention of attending the meeting, but Aunt Matilda unexpectedly stopped by and I see her so seldom. I just didn't have the heart not to spend some time with her. I thought she would leave in time for me to go to the meeting . . ." Never accept a "Ya, but I . . ." in lieu of a signed proxy.

Don't go to the meeting one vote short!

If you're not going to get involved, at least cooperate!

If you're discontented with current circumstances in your CCC, but you don't want to spend your time to help organize the changing of the guard, at least cooperate with those who are taking their time to fix it. Promptly grant your proxy!

❯ *YOU DON'T HAVE TO BE A HOMEOWNER TO ORGANIZE A COUP*

Chris and Cindy Tucker rent a home in a 118-unit townhome community in southeast Aurora, Colorado.

Chris staged a major takeover (a coup). He had to do it twice because the first time he was short the number of votes needed to accomplish the deed.

He tells his story: "We needed 53 votes. The second go round we had 96 votes. Two board members resigned before the meeting to avoid the embarrassment of being removed and we retired the remaining personal agenda board members.

"The second time we were organized with a color coded map showing who were renters, which homeowners were on our side, and which were not." Chris didn't attend the removal meeting because he wanted the focus of the meeting to be about the complex, not on the personal issues between him and the over-controlling board member. As a renter, Chris had no voting rights to help in the coup.

Chris said, "One board member, obsessed with his authority, acted like Hitler. He had undue influence over the president of the board. Anytime he wanted to levy a fine or send a nasty letter he told the president and she did it.

"A little elderly woman planted some aspen trees. When it was hot she would take her very small dog on a leash, sit under the trees, talk to her pet, and relax. 'Hitler' wrote her up for that atrocity and was attempting to fine her. Fortunately, he was removed before the fine was levied.

"A couple who lives at the back of the complex (you can't even see into their yard from the street) had a small plastic swing set. 'Hitler' wrote them up and made them put it away. The only time the children were allowed to play on the swing set was when their father was home and it had to be placed on the cement driveway. It was not allowed on the grass. He didn't care that the children ran the risk of hurting themselves if they fell off of the swing set. In fact, that's probably why he demanded it be on the driveway.

"Another woman, whose front door is on the backside of her unit, put a picnic table outside that door. She doesn't have air conditioning and she enjoyed eating at the picnic table in the summertime with her kids. That didn't matter to 'Hitler,' he made her remove the table.

"He discovered these 'horrible' things because he was under the mistaken notion that, as a board member, he had every right to look over everybody's privacy fences, go into their yards, onto their patio areas, and into their homes. Actually, the common area begins five to six feet from the homes.

"Over and above going into people's yards, he was caught looking in a window at a teenage girl and looking in the windows of several of the older women."

Chris continued: "After our successful coup, 'Hitler' would let his beagle out every morning so the dog could do his duty behind my partner's home, my partner in the coup."

Chris said, "A neighbor ran in one day screaming that my son had almost been run over by 'Hitler'.

"I went down and asked him to come out of his house. He didn't. He called the police. When the police heard what had happened, they talked to witnesses and issued a ticket to him for reckless driving.

"We took him to court. The judge listened to all the witnesses. 'Hitler' was convicted of reckless driving. He was court ordered to pay $5 to each witness."

Chris called me August 4, 1996, and gave the end of the story to me.

"Hitler" sold his home. The residents didn't even know his home was on the market because he didn't allow his real estate agent to put up a for-sale sign.

It was exciting news to everyone when a new homeowner took residence!

It was probably the embarrassment of being impeached that moved "Hitler."

Chris had a very good idea. Color code a map of the complex.

Organizing a coup to reverse a sub-happy situation falls about 5,000 feet short of qualifying as a recreational activity. Just imagine how far down on the list organizing a second coup falls. However, if you happen to be one of those who got siphoned into an ill-fated, unhappy community and realize you probably should get involved in the reversal process, don't shrink back. Start taking action now. Without action, your situation will not automatically get better. It will be quite the opposite. It will keep getting worse until a special someone decides to take the necessary, positive actions to correct the prevailing predicament. That special someone should decide to start the procedure sooner, rather than later. Procrastination compounds dilemmas. There is an urgent need for speed!

The responsibility to take action is the price you will pay for having the audacity to expect to live happily in your home. To keep things hopeful you have to be helpful. Don't give up. The cream always rises to the top.

Motivational trees

WHO?	YES!
WHO AM I?	YES, YOU!
WHO AM I TO THINK?	YES, YOU KNOW!
WHO AM I TO THINK I CAN?	YES, YOU KNOW YOU CAN!
WHO AM I TO THINK I CAN CHANGE?	YES, YOU KNOW YOU CAN CHANGE!
WHO AM I TO THINK I CAN CHANGE THE HOA?	YES, YOU KNOW YOU CAN CHANGE THE HOA!

Great! You've done it. Now you, your neighbors and your homes can smile again.

"It isn't what we get, but what we give, that measures the worth of the life we live."
— Benjamin Franklin

"Sometimes it costs more to do nothing than to do something." — Sam Ewing

So You Want to Be on the Board? Who Are You?

Many clues have been given as to who should and who should not be on the board. There's well over a baker's dozen of the types of people who will vie to be elected. For the protection of the community, before the association members (the homeowners) vote, it is vital to identify the specific character traits of each candidate.

Common sense and good business sense are two attributes that are mentioned. Common sense means the ability of thinking on your feet, thinking "out of the box," and keeping an open mind. It's reading between the lines of what is written and what has been told to you. Common sense allows one to internalize the facts to come up with a solid, revolutionary solution. It's like putting proper data into a computer — no garbage in, only good stuff out. Regrettably, common sense isn't too common. Too many believe they have to get the opinions of everyone they know before they make any decision about anything.

Never rely on a college degree in business administration as a guarantee of either common sense or good business sense. There are those who have never even worked at a "real" job, but who garnered a worthy education from running a tidy ship on the home front or by participating in community and volunteer projects. Many possess more business and common sense than some overpaid, overrated CEOs. Don't label a board contender's cover until you take the time to observe his pages.

▶ THE PROFILE OF THOSE WHO BELONG ON THE BOARD

Ideal board members are those who . . .
- recognize that there is no *fame or glory* connected with *any* position on the board.
- don't even want to be on the board, but are willing to "serve time" to help the association.
- make common sense decisions.
- are willing to perform the many thankless and pay-less tasks as a means to cultivate an amicable neighborhood that favors comfortable living for *all* residents.

- perceive no delight in exercising control over others, who will set aside their own desires, and make decisions that satisfy the needs of the majority.
- respect the rights of others . . . adults and children alike.
- have good business sense.
- understand how to spend and conserve funds wisely and will insist on a proper procedure to protect HOA accounts.
- are thoroughly familiar with using the thinking process to prevent and solve problems, using the rules as guidelines to create a sound, harmonious, well-maintained community.
- believe in adding humane elements to the interpretations of the rules, who consider how to provide legal alternatives to the strict letter of the wording in the Docs to produce an atmosphere of neighborliness rather than one of hostility.

Do those attributes smack of confirmed altruism? They do. *A caring, altruistic demeanor is the only acceptable outlook if one is going to make decisions for the good of the entire community.*

"The person who rows the boat generally doesn't have time to rock it." — Anonymous

Board members who possess such characteristics ask for the homeowners' votes on major issues even when the Docs clearly declare the BOD can make the decision without a vote. It's comforting to them to know that the desires of the majority have been served. They'll ask residents to complete a questionnaire (sample on page V) to learn how they feel about the community. With concern for their neighbors they will gently enforce the rules.

They will be neither intimidated nor influenced by the community's chronic complainers' attempts to keep the board quiet with veiled or unveiled threats to sue if the board makes a decision that is unfavorable to the aspirations of the complainers. That long sentence reminds me of a former TV weatherman who gave his entire weather report in one long sentence without any punctuation other than a period at the end of the show.

If you are fortunate enough to have one or more board member who has any or all of the previous attributes take time to express your appreciation to them. Volunteer some of your time for specific projects. That will be the only pay they'll receive and it could avoid BOD burnout. You want to *keep them there!* You don't want anyone with any of the next types of attitudes infiltrating your board.

❯ *THE PROFILE OF THOSE WHO DO NOT BELONG ON THE BOARD*

Undesirable board members are those who . . .

- are rigid rule enforcers. They will make certain the rules of the Docs are *observed* and *enforced* verbatim to every last word, with no thought of the ultimate effect that iron-handed enforcement creates. They advocate that strict enforcement makes homeowners happy and protects property values. They will feature one rule each month in the newsletter under the headline of *COVENANT OF THE MONTH* to make certain homeowners are aware of *every* rule. After every rule has been spotlighted, they will start at the top of the list and do it all over again, again, and again.
- are on a power trip, are self-serving, and mean. They will control everyone. They

will fine and sue, if necessary, every single homeowner who doesn't rigidly observe the BOD's interpretation of every rule. They say the homeowners knew there were rules when they moved in and they can darn well learn to follow them or move out if they don't like them. Once elected they will set all the proper procedures into place to fit their own needs. They have no regard for others.

- don't believe children or homeowners have individual rights. They'll use their powers to get their concerns handled "properly," *their way*. They'll put a stop to the kids playing on the common areas and having too much fun.

- are steeped in the belief that everything in writing is true, valid, and unchangeable, especially if it's written rules.

If they have just read a magazine or newspaper article that very convincingly declares that *whatever* is required in the Docs is for the good of all the homeowners, they will likely believe that every word in the article has to be true because it's written. Untruths are just not put into print. They will put that article right next to the Docs and proceed from there. They will proudly offer to give a copy of the article to you.

The author of that gospel article has probably never even slept one night in a CCC. Let alone *ever considered living* in such a place. That bit of knowledge wouldn't sway those board contenders. They are firmly convinced that you too will believe once you read the article.

- are strict, mean, and lazy, rigid rule enforcers who want *everything* covered in the HOA dues because they do not want to lift one irresponsible finger to do anything. They would never taint themselves with work.

HOA dues will spiral upward as more and more services are added. They'll make their strict and mean decisions and turn all the work over to an equally strict and mean management company with instructions to whip the homeowners into bite-sized pieces.

- are bent on a single-issue and are self-serving. They just received a citation for an infraction of a regulation. They want to be on the board to change that one specific rule. They wouldn't move one inch to work for anything other than "healing" that one issue. When they got called about the violation the first words out their mouths were, "How do I get on the board?"

- are just lazy. They only covet the prestige that they believe comes with the title of being on the board of Just Another Homeowner Association. Their sole purpose is to gobble up every morsel of imaginary fame and glory. Beware of planting a North American social climber on the BOD.

There is no connection whatsoever between being a board member and the kudos of fame and glory. Go to any place of your choice and say, "Do you know who I am? I'm the president of the Just Another Homeowner Association in Apathy Ville." That disclosure and a $50 bill won't influence even the maitre d' at a crowded McDonalds restaurant to give a good table to you. Just order a Big Mac to go and ask them to hold the glory.

If there's no glory and no fame, what is there? Work. Only work.

Contenders with *any* of those tendencies better tailor new attitudes. The process of thinking is foreign to them. With an inch of knowledge they will make decisions by the yard, with careless abandon. That inch contains all the knowledge they need to execute their personal preference schemes.

With their blinders and earplugs firmly in place, they wouldn't want to see or hear what other residents may want, they will rush ahead to ensure there will be *no* deviation from the fine letter of every trivial rule. The rules shall reign supreme! Who could blame them when all they plan to do is authoritatively enforce what is written in black and white?

Can't you just see them sitting for days at a stuck stoplight? They would sooner die before they would even consider going against what's right and written.

While those candidates may voice and have similar goals, each will have a variation of individual tendencies. The prospect is severely shaky for any of them ***making you happy*** and protecting your property values. They are the types who will build a dictatorship.

KEEP THOSE PEOPLE OFF THE BOARD. THEY DO NOT BELONG.

With any of those people on the board residents' freedom and individuality will go up in smoke. Pride of ownership will atrophy and vanish. Property values will follow suit.

Have you been keeping count? Which verse of this song am I on now?

It's possible to rule with self-serving attitudes for a while. Sooner or later, a David will buy a nest in the unhappy little tree. The next thing that will transpire is the offending Goliaths will find a big rock right in the middle of their self-serving BOD foreheads. Davids just won't live under a dictatorship for long.

If you have one or more board member who fits any or all of the profiles of those who do not belong, become a David. Start the wheels of a coup d'état rolling (chapter 6).

Look for the responsible person who doesn't want to be on the board

Shirley Gardner, Miami, Florida shared her opinion of how to select members for the board.

"The only contenders who should ***ever*** be considered are those with a true desire to develop or maintain a comfortable community, those who *don't want* to be on the board and still vie for the position. They have their own lives.

"Self-serving people grab at the chance to be on the board as a way to control. They see it as a way to give 'importance' to their fractured egos.

"How do you know what they're really like? Get to know them. Ask them, not only their qualifications, but also what they intend to do when they sit on the '*royal*' throne'. If they've been on the board for years, examine the results they have produced rather than be persuaded by longevity."

Associations can get mired down in politics

Dennis Hankey lives in a condo near Granby, Colorado.

Dennis said, "I have found that those individuals who volunteer for board positions are not always the ones best suited for the job.

"More often than not, seeking out qualified persons among the owners can prove rewarding. Generally my experience has been that those who do accept tend to be reliable and meet their commitments. The job is not their claim to fame.

"One of the difficulties is that associations tend to be political. Most people who are asked to serve think in terms of getting the job done and would rather not get mired down in politics. They are interested in governing the affairs of the association in the most economical and efficient manner, spending no more time than is really needed."

Shirley and Dennis stated their sound advice quite clearly.

Unsavory inclinations have been known to be disguised. If you have advance notice of who the candidates will be, observe with whom they pal around. Someone is bound to blow the cover. You know the bit: You can fool some of the people some of the time, but you can't fool all the homeowners forever.

Information needed from BOD contenders — ask these questions:

- In general, what do you like and dislike about this community?
- What are your qualifications to be a board member?
- What do you like about how the complex is being governed now?
- What would you do to continue that type of governing?
- What do you dislike about how the complex is being governed now?
- What changes would you make to administer the complex better?
- What would your policy be on rule enforcement and fines?
- Do you feel the HOA fees cover adequate services for the residents?
- What services would you remove or add to be covered by the HOA?
- How do you perceive the BOD's relationship with the management company?

Those are essay type questions. Either give them a form a week or so before the meeting to write their answers or let them speak their replies at the meeting (preferred). If you choose to send the forms have each candidate read their responses at the meeting. Don't accept short, vague, hazy, or political responses. Press the issues until you acquire a clear picture of that person. The more they talk, the more the real person will be revealed. Watch for even the slightest signs of chronic power-itis. Listen for a sign of benevolence in their hearts. Just a smidgen of benevolence isn't enough. One smidgen falls about 20 smidgens below the minimum RDHOAA (Recommended Daily HOA Allowance).

If a nominee has intentions to make a lot of changes to reverse the way the community is being run, and a reversal isn't fitting, quickly nominate another homeowner from the floor. You don't want to see pride of ownership and the integrity of your community destroyed.

Pride of ownership is the quality that creates better subdivisions

Momentous concepts have slipped right by me until I heard them the third or fourth time. With that reality and my father's advice, I installed redundancy software into my computer.

I realize that I may even be stretching my father's advice. However, I will have fallen short of my goal if, by the time you've finished this book, your brain isn't saturated with this and a couple other extremely necessary premises. So don't stop me if you've heard these songs before. I may be getting fairly close to the last verses.

If you want to help encourage communities to stop crying and to start singing happy songs, assist in making an impact on developers to update, simplify, and humanize governing restrictions for their new developments. Even if you don't want to buy a home, you can *pretend* to be a potential buyer to help speed up the movement. Either way, visit new developments. Urge the builders to make allowances that will generate residents' pride. Tell them that pride of ownership only comes from the heart of self-respect. Tell them no matter how lovely their homes are, their documents are miserable. Ask them if they've ever lived in one of their raging CCC hornets' nests. Tell them that you wouldn't even consider buying into their complex until they humanize their Docs.

You can also make an impact in your community. Encourage modification and sensible interpretation of the rules.

A good plan

Never sit still for the authority of anyone signing the checks if they are also in charge of writing the checks! Insist on two board members' signatures on all checks. If the checks are written by the board treasurer, the treasurer should *not* be one of the approved signers. *No less than two board members should always review the bills and the corresponding checks.* That practice creates a practical cross-check. If there is a management company, they are *only to coordinate the bills* and *write the checks*.

Before all of you management companies get too upset, especially those who have your hands on HOA bank accounts, hold on to your ire for a few more pages until you get to the part that explains why I want to change your names. At that time you can total up your entire outrage and just have one big, worthwhile snit. It may appear as though I'm down on *all* management companies. I'm not. A good, caring management company can be essential.

Two constantly outvoted BOD renegades and an attempt to control proxies

W.N., who lives in a small complex in Colorado, under 100 units, prefers to remain anonymous to avoid possible backlash.

W.N. said, "The majority of the board preferred to rule like a true covenants 'Gestapo'. One big problem was in the summer when they took pleasure in telling people they couldn't be in the pool. There were two of us on the board who kept trying to further more relaxed policies and attempted to make decisions for the overall good of the complex. The president always pushed to satisfy her personal aspirations rather than an outcome for the community. The other four board members just rubber-stamped her requests. We were the two renegades who were constantly outvoted by the other five board members. I was on the board for a three-year term and then chose not to run for a second term."

W.N. offered, "We are fortunate in that we've always had a good management company. A lot of the homeowners, including me, really got upset when we received an announcement that stated, 'Send your proxies to the secretary of the board, not to the management company. Because it's a small community, the board knows just about how each homeowner votes. If the board received the proxies, they would have prior knowledge that, perhaps, they needed to stir up more votes and proxies. We didn't mind sending proxies to the management company because they were neutral. They didn't have an ax to grind as to who was and who wasn't on the board."

W.N. said, "When I called the secretary to inquire why the new mandate, he said, 'That's the way it's always been.'" W.N. said, "That's not true and there are many who don't want to mail them [the proxies] to you.

"Our management company resigned. They said they no longer had enough time to work with us, but I'll always believe the real reason was they no longer cared to deal with all the petty problems we had that were caused by the board.

"Everything has settled down now. We have a new, conscientious board and another good management company. Everything is running smoothly. Our neighborhood now offers a very congenial atmosphere for living comfortably."

❯ *MORE ABOUT VOTES AND PROXIES*

Sadly, many homeowners neither attend meetings nor send their proxies to the meetings. There are those who don't even understand the significance of a proxy.

A proxy is your right to vote given to another person to vote in your stead. In the context of an HOA meeting, it's your bit of voting power for the benefit of you, your neighbors, and your mini-government. If you can't or won't be at an HOA meeting in person, make certain your vote is. Be cautious about whom you choose to exercise your right to vote. Assign your proxy to a person you trust and you know *will attend* the meeting come high water or Aunt Matilda. A person whose attitudes and ideals are much like yours and who will vote as you would. That person will likely be a friendly neighbor.

Proxies are to be registered with one entity sometime prior to the voting process. That entity can be a board member or the management company representative. You can give your proxy directly to the person you have chosen to vote for you. They can register your proxy prior to the start of the meeting. If you haven't been thrilled with the HOA's disposition, for goodness sake, don't give your unassigned proxy to them to "cash" your vote. *Never, never sign a proxy that doesn't have a date limit!*

❯ *THE POWER OF VOTES AND PROXIES CAN AUTHORIZE A DICTATORSHIP*

Many CCC dictatorships have been built with the power of proxies.

You receive your announcement of the upcoming meeting with a proxy enclosed. The announcement says, "Sign your proxy and return it to the BOD (or maybe specifically to the president, vice president, secretary/treasurer, or ???)." So you sign it and return it.

> We're getting real foxy
> by requesting your proxy,
> but, we see it no sin
> to make certain we'll win.

The meeting takes place and magically every decision matched the outcome that the BOD wanted! You and other homeowners willingly gave the power to the BOD to form a dictatorship by presenting them with the majority of the votes. Too many of you merrily mailed your signed proxies and neglected to do one vitally important step. Read this twice and very slowly: You didn't fill in the portion that asks to whom you assigned your proxy.

The apathetic homeowners who did absolutely nothing are nonetheless at fault. Maybe they read the announcement and just ignored the contents. Maybe they didn't even open the envelope. They have a song all their own: "Apathy, apathy, apathy seems to work for me."

▶ *SAME SCENARIO — DIFFERENT DICTATORS*

Your announcement of the meeting states, "If you can't attend the meeting, sign your proxy and return it to the management company." The meeting takes place and magically every decision matched the outcome the management company wanted! They had the majority of votes this time. Please remember this: The management company does not have a vested interest in you, your happiness, or your community's happiness. They only have a vested interest in *their* happiness and fattening *their* bank account.

Important step

Assign your proxy to one who will definitely attend the meeting. A neighbor who thinks very similarly to the way you think and will vote the way you would if you were personally at the meeting. Check your documents. Assignment of proxies may not be limited to members in good standing with the association. Some documents allow assignment to anyone of the voter's choice — a non-member of the association. Put that trusted person's name in the blank where it says, ". . . I give my proxy to _____."

Neglecting that important step is tantamount to signing a blank check. Anyone can fill in an amount (a name) and cash it. Your vote may be cast exactly opposite of the way you wanted. *Even if you have filled in that important assignment portion* there is *a strong possibility that your proxy will never reach the proper hands* if you mail your proxy to a nefarious BOD or management company. Given that situation, I would give my proxy directly to the person to whom I had assigned my proxy.

Sample proxy with a date limit

NEIGHBORLY VILLAGE HOA PROXY
YOUR VOTE COUNTS!

I, _____, residing at _____
     (Your name)   (Your address)

give my proxy to _____ to vote in
               (Trusted-person's name)

my absence at the HOA meeting on _____
                                  (Date of the meeting)

_____
(Homeowner's signature)   (Date)

Assigning your proxy is not like giving your first-born child away. It is just an assurance that your vote will be counted. Should you decide at the last second to go to the meeting, your proxy will be given back to you and you can still do your own voting.

You're exceptionally fortunate if the decisions to be made are listed in detail and there are provisions to choose either to give your proxy or to vote by mail (absentee). To vote absentee is almost as good as your being at the meeting. Read the issues and quickly vote absentee.

Not assigning your proxy is like not guarding the candy store. You deserve to be robbed by the Sweet Tooths' Gang. Now that you've heard several verses of this song, you know this is another important premise *always* to remember.

Check who's controlling the votes

Jim lives in a small town in Colorado in a complex of mobile homes on permanent foundations. The lots are owned by the residents.

Jim said, "The developer created a problem for the homeowners when he filed a plat for two phases (90 lots in the first phase, the one that has been developed, and 165 lots in the second phase, not yet developed). He made unilateral decisions without telling the homeowners. When we asked why he didn't consult us he said he didn't have to because he held the majority vote — the 165 votes for phase two. We tried to negotiate with him, but he would only have it one way — his way. He turned the sprinkler system off and just stopped mowing the greenbelt area.

"We have a requirement in our covenants to have an annual meeting. The developer refused.

"He controlled the votes, the HOA funds, and consistently denied our requests to see a financial statement. The dues were low, only $53 a year with a built-in 50 percent annual increase. In ten years the dues could raise to $255 a month!"

Jim said, "For over 11 years the HOA was nothing but problems. We elected officers, but the developer still claimed the quorum because of phase two."

Finally the homeowners and the developer agreed to part company and dissolve the entire HOA. It was the only viable solution.

Jim continued, "The HOA did nothing for us except collect our dues. There wasn't one covenant that wasn't already covered in the town's ordinances. The problem is the town isn't effective at enforcing regulations. The town attempts to substitute the police department in place of a code enforcement officer. It doesn't work. It only makes the police department cranky. They have better things to do than tell someone they can't paint their house furious fuchsia. Of course, the HOA never enforced the rules either.

"The town's officials periodically introduce new ordinances. The ordinances have the look of importance and legality. Ordinances are supposedly created specifically for the particular town or community. Right? Wrong! You would be shocked if you knew how many 'customized' ordinances I've read where the official neglected to even remove the name of the other town. What other town? The town whose ordinance was copied.

"I've learned a lot since I moved here. The main lesson: Check *everything out thoroughly before* you buy!"

Jim and his neighbors turned off the developer's oven. They were weary of being *road-pizza* for his personal taste buds, profit, and pleasure.

Until I talked to Jim I didn't know that towns could be on the same circuit as CCCs with the pollution of off-the-rack ordinances!

> Judy Weinstein, owner of several properties with HOAs said, "The six-member board in one of HOAs claims that they hold the majority of the proxies. When they count the votes there is no confirmation of the validity of the proxies!"
>
> Judy continued, "Meetings were held at 7:00 a.m. to discourage homeowners from attending. When that little game didn't work, the board banned homeowners' attendance. Sometimes the BOD issued an invitation to a specific meeting." She said, "Some get on the board to institute their own personal agenda. The board has changed the rules and regulations to fit their own needs."

A six-member board? That's a perfect number to get go-nowhere-deadlock votes. Always verify by asking to see the proxies if you sense a dictatorship is in charge. Among other states, Colorado has prohibited the practice of banning homeowners from board meetings.

A short stroll down the levity path

There are all kinds of HOAs, boards of directors, attorneys, judges, and management companies. You've heard the phrase, "It takes all kinds." I prefer the one that I heard many years ago, "It doesn't really *take* all kinds, it's just that there *are* all kinds." The prospect of eliminating a *few kinds* would not bring a single tear to even one of my eyes. Some people make me want to ask, "Excuse me, did your mother ever have any children?"

I heard a great suggestion. Provide motorists with "dumb-darts," darts that would only stick, not wound. Every time a motorist observes another driver doing a dumb thing, he is to shoot a dumb-dart at the vehicle. The owner of any vehicle sporting three dumb-darts automatically earns a "three-dumb-dart" fine.

A variation of that process would be to give every person a limitless supply of mean-darts, darts that will only stick to mean people. Three mean-darts and the person vaporizes.

‣ *WHAT'S IN A NAME?*

Words have power. People have a tendency to label according to the meaning that a word implies.

Anytime the word *CONTROL* appears, such as in covenants-***controlled*** community and architectural ***control*** committee, insert some derivative of ***protect*** or ***protection*** in place of control. Mr. Webster supplies the differences in the meanings.

> **CONTROL** *vt. -trolled', -trolling* **1.** orig. to check or verify (payments, accounts, etc.) by comparison with a duplicate register **4.** to exercise authority over; direct; command **5.** to hold back; curb; restrain *(hold your grief)* — ***n.*** **1.** the act or fact of controlling; power to direct or regulate; ability to use effectively [per *control* over her passions, the violinist's *control of his vibrato*] **2.** the condition of being directed or being restrained **3.** a means of controlling;
>
> **PROTECT** *vt.* **1.** to shield from injury, danger, or loss; guard; defend
>
> **PROTECTION** *n.* **1.** a) a protecting or being protected b) an instance of this **2.** a person or thing that protects **3.** a safe conduct or passport

How about *covenants-protected community* and *architectural protection committee?* The name changes alone could make an enormous difference in attitudes. Read further about service companies as opposed to management companies. You make your own determination about changing *control* to *protected or protection* and *management* to *service.*

▶ WORDS <u>DO</u> HAVE POWER

There are many types of management companies just as there are good and bad, and in-between calibers of communities, BODs, and architectural committees.

Good companies know they are good and they know the names of most of the bad companies in their area.

Bad companies have their heads buried so deeply in the sands of selfishness that they neither admit nor recognize that they *are* bad. Their philosophy: "If we're making money we must be good. If we're making a total ton of money we must be fantastic." Possibly one of the reasons they are bad is that they have fallen in love with and fully believe in the label of *management* in their names.

If the management company is managing the complex, the BOD has turned over their accountability and elected decision-making powers to the *management* company. Shame, shame, shame on the BOD. It's the elected duty of the BOD to make final decisions with a majority vote of the board members.

One scenario: The management company, without thinking about it, is so carried away with *management* being a major portion of their name their original intentions have slowly eroded away. They no longer remember their real purpose for the HOA.

It's difficult, if not impossible, *not* to think of one's self as a manager when one owns or works for MNO *Management* Company. It's equally as difficult for some board members not to *feel managed* when they have just contracted with MNO *Management* Company.

Takeover by management companies of the BOD's elected decision-making powers happens automatically when board members are only after the imaginary *fame and glory* and had no intention of sullying their hands with HOA work.

Another scenario: Management company takeover has even happened to BODs with the loftiest intentions of fulfilling their elected duties. That occurs when the BOD believes the mislabeling of *management* in MNO *Management* Company's name and believes the words of a clever, determined, and manipulative management company. In either scenario your BOD has just become a puppet BOD.

The word *management* in management company, when the company is working for an HOA, is a mistake. It is a misnomer. *Service* company would be much more appropriate and descriptive of their duties.

Indeed, what *is* in a name?

> **MANAGEMENT** *n.* **1.** the act, art, or manner of managing, or handling, controlling, directing, etc. **4.** a) the person or persons managing a business, institution, etc. b) such persons collectively, regarded as a distinct social group with special interests . . .

SERVICE *n.* **3.** b) work done or duty performed for another or others **6.** a) an act giving assistance or advantage to another b) the result of this; benefit; advantage c) [*pl.*] friendly help; also professional aid or attention

Enough said? When a company is an independent contractor for an HOA, which definition do you think is closer to painting an authentic portrait of a company's duties?

In my book, pun intended, the name service company is far more appropriate than management company. What *is* in a name? If I had a magic wand I would gather up every company that deals with HOAs and make a global zap of *service* in place of *management* in every company's name.

Chances are probably slim and dim to have a global name change take place. Nonetheless, I'm writing this book. For the remainder of it, good companies will be referred to as *service* companies. The term *management* company will only be used as an editorial comment to describe a company that uses manipulative methods — a bad company. "Management" will still be used when it is part of the name of an actual company.

If you're in agreement with me, you can make certain your management company comprehends that they are now recognized by the BOD and the homeowners as your HOA's *service* company. Explain to the company why you've chosen to make this change in the distinction about their name. It would be outstanding, but not necessary, if they agreed to make a formal name change. In the absence of that happening, inform them that all future correspondence and verbal reference to their company must contain a reference to *service*. Something equivalent to "your friendly service company" must follow their management company's name or "service representative" must follow the representative's name. They are a true *management* company if they fight you on that issue. Exercise your 30-day "write when you get work" clause and get a real *service* company.

Example of a declaration of being a service company

GOOD MANAGEMENT, INC.
1234 West Cooperation Parkway • Pleasant Towne, OH 43500 • 333-555-6666
Your Friendly Service Company

Dear _____ ,

_____

_____

_____

_____

Sincerely,

George Bookkeeper
Green Valley Townhomes' service agent

Don't take any pushing around by *any* management company. You aren't their slaves or flunkies. *They work for you.* You, the board, make the final decisions. Any other profile is not acceptable.

No company should *ever* be in a position of feeling they're managing the homeowners.

Homeowners are not tenants. Even if a homeowner hires your HOA's service/management company to manage his rental unit in your complex, management stops at the door of that one home.

The company is only to perform SERVICES for the HOA. If you have one tiny tinge of feeling managed, read this portion over and over until the feeling and the management company go away.

When this whole revelation hit me, I called the owner of our service company. (Actually, management is still a part of their name.) Here is the content of our conversation: I told her about my new awareness that management should never be in the name of Whatever Management Company whenever that company contracted with HOAs because the company doesn't manage in that situation. She said, "Oh, yes we *do* manage." Then I explained to her that the company *only performed services* for the HOA. Later I learned, to my dismay, that a lot of companies *do* get away with a managing act.

At that point, she said that it is necessary to have management in the company name in order for the IRS to consider them an outside independent contractor. My comeback to that was something like, "Oh, fluffy cow feathers! Our lawn service is an outside independent contractor and their name is not Lawn Management, Inc. to retain their present status with the IRS. I then asked her how much managing she had ever done in our complex. Of course, her answer was, "None." We understand each other now.

▶ MANAGEMENT COMPANIES

Vicki Ferguson and her partner own nine rental properties: three single-family homes, three condominiums, and three townhomes.

Their first experience in owning in a covenants-controlled community was when they purchased three condos in Americana, a complex in Aurora, Colorado.

"Westwind Management handles everything professionally, proficiently, and promptly in an honest, caring manner."

Vicki said, "It had been so easy and such a pleasant experience with those three units that we were under the illusion that covenants-controlled communities were the only path to take. We believed it made life easy. We promptly proceeded to purchase three townhomes.

"This is where our fairy tale ends. Easy quickly reverted to a migraine.

"We are tormented with constant problems with one of the three townhomes. They take our management fee and give us nothing in return except headaches and a canceled check. I'm not saying condos are good and townhomes are bad. Some boards and/or management companies are sound and some are rotten.

"One fairly minor, but irritating townhome incident: Our tenant, in pulling out of the garage barely nicked the trim around the door, about a one-to-two-inch piece. The renter, being responsible for repairing damages, called the management company. They scheduled a *handy*man to give an estimate — $50 or less. The renter said, 'Proceed.'

"When the *un*-handyman arrived to perform the duty he found he couldn't match the existing trim, so he tore off all the old trim and replaced it with an entirely different style. Without getting a higher amount approved, he billed $113 — $35 for materials and three hours labor.

"My partner, who is in construction, said he could have fixed it in a half an hour with wood putty and painted it to match. Now our garage door trim is unlike that of the other three units in our building. It doesn't much matter though, because the complex is so run down due to bad management and, obviously a feeble board, what difference is a mismatch?

"Speaking of the board, one board member was honest in stating that the whole job should have been less than $50. He was overruled by the other five board members." [Another-six member board! With any luck, they can get three for and three against and never get anything accomplished.]

"I won't belabor the point with all of our tales of woe," Vicki said, "we do have a multitude of them."

Vicki went on to offer, "Too many times board members are naive, with no business sense. They are there only for the glory and power trip. It seems to be the only claim to distinction in their lives. It's pathetic. At best, it's hollow glory.

"We have learned you can have a good management company and a good board of directors — the ideal situation. You can also have a good board and a bad management company, a bad board and a good management company, a bad board and a bad management company. The last combination really causes problems."

Usually the BOD and the management company are like bookends, a matched set. A good board will not intentionally retain a bad company. The BOD may have been conned into believing that Good Service Company really was good and later discovers Bad Management Company was disguised in Good Service Company's clothing. A good BOD will hand Bad Management Company their running papers as soon as the contract allows. Never sign a contract that doesn't have a decent (nothing over 30 days) "never-darken-my-doorstep-again" clause.

Usually, a bad BOD doesn't even recognize a good company from a bad company — although, sometimes they accidentally bumble onto to a good one.

A good service company will *cancel their contract with a bad BOD!*

Basic services performed . . .

. . . by service/management companies can include the following and more:

- Consulting.
- Obtaining bids.
- Coordinating outside contractors such as lawn maintenance, snow removal, and so on.
- Coordinating maintenance and repair work, with the board's request and approval.
- Performing secretarial services.
- Collecting HOA dues.
- Providing bookkeeping services.
- Help in making budget projections.
- Writing checks. *Never signing checks.* At least two board members must review and approve the bills and the checks, then two board members *sign the checks.*
- Producing newsletters and special announcements from information supplied by the BOD or a newsletter committee, mailed only after final approval by the BOD.
- Receiving phone calls from homeowners, unless the BOD wants to keep personal contact with the residents and requests residents make all calls to a board member.
- Relaying information from such phone calls to at least one of the board members.

- Verifying the validity of reported infractions.
- Making phone calls and sending letter(s) to homeowners who are at fault with a verified infraction of a rule, with the board's request and approval of the letter.
- Inspecting the complex for needed maintenance.

Some questions for the BOD to ask the company's representative
- What is your perception of your role with the board?
- Will you submit a written proposal to our board?
- What are your charges?
- What services do you perform for those charges?
- For what services do you charge an extra fee? How much is the extra charge?
- Do you attend all meetings?
- Do you keep and record the minutes of the meetings?
- Traditionally, how many bids do you obtain for repairs and improvements?
- Plus, any other questions you can think of.

If the company doesn't promptly return calls from the HOA, replace them with a good service company who will. We fired a company before they were hired due to their not returning a message for two days.

Good points for the BOD and homeowners to remember
- *Never* sign a contract with any company that does not contain a 30-day written notice, without-reason cancellation clause.
- *Never* allow the service/management company to decide which company will be hired to do various work in your complex. The BOD should *always* make the final decision.
- *Never* allow a puppet BOD to remain in power.
- *Never* give your signed proxy without verifying the person you have designated will indeed attend the meeting and vote as you would.
- *Never* allow checks to be signed by the management company. Ed Perlmutter, Colorado State Senator and an attorney, told me that it has been his experience that *most* HOAs turn the *whole financial process* over to their management company! An extremely unsound practice. While it's not a written-in-stone given, it's usually much easier to make thoughtless, costly, money-spending decisions when it's someone else's money one is spending. Too many BODs stand backstage and let the company run the whole show.

Another source of that perception: The owner of our lawn maintenance company and I were inspecting the common areas. As the usual spokesperson for the BOD, I explained to him what the BOD expected him not to do, to do, and a few ways we wanted him to do it. He looked at me, grinned and said, "I call this *Joni's Complex,* there's another one I call *Roy's Complex.*" Tradesman will work every angle to intimidate an involved homeowner in an attempt to set an easier routine into place. It's easier for tradesmen to talk only to the management representative. They don't get as much guff from them because they aren't as concerned about the work or as familiar with the complex as a homeowner is. When a homeowner is involved it means the tradesman has to think about what one complex wants as opposed to another one on his list. A cookie cutter operation is so much easier for him.

HOA management companies are given positions of controlling enormous sums of others' money. They can assert too much power over too many lives. Such influential positions should not be unregulated. Colorado requires a real estate license only if one or more *rental properties* is managed for someone else. Working with HOAs doesn't count. HOA management companies are totally unregulated in far too many states.

If that is the case in your state, pressure your state representatives to require regulation under the Real Estate Commission or another regulatory agency. Such regulation would allow wrongful acts by management companies to be reported and the company reprimanded without expensive litigation. No attorneys would have to be involved.

Florida passed legislation that requires a license for anyone managing five or more units. Approximately 10,000 Community Association Management licenses have been issued since the statute went into effect in July 1988. (*The News*, Boca Raton, Florida November 8, 1996.)

If you're plagued with a bad management company, don't petition the BOD to fire them. Reports of failures from a legion of residents confirm that process is rarely effective. Seldom do the Docs specify that the BOD must comply with petitions. It's folly to waste your energy and your momentum to win a skirmish and lose the battle. The BOD will deny your petition. While you're all fired up and organized, accomplish the real task at hand. ***Do a coup. Petition to remove the BOD. Then hire a good service company.***

Contact all absentee owners. Get their proxies. If you don't take this vital step, the BOD or the company will defeat you with those proxies that you didn't take the time to obtain.

Homeowners, if you perceive your BOD has turned over even one of their elected powers to a company, even if you perceive the company to be a good service company, immediately start the coup process if the BOD refuses to take their elected powers back.

Example of a good service company's approach

Vicki Ferguson was quoted earlier in this chapter, "Westwind Management handles *everything* professionally, proficiently, and promptly in an honest, caring manner."

Tim Larson, owner of Westwind, shares their business philosophy.

WESTWIND MANAGEMENT GROUP: OUR APPROACH TO MANAGEMENT

Often Westwind Management Group is asked to submit a proposal to manage a specific homeowner association. From the time of our inception, limiting our geographical area of operation has been very important to us. We specifically manage properties in Aurora, Colorado. The reason for this limitation is service. By creating geographical boundaries in an area rich with homeowner associations, we can focus more time on our communities instead of more time enjoying the many highways within the metro Denver area. No property managed by Westwind is more than 20 minutes from our office, and often we will have two or three communities side by side that we manage.

When a community decides to make a change, there are generally reasons for that change. Most reasons focus on service and response by the management company currently in place. Our interviews with prospective clients are in depth, so we understand the concerns and priorities of that specific client. Each community is different, and each community has its own idiosyncrasies due to original design, owner/renter ratios, economic levels, etc.

Once a management contract is awarded to our firm, we spend a significant amount of time listening to our clients to determine exactly how they would like us to administer the day-to-day business associated with that community. Once we have listened to their desires, we make suggestions to the board of directors regarding primarily procedural functions for that community. Our company and the board need to be on the same page, working together instead of apart. Often directors consist of professional business people as well as nonprofessional business people. We will spend as much time as necessary in education of the board of directors regarding their fiduciary responsibilities as well as financial statements, checks and balances, etc. We do not make business decisions for the board of directors. Whether an individual has extensive business acumen or not, we feel that if we provide the appropriate information for a specific subject matter, those directors will make an appropriate business decision based upon the facts, the figures, and common sense. This is, in fact, their community; not a community owned and operated by a management company. From time to time, individual directors will make decisions based upon other factors that may be self-serving. Occasionally, a one-issue individual will become a director to accomplish one item and then leave the board.

When a business decision is made that, in our opinion, does not make good business sense, we will express our opinion and note that opinion in the minutes. The final decision, however, does rest in the hands of the board of directors. As long as that decision is not of a criminal or negligent nature, we will administer that decision to the best of our abilities.

We consider long-term business relations with our clients to be extremely important. We feel that when an association's funds are being spent, not a penny of those funds should be wasted. In that vein, we spend a significant amount of time preparing specifications that are reviewed and approved by the board of directors, and a significant amount of time is spent supervising contractors completing work on communities within our portfolio. For instance, three detailed inspections are completed during a painting job to insure proper preparation and application. Materials are inspected and spot-checked to make sure that we are getting what we are paying for, and surprise inspections are made to insure full compliance with our contracts.

A relationship of trust comes with time. However, proper education of directors and giving them the tools necessary for them to understand the industry and the business is key to accelerating that trust and appreciation for what we do.

Thank you, Tim Larson. Westwind sounds like a certified, card-carrying Service Company, regardless of the company's name. Their attitude is one of caring for the HOAs. *"This is, in fact, their community; not a community owned and operated by a management company."* That could not have been said better. As long as that attitude prevails, Westwind and their clients will continue to prosper. A suggestion if you're opposed to taking the giant step of changing your name to Westwind Service Group, or Westwind Management Service Group, at least consider changing "our approach to management" to *"our approach to SERVICE."* Service is what you're offering. Flaunt it!

If you're a board member and your HOA's service/management company doesn't quite match Westwind's vowed integrity, consider interviewing other companies.

Those involved with HOAs, from management companies to homeowners, can access professional advice and find an excellent selection of tools and forms on AMPL, Inc.'s Condo-Info Web site http://www.condo-info.com. They offer tried and tested forms, letters, notices, and sample specifications that they state are updated weekly.

As you search for a service company, don't judge them by size alone. We have a very small service company and they are first rate. We appreciate their attitude, the services they perform, and the manner in which they perform those services.

Many times, very large companies demonstrate about as much caring service as a deceased doorknob. There are several extremely large management companies in the Denver area that are infamous for displaying all of the bad elements previously described as the composition of a bad management company, and more.

There's a terrifying tale about one huge management company that found naughty deeds to do that surpass the roguish traits that I listed. I can't conceive any company even thinking of such abominable acts, let alone putting them into practice. You be the judge.

The board member in this tale asked that he and his complex remain anonymous. We'll call him Arthur. Arthur was investigating some charges to the HOA by the management company. He suspected some services that were to be performed by another company, *owned by the management company*, were never completed. *Never allow services to be contracted through a company that's less than an arm's length away from the management company*. Then Arthur unearthed another clever scam. When he asked Bad Management Company about the unfulfilled services and a charge for the company's CAI (Community Associations Institute) membership dues he received a mumbo jumbo, B.S. answer. Arthur realized they were obviously charging every client the same membership fee. The company paid only one membership fee even though they handled 83 complexes. They were just merrily pocketing the fees from the other 82 complexes! Clever? Maybe. Dishonest? I would say so.

When Bad Management Company discovered they were about to be replaced by Good Service Company they used clever fairy tales about the board members to convince three adaptable homeowners to circulate a petition to call a special meeting to remove and replace the board. Bad Management Company sent notices of the meeting to **everyone except the BOD!** Ultimately, Bad Management Company's attempted coup was discovered and squelched.

That is a prime example of a good BOD getting conned by a bad management company.

It may sound as though I'm down on big companies and up on small companies. I'm not. Small companies are not immune from being unscrupulous either. Big, small, expensive, or economical does not translate to either good or bad.

It is paramount to eliminate any possibility of hooking up with a takeover management company.

Beware of those who use professional chutzpah, self-promotional B.S. You know the kind. They have a quick answer for everything, whether they really know the answer or not. It's a face-saving device. Most people have a B.S. line. Some don't recognize when they've crossed their own line. Others just cross their figurative fingers and fervently hope their victim doesn't figure it out. Board contenders have been known to use those tactics too.

Those who actually believe their own B.S. are very dangerous. Worse yet, are those who know it's B.S. and shrewdly use it to manipulate.

Ask the company for names of two to ten complexes that they manage. The smaller the company, the fewer names you'll need. Opinions you get from specific board members given as references by the company have the potential of being slanted. Without exception, you'll get twisted opinions if you contact a puppet board member. If you're exceptionally dedicated to acquiring authentic information, as you should be, knock on a few doors of homeowners in two or more of the complexes that the company handles.

▶ *IS THE BOARD OF DIRECTORS REAL OR LET'S PRETEND?*

A real board retains all of their elected powers and performs their elected duties.

Be assured that the board is real if the community is handled with care and compassion.

There are several scenarios that will create a Let's Pretend board.

• The majority of the board may always say "Yes" to the edicts of one or two members. Or the whole board may dance to the management company's desires. However board members relinquish their powers, they are a Let's-Pretend, puppet board.

• Strict enforcement is no assurance the BOD is real. They could still be Let's Pretend. If you feel choked by a Gestapo Land environment, it's imperative to determine who is actually making the enforcement decisions. Minutes of the BOD meetings *should* reveal that information. Make certain the board is following the decision-making procedures in the Docs. Your Docs are unique if they don't call for a majority vote by the BOD. If only one or two members have been making the decisions, it's possible that a majority vote would reverse the disposition of enforcement policies from unpleasant to humane.

Let's-Pretend, puppet BODs spawn the unacceptable practice of decisions being made by the management company.

• Here is a scenario that has happened more than once: A deceptive management company convinced the BOD that the company has *management obligations*. They informed the BOD that the company's expertise in the field was obviously superior to that of any of the board members. They would take all undue pressures off the BOD. With their superior qualifications they would make all the professional decisions and take care of every important detail for the community. The BOD could just lie back and enjoy their moments of glory. They would only need to be present at meetings and announce this, this, and this. The company would supply the "this" list and *manage* all the laborious details.

The company extended that easier way of decision-making to set up the easiest-to-handle business advantages *for the company*. It maximized the use of the company's time. It gave them more time to spend gathering more HOAs into their fold. Bill-fold, that is. The company will keep the BOD and the other homeowners *easily* in their places. The company can now very effortlessly raise the HOA dues, levy special assessments, and raise the fees paid to the company. The HOA may not even be able to fire them if the company has manipulated control of the majority of votes via homeowners' proxies.

The BOD may merrily go along with everything the management company says and does, because the BOD has been manipulated to have the mindset of *that's the way the system works*. Indeed, *what is in a name?*

• This is another interesting scenario: The members only wanted to be on the board for the element of prestige. Work? Make decisions? Oversee finances? No way!

After they were elected they could barely get to the management company fast enough to present their newly gained powers on a shiny, silver platter. The company happily accepted the gift and immediately attached the marionette strings to each board member. They didn't even have to dust off their manipulative dialogue.

Unless the company has acquired a vested interest in the HOA's bank account, God forbid, neither a service nor a management company has a vested interest in your HOA funds. They do not share the same concerns for your community as those who own, live there, and pay the bills. They absolutely aren't affected by special assessments and raises in the HOA dues. They don't pay them! That applies even if the wonderful service company is owned and operated by Little Red Riding Hood's loving, cookie-baking grandmother.

One of the results of a Let's Pretend BOD is Takeover Management Company may make willy-nilly decisions for the HOA. When a problem arises from a lame decision, Takeover Management Company takes a big step back, points a finger at the BOD, and shouts, "It's them! It's them! It's the BOD's responsibility. They're the ones with the elected powers. We just work *for* the BOD." The BOD has no recourse because it's true. No matter who makes the decisions the BOD holds 100 percent of the responsibility. For a BOD to let anyone else make HOA decisions is like allowing an unlicensed driver to drive your car. It's as bad as handing out blank, signed checks!

It's a popular, mistaken belief that first on the HOA tree of command comes the management company, next the BOD, and then the homeowners. If the homeowners in *all* CCCs were surveyed, I speculate a minimum of 80 percent would place the management company as first in the pecking order. A like survey of all HOA management companies would feasibly show close to 100 percent saying they manage the HOA as opposed to performing services *for* the HOA.

The value of **what's in a name** and **the power of words** is not even close to an over exaggeration. The name management is a real influence in the thought process of homeowners, BODs, the companies, and the representatives of the companies.

We instructed our management company that *all* contact with homeowners and the BOD is *always* to include a **service representative** disclaimer: "Your service representative" or "Pleasant Valley Townhomes' service agent". We've also taken the word control out of our vocabulary.

Before we instituted that procedure a past board member approached me with, "I don't think you can do anything about this but . . ." For the first time in over nine years she was late paying her monthly HOA fee and received a late charge notice from the management company. I said, "No problem. Last year the board made a decision to waive the late fee for another homeowner who was late for the first time. We'll waive yours."

At that time, I projected that more than 40 homeowners in our 51-unit complex were under the mistaken belief that the whole HOA was **managed** by the management company. We weren't managed then and we are not now. The present BOD has never spent one nano-second even considering handing over one of our elected duties to anyone.

Institute the service representative disclaimer procedure and you will upgrade interactions with your company's and homeowners' understanding of **how it really works** in your HOA.

How to Get Special Assessments and Increase Dues

You live in Sedated Townhomes. Everyone depends on Susy, Steve, and Sarah, the board members, to handle the whole shebang appropriately. Years ago the BOD contracted with Bizzi Management, Inc. to perform services for your HOA.

All the units in Sedated are in need of painting. Bizzi Management, Inc. is absorbed in doing service work for numerous HOAs. Like their name, they are *busy.*

▶ GETTING BIDS — A SKETCH OF WHAT CAN HAPPEN

The BOD expressed to Bizzi Management, Inc. that the last painters did a lousy job. This time Sedated Townhomes wants the paint to last a reasonable time.

Bizzi is busy, too busy to get multiple bids. Besides, Bizzi knows all about Prosperous Painting Company. They know that they do a superb job of painting. Unfortunately, they also do a superb job of billing. Bizzi Management told the BOD that they knew Prosperous Painting Company would do a good job. Prosperous painted Sedated.

Another sketch of what can happen

The BOD of Sedated Townhomes expressed to Bizzi Management, Inc. that the last painters were too expensive and they took too long to complete the painting. This time Sedated wanted to pay less and wanted the painters out of their complex as soon as possible, if not sooner.

Bizzi was busy, too busy to get multiple bids. Besides, Bizzi knew that Speedy Spray Company was always lower priced than other painting contractors and they sprayed the paint rapidly. Unfortunately, the life of the paint was comparable to the length of time it took Speedy to spray the paint.

It was only two years later when Sedated Townhomes had to paint again. That wasn't enough time for the funds to build to pay for the next painting project. A special assessment had to be issued to the homeowners. So much for Sedated's plan to save money and time.

Bizzi was not being malicious when they didn't get more bids. They were busy. No one, apart from the homeowners, has the same degree of concern about the HOA's pocketbook as the homeowners do themselves. It's no epidermis off Bizzi's proboscis to have dues raised and special assessments issued. You can bank on that!

All along, hanging in the wings . . .

. . . but never contacted to present a bid, was Expert and Reasonable Painting Company. Yes, they take a little longer. They make needed repairs, properly prepare all surfaces, prime, brush (not spray) with high quality paint, the paint lasts, and they are reasonable.

When one is too busy, lack of time sometimes precludes looking over past records or sorting through the yellow pages or classifieds to find an expert and reasonable company.

We've encountered both Speedy Spray Company and Expert and Reasonable Painting Company. Speedy was rounded up by the previous BOD's management company. They will never enter our complex again unless it is to purchase a home with a for sale sign.

It's often a good idea for the BOD, a volunteer homeowner, or a committee to help obtain bids. The dollar amount alone of a bid doesn't translate to the best deal. Neither is it an assurance of a company's mastery, proficiency, nor financial soundness. Thoroughly investigate all companies, especially on large projects. Make certain the company is reliable and will still be around when you need them. Don't rely on warranties to save you.

Warranties can vanish!

BOARDROOM DISCUSSION
❖ Published by the LAW FIRM OF WINZENBURG, LEFF, PURVIS AND PAYNE, LLP ❖
● 1660 Lincoln Street, #1750 ● Denver, Colorado 80264 ● 303-863-1870

LEGAL TIP: September/October 1996

Warranties by a contractor (or manufacturer) are only as good as the financial status of the company. Be sure to check on every contractor's financial stability before signing a contract, especially if you plan to rely on the contractor's warranty.

Usually roofing warranties are of two types:

1. The roofing contractor warrants labor for one to five years.

2. The roof manufacturer warrants the roofing product, typically 15 to 30 years.

LEGAL TIP: January/February 1997

When a problem arises, begin by reviewing the warranty! If required, **send written notification and give the contractor a chance to correct the problem.** If you send a handyman or roofer to repair roof leaks on a roof installed by a different contractor, **it might void the contractor's warranty on the entire job.**

Another plot

Morris Morecash and Gladys Gotfunds have the mindset that every exterior obligation is supposed to be paid by the HOA. They prefer not to lift one affluent finger to pull a weed, pound a nail, or take care of any other homeowner responsibilities. They have deep pockets and the amount of the HOA dues is absolutely of no concern to them. That plan will cause an increase in the HOA fees.

Morris and Gladys have every right and the ability to hire all the extra "dirty" tasks to be done for them. That would give them direct control and they won't need to complain to the BOD about inferior workmanship. With that plan they will only add to their own individual monthly expenses. It will not increase the dues for homeowners who perceive better ways to spend their money and who are willing to accept some individual responsibilities in order to keep the dues realistically low.

The prospect of having the HOA pay for everything may even sound tempting to those who have less than affluent incomes. Those who have to budget carefully and who want all of their discretionary monies to go toward personal, people-pleasures rather than toward the mundane and the trivial. You are wrong if you believe everything covered by the HOA will keep your financial burdens at low tide. Think about it. Would you personally hire a bunch of extra deeds to be done? Would you want to pay for them out of your own pocket? If not, the extra services don't belong in your HOA fees either. The fact that the HOA pays for a service *doesn't make it a free service* for you. Your fees will increase as services are added! Remember HOA money is *your* money. The HOA is just the middleman between your cash and the paid service. Somewhat like being your bookkeeper.

Envision just one icky deed added to the HOA. All the weeds will be eradicated from the front lawns by the lawn service with no raise in the HOA dues. Ha!

The real world . . .

- The lawn service company will come to your complex, perform the extra duty, and charge an extra per-hour fee.
- There will be complaints from some homeowners that their lawns still do not look like weed free, Japanese gardens.
- HOA fees will go upward. There will be a lot of unhappy dudes and dudettes.

Weeding should take each homeowner five to ten minutes a week to weed the lawn area around their home. Is saving ten minutes a week worth having the dues increased $5 to $10 a month? Imagine how many other items you could add to be covered by the HOA. Add another $5 to $15, or more, a month to the dues for each additional service.

Some residents keep clinging to the myth that the fewer personal obligations they have and the more services covered by the HOA, the better. The reality check comes when their fees sail out of sight. Make it your goal to maintain slim dues and healthy reserve funds. Encourage the BOD and other homeowners to do the same. If your dues seem high, it may be time to investigate ways to trim excessive services that are now covered by the HOA.

Don't let Morris Morecash and Gladys Gotfunds cause an increase in your dues. Don't you cause an increase either by shirking responsibilities. Help keep those dues low and avoid special assessments. Even if all the grounds are common area, pluck that weed and lift that trash into the nearest litter bin, no matter whose trash it is!

Other than an abundance of amenities and/or just plain bad financial management, HOAs paying for an overflow of trifling services is the primary reason so many CCCs have such exorbitantly high fees.

Take responsibility, but don't step in hazardous territories

BOARDROOM DISCUSSION
❖ Published by the LAW FIRM OF WINZENBURG, LEFF, PURVIS AND PAYNE, LLP ❖
• 1660 Lincoln Street, #1750 • Denver, Colorado 80264 • 303-863-1870
September/October 1996

IS OUR ASSOCIATION EXPOSED TO LIABILITY IF WE USE VOLUNTEERS?

Many Associations rely to some degree on volunteers. The following are some guidelines to consider when using volunteers to perform Association-related activities.

- Associations may be held liable for injuries suffered by a volunteer while performing services for the Association.

- Many worker compensation insurance policies do not cover volunteers. Does your policy cover injured volunteers?

- Do not use volunteers for hazardous activities, or for activities that involve physical strain (such as roof repair, painting of buildings or using power machinery or equipment).

- Volunteers should not perform tasks that require a licensed professional (such as plumbing or electrical work).

- If volunteers maintain the common elements, the Association should supervise the work. Most Associations have a duty to maintain and repair the common areas, and may be liable for breach of its duty if they are not maintained adequately.

- Develop procedures and guidelines for committees. Monitor each committee to ensure that it does not exceed its authority. Committees should make recommendations to the Board, instead of having actual decision-making authority (though many architectural control committees are authorized to operate with great independence).

Pulling a weed, picking up trash, or pounding an occasional nail requires neither a hard hat nor goggles.

Group rates can save the HOA money

HOAs get group rates for many services. Group rates are often much less expensive than individual rates because the company doesn't have to deal with a pack of people.

A few services where group rates can apply are

- Hazard insurance
- Painting
- Roofing
- Trash removal
- Lawn mowing

However, note this cautionary tale about group water and sewer rates. The water and sewer district for our complex gives a special rate even if it's only two homes per meter. The first water rate is up to 30,000 gallons (as it is for a single-family home). With more than one home on the same meter an additional 13,000 gallons is added (per home) to be billed at the lowest rate. So with four attached homes 69,000 gallons would be at the lowest rate. They give like consideration for sewer charges. That's the way it should be.

Some water/sewer districts treat multiple units as if they were billing one single-family home. Clearly unequal treatment. Those in attached homes do not use as much outside water as single-family dwellers. Jay Cusimano, an attorney in Cleveland, Ohio said, "An association of 200 units could probably save almost $10,000 a year if the units were treated more fairly for billing purposes. Water rates more than double and even triple as usage goes up."

Another caution is *never* sign a contract with a company (such as a trash or a laundry company) that has a provision that *they* have the option to restart the date-clock running on the contract. Such provisions will look something like . . .

- If written cancellation is not received 30 days prior to the termination date of this contract, the contract will automatically be in effect for an additional five (or however many) years. (You have to mark your calendar — they do not have to remind you of the time-window for you to terminate the contract.)
- If we replace a washing machine (or a "whatever") the length of the contract starts over for another five (or however many) years.

DO NOT SIGN SUCH CONTRACTS. They protect the contractor, not your HOA.

Another way homeowners can save money

In our complex we are each responsible for the upkeep of our own driveways. The HOA needed some cement work done on the street curbs. Several homeowners were in need of some driveway maintenance. The HOA obtained a lower rate for the residents by using the same contractor while he was completing the HOA's project. The contractor gave individual bids to each resident. The HOA coordinated the work and collected the money from the homeowners, prior to the work being done. The HOA paid the contractor.

Time for a short vacation

Read this paragraph very slowly. Visualize a peaceful blue ocean. Observe the occasional, lazy whitecaps softly rolling toward shore where palm trees gently sway. Catch a glimpse of the majestic snowcapped mountains in the background as billowy white clouds drift leisurely overhead. On the beach is a proud ostrich with its head buried deeply in the sand.

❯ *HOW NOT TO KEEP DUES LOW*

Years ago Ostrich Townhomes planted their head in the sands of foolishness. They refuse even to consider taking a peek at the firmament of common sense.

Ostrich Townhomes are attached with four units per building. The redundancy bell chimes. All townhomes are attached. It's the aspiration of a townhome to be attached. They wouldn't have it any other way.

Ostrich Townhomes is a small complex with unheard of low *disclosed* HOA fees of $60 a month. I can't testify for your territory, but in the Denver area that's a foot or ten below the level of reality. You'll soon see how their fees may actually be $100 or more. The exact amount is *undisclosed*. The BOD is determined not to do anything that would cause the disclosed dues to climb.

"Isn't that an excellent goal?" *NO! Some major services should be covered in the HOA fees on attached units.* Residents should not be *individually responsible for*

- Exterior painting
- Roofing replacement and repairs
- Hazard insurance on the structure

Ostrich Townhome residents are not enjoying the advantages of group rates for painting, roofing, or hazard insurance. By keeping the disclosed dues low, the BOD causes the homeowners to pay more than they would if those services were covered in their HOA dues.

Further, the homeowners are forced to issue self-imposed special assessments on themselves. When it's time to paint the exterior and repair or replace the roofs, they have to come up with a lump sum of money. Those expenses could be spread out in their monthly dues.

Of course, homeowners have every right to sock money away in anticipation of the costs of the inevitable maintenance. Most people are not very disciplined with that course of action. Tomorrow is always a better time to save than today is. If they do put money away for the rainy, self-imposed assessment day, a preempting emergency invariably occurs. It seems the funds just dwindle away. When the assessment day comes, they just aren't financially prepared. Many have to borrow the money, adding more to the **undisclosed** HOA fees.

Ostrich's board uses sleight of hand, mirrors, and is quite proficient at the old shell game to make it look as though the dues are low. They continue to opt to keep the disclosed dues at the current $60 rather than increasing them by a possible $15 to $20 to add other major services. Notice the operative word "major," *not* trivial services.

The homeowners continue to pay an extra $40 to $50 a month, or more, for maintenance, repairs, and individual insurance policies. That same additional amount would become more cost effective if it were paid in HOA fees. It could build a reserve fund that would prevent special or self-imposed assessments.

Many insurance companies will not accept less than a three- or six-month premium from individuals and most charge an extra service charge for paying less than a full year's premium. The homeowners could effectively have the benefit of paying their insurance premiums monthly, in their HOA fees, and get the six-month or annual premium advantage. They would also gain the perk of a lower group rate premium.

When common catastrophes occur . . .

The undisclosed-dues practice causes another dilemma in attached-home communities. Imagine when a hail storm or another common catastrophe strikes the community. Picture the pure joy of coordinating umpteen insurance companies and a multitude of painters and/or roofers stepping all over each other. Worse yet, how about the homeowners who insist on *doing the work themselves!*

There are other undesirable scenarios that can transpire.

- Some homeowners may not get around to contacting their insurance companies.
- Other homeowners, who do report the damages, may receive their checks from their insurance companies and not have the repairs completed.

When regular maintenance is needed . . .

Imagine what can happen when it's merely time to paint, not to mention roof repair.

In one four-unit building, Sally Slick lives in one unit, Bob and Betty Broke live in another, Gary Gotbucks lives in the next unit, and Alice Average lives in the fourth.

Bob and Betty are broke and have no means of paying for painting even if they do the painting themselves.

Sally, Gary, and Alice are amenable to painting, but they can't agree on a painting contractor.

Comprehend the sheer thrill it is for a painter when the homeowner gives the instructions, "Charlie, my unit is from this point to this point. I want my paint to match the shade of my neighbor's home to the north. Forget about the unit south of me. He's never done a thing to his unit and I don't know if he ever will."

Ostrich Townhomes are all painted the same army-barracks beige. Can you imagine how many shades of that one specified color are going to appear as each painter "matches" the paint? They are already accelerating in achieving a reputation of being unique. Defined lines of different hues are apparent on every building. Exterior paint shades and roofing materials are causing a striped effect. What do you think is happening to their covenants-protected property values?

There are Ostrich homeowners who perceive the errors in this don't-raise-the-dues program. They understand the concept is not only a bogus way to "save" it's an absolute mirage. The proponents of don't-raise-the dues will not budge.

The homeowners and the BOD are locked in a battle of the budget.

A suggestion for Ostrich homeowners who perceive the faux pas: Petition and compel the BOD to get their proud heads out of the sand and enter the real world. Do a coup, if necessary.

I keep saying, "If it isn't working, do a coup." I am a pacifist, not a militant. I just want CCC homeowners to have the freedom to enjoy their homes and to support equal freedom for their neighbors. That can only be accomplished with reasonable BODs.

There's more than one way to create undisclosed dues

The *management company* of Mammoth Townhomes, a very large complex, decided to have each homeowner individually contract for trash removal. That not only loses the group rate advantage, it gains the disadvantage of multiple weighty trash trucks promoting street damage. Oh well, HOA fees can be raised or special assessments can pay for the damage.

You can probably conjure up more dilemmas that silly practices can cause. Hopefully, you don't have firsthand knowledge of additional predicaments by virtue of residing in Silly Practice Townhomes.

▶ *BEWARE OF PHONY LOW DUES* ### *BEWARE OF EXCESSIVELY HIGH DUES*

If your dues seem unusually low or uncomfortably high for the norm in your area, investigate now. If you decide to sell, low dues are suspect and excessively high dues are frightening. Either can deter your sale. Don't assume a snail's pace. Research and encourage your community to correct possible pitfalls and institute reasonable financial procedures.

- Know what services are actually covered by the HOA dues.
- Are funds being handled prudently?
- Is the advantage of group rates being utilized on necessary and major services?
- Are fees swelling because too many trivial services, such as weeding homeowners' lawns, are the responsibility of the HOA?
- What are the actual monthly or annual HOA bills?

- What amenities are in the complex? Do the fees include maintenance of extensive common areas, heat for the individual units, pools, saunas, exercise rooms, property taxes, and so on? Those dues are naturally going to look as though they are excessive compared to dues in communities with few or no amenities. It is written, "Compare an apple only to an apple. An apple can never parallel a pear."
- What provisions are in the Docs about the amount allowed for increasing the dues and what is the frequency allowed for such increases? Historically, what has the pattern been?
- Is money being added monthly to reserve funds and do the reserve funds seem healthy enough to prevent special assessments?

  If reserve funds are low or nonexistent, quickly boogie out of that complex. They're destined for special assessments and colossal increases in the monthly dues.

- No matter what amount is in reserves, infallible control of the funds must be firmly in place. If the funds appear a wee bit plump and without proper control measures, what assurances do you have that the HOA funds aren't planning a trip to Switzerland when the account gets to massive weight? Make certain funds are protected and not just waiting to provide a board member or management company's representative a comfortable retirement in another country.

  High fees and large bank accounts don't categorically proclaim wicked intentions. Do investigate.

- Are the books reviewed or audited annually by an outside, independent firm?
- Don't make assumptions or rely on hearsay about the HOA's finances. Obtain verification from the HOA or their service/management company, preferably *before* you buy.
- *After* you buy, attend the meetings to help thwart any silly, false attempts to keep dues low. Sing the praises of the value of group rates. Make every effort to prevent all attempts to add too many extra services to the HOA's obligations that will increase the dues.

We include the premium for a blanket insurance policy in our dues, as any rational HOA with attached homes would. We print this mini-budget on the back of our community phone directory as a constant reminder of the destination of the monthly HOA dues.

Our goal is to develop and maintain the advantages and serenity of single-family home communities, while minimizing maintenance costs with a balance of resident participation and HOA group rates. How are your HOA dues spent? A mini breakdown follows . . .

What we would pay in a single-family, detached home	Service	Average dues in Colorado are *OVER* $125! OUR $90 MONTHLY DUES PAY FOR . . .	
$11.00 to 21.00	Trash Removal	$ 6.70	$24.70 is left for common
(Approximately) 30.00	Homeowner's Insurance	16.20	area maintenance, exterior
(City's average) 34.62	Water and Sewer	23.70	maintenance (painting, roof
60.00 to 75.00	Mowing and Snow Removal	11.70	repair, front lawn mowing),
-0-	Service Company Fees	7.00	water and sewer, office supplies,
$135.62 to $160.62 PLUS other expenses	← TOTAL →	$65.30	street maintenance, and capital improvement funds.

If you discover mindless decisions about the HOA fees are being made by those on the BOD run to a petition maker, a really good attorney. Get those members off the board *now!* Do not pass GO and do not linger at Park Place to smell the pretty flowers.

You may plan just to sell your home, if necessary, to get away from excessively high or mindlessly low HOA dues. Unduly high or low dues can cause a slow to no sale. Buyers will compare your home with other properties. They are more likely to choose to purchase a home in a complex with more practical dues.

Your prospective buyers will investigate thoroughly if they've read this book.

A little about insurance

- An HOA blanket hazard insurance policy covers claims of common disasters for an entire building or the entire complex (primarily exteriors), and for specific disasters to individual units.
- A resident-paid content insurance policy covers items inside the home which are not covered under the blanket policy.
- A homeowner's hazard insurance policy, usually only carried on single-family detached homes, covers damages to the inside, the outside, and the contents of the home.

Guard against a gap or an overlap of coverage between the HOA blanket policy and your content policy. Specific items covered by insurance companies vary from company to company. Verification of exact coverage is the responsibility of the homeowners.

Add this coverage to your insurance policy

BOARDROOM DISCUSSION
❖ Published by the LAW FIRM OF WINZENBURG, LEFF, PURVIS AND PAYNE, LLP ❖
• 1660 Lincoln Street, #1750 • Denver, Colorado 80264 • 303-863-1870

July/August 1996

LOSS ASSESSMENT INSURANCE COVERAGE

Loss assessment insurance coverage is often not added to a homeowner's insurance policy. If an Association levies special assessments to the owners as a result of a direct loss or a liability, such coverage will provide for payment of special assessments. Under most circumstances, homeowners can secure an endorsement that insures loss assessments.

When is this a valuable coverage? Since most policies do not provide coverage for floods, mud or earthquakes, unit owners without loss assessment coverage would not be covered for special assessments levied as a result of such problems.

Therefore, we recommend that you encourage all unit owners to discuss "loss assessment" coverage with their individual insurance agents at the owners' earliest convenience.

Companies know how to charge more for more services

Services, such as lawn maintenance companies, understand charging more for added services. The BOD says, "We had sod put on five areas that were xeriscaped. Include those areas in the weekly mowing and trimming." The lawn service owner quickly replies, "We'll be glad to include those areas. That will be an additional $100 a week."

Companies don't know how to charge less for fewer services

Evidently there's something extremely simple about the mathematics of adding and something radically complicated about subtracting. Some companies become absolutely incompetent at reducing their bill for performing fewer services. "Remove these five areas of lawn from the weekly mowing and trimming. We've decided to xeriscape them. How much will that reduce our monthly bill?" The lawn service owner says, "Oh, no adjustment, the bill will remain the same." If you encounter a similar circumstance, hire a different lawn service or whatever type of company that applies to your specific situation.

That popular practice reminds me of when the cola industry raised cola prices in the 1970s due to a sugar shortage. Sugarless cola prices rose right along with sugared cola prices! The price of sugar went downward. The price of cola didn't. Once they (whoever they are) get the taste of higher prices, they regard lowering the price as diminishing their profits. Greedy blinders prevent them from recognizing that when their cost factors go down, they can lower their prices accordingly and their profit margin will remain the same.

A *classic example of how negligence and a management company's dictatorship can cause special assessments and raise the dues.*

I was going to reprint an article about this nightmare. A real estate broker who is very familiar with the whole mess said, "I wouldn't if I were you. You would have to print every name and that might not be a healthy course." That sounded too Mafia-like for my comfort. I prefer Birkenstocks to cement shoes so I contacted homeowners in the complex. They gave the following accounts starting in June 1995. Pseudonyms and initials are used.

A potpourri of information from residents of LovingWay Condos

D.B. said, "This used to be a happy community. Now it's turned into a battle zone. It all started about two years ago when the management company, with the board's sanction, proposed a special assessment of up to $10,000 per unit to repair or replace the outside stairs!"

The proposal was defeated by a majority vote of the homeowners. The unpopular proposal was repeatedly added to the ballot and it finally passed!

Residents said the board and the management company gathered proxy votes from absentee and other owners. They claimed that Anna Salt, representative of the management company, enclosed a letter that had altered facts about the undertaking when she sent the requests for the return of the signed proxies.

Between the defeat and the "victory" of the special assessment, empowered by the condominium bylaws, the board raised the monthly homeowners' fees.

Opponents of "project stairs" suggested a repair or replace as needed process using the increased monthly funds rather than the Blitzkrieg, do-it-all-now approach.

Anna Salt told the residents that it was imperative that the stair problem be handled immediately because the city was about to condemn the entire community if the stairs weren't repaired or replaced. She told them that complete replacement was the better way. It would protect the residents' safety."

D.B. said, "That was a bunch of rotten garbage. Anna doesn't care one bit about the residents' safety. And when we called the city they had no knowledge of any plans to condemn LovingWay!"

Repairs on the stairs could have been paid for with funds from the ten-year home warranty. Several other Colorado communities built by the same developer took advantage of their warranties. LovingWay Condos ran past the deadline of the claim period.

Several homeowners obtained bids as low as half the bid of the contractor recommended by the management company. Anna Salt told the homeowners that none of those other companies were fully professional.

The entire "project stairs" will cost well over two million dollars!

Sally Sweetheart's monthly association fee leaped from approximately $105 to $135. She said, "If I choose to pay off the assessment in installments my fee will soar to about $300 a month. Either way, I can't afford it."

Some homeowners charged the board and Anna Salt of lying, spying, prying, intimidating, manipulating, and sabotage.

"We thought we had won, then they came back two more times for a new 'vote,'" said LovingWay's resident, Steve Sensible. "You can't win when they have the majority of votes via proxies in their hands. Yet, we never actually saw the controlling proxies, we were just told they existed. Most here are middle-income residents. There are many who aren't able to handle this financial burden. They will be forced to sell or abandon their homes."

One resident of LovingWay said, "Before Anna Salt arrived on the scene, everyone was content. We had an on-site manager and maintenance person. We could put our trash out in front of our building any day of the week and the maintenance person would take it to the trash dumpster. There is only one dumpster for almost 300 homes. They [the BOD and the management company] changed our convenient trash pickup system to one specific day that we are allowed to put our trash out. A week's worth of trash overtakes our small homes. Yes, we can take it to the dumpster ourselves. Many senior citizens live here. It's a real burden for them to do that, especially on snowy or rainy days.

"When a neighbor returned from a trip, she had a citation and a $50 fine for having put her trash out on the wrong day. She called to explain that since she wasn't even in town, it couldn't have been her trash. Not taking her word, they scheduled a hearing before the board and the management company. Both the board and Anna Salt, with her 'Gestapo' tactics, insulted and interrogated her. Finally they did waive the fine but informed her if it ever happened again the fine would stand!

"I like my place but, since the management company has taken over I don't feel like it's my home anymore. I feel like an unwelcome guest.

"Over the years, while fighting the special assessment, we've lost a lot of support as people bailed out of the complex. Many have rented their units, some have sold, and others have simply walked away and let their homes go into foreclosure. It's becoming a rental city.

"It's been a real struggle.

"We have a blanket liability insurance policy and the board hasn't even pursued the possibility of the insurance company paying for, at least, part of the stairs. Hail damage or whatever is a possibility. It seems it would be worth checking out.

"Anna Salt tells everyone just how it's going to be and what the homeowners will and will not do. She has somewhat of an answer for everything, whether she knows what she's talking about or not. She changes her story to fit the end result she wants. I don't like dealing with these jerks.

"The board doesn't listen. They don't care. They harass everyone they don't like with fines.

"At meetings the board and management company ridicule homeowners. They laugh at them and belittle them. They are rude and insulting. They act as though homeowners are imbeciles.

"Emergencies have to be scheduled at the management company's convenience! Did you ever try scheduling your emergencies?

"One couple had a hot water heater that was about to blow. They had a plumber bring a new hot water heater. When he couldn't find the shut off valve they called Anna Salt. They were informed by Anna that she wouldn't give out that type of information just any time of the day. They would have to schedule time with her. After a phone screaming match Anna finally gave the location of the valve to the plumber. Anna is a royal bitch.

"They got the special assessment passed with the votes they controlled from absentee owners' proxies. Anna is very good at altering facts to manipulate her way around people. Absentee owners obviously just don't care.

"Anna Salt is in complete control of the board and this whole complex. The president even gives *signed blank checks to Anna!* There's something in the woodpile here that doesn't have the right odor. It's scary."

That was a close up view of the *power of proxies*. A dictatorship was handed to the management company by the BOD and homeowners' signed proxies! Perhaps there were a few homeowners' signed "blank check" proxies involved too, assuming the signed proxies ever really existed.

For two years the special assessment issue kept reappearing on the agenda. Defeating an issue once doesn't guarantee it's a done deal.

Even without the ignored warranty, the whole expensive mess could have been avoided. Continuing preventive maintenance is an absolute necessity to avoid emergency measures. The current omnipotent powers don't seem to comprehend *do it before a crisis occurs*. They need to take Preventive Maintenance 101, 102, and 103. But first, they need to stop playing marionettes for the entertainment of the management company and escape from the puppet strings that Anna Salt holds.

In their exalted "place of honor" the BOD was blatantly negligent in not noticing the crumbling stairways long before the ten-year warranty expired. Suddenly, they happened to notice the stairs are falling. The stairs are falling. That scene smacks of Chicken Little's announcement, "The sky is falling. The sky is falling." Residents at LovingWay better keep a watchful eye on needed repairs.

The management company has all the qualities of Bad Management Company plus a string of pure evils they must have learned at the "University of Hitler."

The homeowners offered more reasonable bids. They also suggested that by staggering the reconstruction of "Project Stairs," the increase in the monthly dues would cover the costs. The *management company turned both proposals down* and *insisted* LovingWay use the construction company recommended by them! Could it be that someone may be getting a kickback from that construction company?

Steve Sensible told me that the residents petitioned the BOD to change management companies. The petition had more than the required number of signatures. The BOD denied the petition. That decision was defended with the interpretation that the bylaws state that the BOD has the power to hire and fire management companies.

An error lies in the intent of their petition. The petition should have been a petition to relieve the BOD of any further duties. With the transplant of a new BOD, they could have performed emergency bypass surgery and hired Good Service Company, Inc.

"Anna is very good at altering facts to manipulate her way around people." Steve Sensible told me that recently he contacted the absentee owners and discovered exactly how the facts were altered to hoodwink those homeowners. They were told that they were sending their proxies to board members who *represented the sensible group*. Nefarious, desperate people will stop at nothing to get their way.

With the gigantic "Project Stairs" facing the complex, there's a chance other needed repairs will take a back-seat until suddenly neglected repairs become the next big project(s). As synthetic emergencies devour fat funds, a genuine calamity could strike that truly will require immediate, expensive attention.

The preceding paragraph was meant to be a prediction. Look at what just came to light: The funds from the special assessments are *not being used for the dire stairs problem!* Steps and railings are being repaired on an ***as-needed basis.*** The residents were told that suggestion wouldn't work.

Now more money is going toward replacing some of the cement balconies and patios than is going to fix the dreadful stairs problem. The cement has been identified as the real dilemma. It seems that the balconies and patios were installed wrong and cause a water flow problem. Someone is playing the shell game with money from the special assessment. Could it be that there never was a true need to levy a special assessment? Is either "Project Stairs" or "Project Cement" a genuine emergency or could both be fixed on an as-needed basis? Will the assessment money ever even be in the hands of a construction company? It's worse than a soap opera.

Does LovingWay's BOD make Watergate-like decisions?

BOARDROOM DISCUSSION
❖ Published by the LAW FIRM OF WINZENBURG, LEFF, PURVIS AND PAYNE, LLP ❖
• 1660 Lincoln Street, #1750 • Denver, Colorado 80264 • 303-863-1870
Reprinted with the permission of *Common Ground* ©*1986* Community Associations Institute

UNANIMOUS DECISIONS CAN LEAD TO TROUBLE   August 1992

What do the following events have in common?
• The disastrous launch of the space shuttle "Challenger"
• The Watergate break-in and cover-up
• The Bay of Pigs invasion of Cuba

All were consequences of unanimous decisions called Groupthink by psychologist Daniel Goleman. According to Dr. Goleman, Groupthink is a way for groups to protect themselves from such unpleasant things as disharmony and strife, *overlooking any facts or feelings that might threaten unity.*

Board members can avoid this trap. If you need more information, disagree or have doubts about a certain decision or topic, make sure your comments are heard *and* included in the Minutes of the meeting. You owe it to yourself and to the Association not simply to agree with every decision. If the meeting has gone on too long, postpone the discussion until the next meeting rather than rushing into an unanimous decision for the sake of concluding the meeting. You can disagree or object in a friendly way, says Dr. Goleman, but *you must be courageous enough to state your convictions.*

By seeking all the facts and considering every point of view, Board members will be better able to make good decisions.

"We find comfort among those who agree with us — growth among those who don't."

— Frank A. Clark

LovingWay homeowners, look at the minutes to see how decisions are made

BOARDROOM DISCUSSION
❖ Published by the LAW FIRM OF WINZENBURG, LEFF, PURVIS AND PAYNE, LLP ❖
● 1660 Lincoln Street, #1750 ● Denver, Colorado 80264 ● 303-863-1870

July 1995

PREPARING BOARD MINUTES

When Boards authorize unusual actions or high expenditures that might be challenged by present or future owners, take care in preparing Board minutes. For example, let's say the Board approved Roofing Contract for work in excess of $50,000. The resolutions approving the agreement should

● *Clearly identify and approve the agreement.* Identify the agreement so there will be no confusion concerning which agreement was approved.

● *Indicate the basic purpose of the agreement.* Sometimes Board members are familiar with the general nature of the contract, but haven't read the agreement. Clearly state that the Board members were aware of the substance of the matter on which they acted. If there is any dispute about this, it could cast doubt on the validity of the Board's action and whether they complied with their fiduciary duty of care.

● *State that the agreement has been reviewed by the Board of Directors.* If an agreement is materially changed after submission to the Board, the agreement may have to be resubmitted and approved before it can be executed.

● *Authorize the proper persons to execute the agreement by preparing resolutions specifically authorizing execution.* To remove any doubt concerning execution and delivery, the resolution should expressly state which Officers are authorized to execute the agreement.

Before the special assessment "passed," homeowners who were selling their homes were uncertain as to what ranked as honest disclosure to the buyers. ***Because the special assessment had originally been defeated by the homeowners, some sellers made no disclosure.*** Other sellers tried to compensate the buyers for the unresolved, special assessment. Buyers received $2,000 to $5,000 and who knows what other deals were made? One resident likened the stairs-are-falling mess to the many faces of Dorian Grey.

Multitudes of sellers, buyers, and real estate brokers have been financially injured along the path as the unsettled assessment continued to lurk just below the surface. There are still lawsuits and financial litigations pending.

LovingWay homeowners, keep a watchful eye on funds, your BOD, and management company. This could be the start of serial assessments by the raise-the-fee's stalker.

Just a reminder . . .

- *Never* allow the service/management company to decide which company will be hired to do various work in your complex. The BOD should *always* make the final decision.
- *Never* allow a BOD to remain in power if they are uncaring and dictatorial or if they are a mere puppet of the management company. Do a coup of the BOD.
- *Never* give your signed proxy without verifying the person you have designated will indeed attend the meeting and vote as you would.

- *Never* allow checks to be signed by the management company. *Always have the BOD review the bills and two members of the board sign the checks.*

Some HOAs try a little of everything to keep raising the dues

Bob Waber posted a fact-filled, two-page announcement to inform other residents in his townhome community in Boulder, Colorado of the unsavory activities and non-activities of the board that defy financial prudence. An abridged version follows.

Unofficial Newsletter   No. 1 - Nov. 13, 1996

TO ALL PROPERTY OWNERS AND RENTERS

Have you ever wondered how your dues (your money) are spent? Have you ever wondered why our association's dues keep going up so rapidly?

The board spends our association's dues senselessly.

- A street light, for crime prevention, cost $1,534. It *only dimly lights one tiny corner* and is *not even on our property!*

- Recently, repairs for structural rotting on one unit cost $2,000. The repairman determined the underlying cause was lack of proper outside maintenance to prevent infiltration of water. Preventive maintenance would have cost about $100. Approximately $1,900 of our money could have been saved.

- A rainstorm caused flooding in at least two units. A city official of Boulder, a civil engineer, determined the cause was lack of proper drainage. Since January, 1992 the board has received notification, verbally and in writing, that the drainage problem is causing serious damage to units. The board under-reacts by continuing to neglect and ignore preventive maintenance.

- The board hired a management company that charged roughly double normal management fees. After $56,000 was discovered missing from the funds of another complex in the area, the company resigned their position at our complex and left the state. Some of our records left with them!

- My roof was leaking. A roofer told me the roof was fine. The leak was caused by deferred maintenance on the chimney flashing. *Sometimes the board overreacts.* They fixed my problem by paying *$28,000 to replace all the roofs!* About three months later the wind blew off a large portion of the new roofing. The underlying, old roofs remained in place. The roofer refused to honor his warranty so our insurance company paid for roof repairs, then raised our premium!

- I asked the management company why deteriorated siding was not being repaired and why dirt and debris were not removed before painting the complex. I was told that all we could afford was a Band-Aid solution. Paint is meant to preserve siding. Some of the *paint couldn't get past all the dirt and debris even to touch the siding.* How much of our *$33,000 went to paint rotten siding and dirt?* That "money saving" procedure will only hasten the need to paint again!

- Many trees and shrubs have died due to lawnmower damage. Some owners put barriers around some trees to keep the mowers away. *Management told them to stop!* Trees are very expensive to replace. Aesthetically, the loss of trees can reduce property values. The lack of shade will decrease residents' comfort.

Conditions could get much worse with disastrous effects on our property values and quality of life. Dues will go higher and higher as deferred maintenance and negligence cause the urgent necessity of expensive repairs.

I call upon the board to start maintaining our homes properly and stop squandering our money or step down so we can elect those who will do the job right. Two of our current board members are absentee landlords — they are rarely even seen in the complex. They don't care as much as those of us who live here.

The main priority of the board should be to preserve and enhance our investments. Many, as I, invested our life's savings to buy our homes and we hate to see our community continue to deteriorate.

It's time this dictatorship be replaced with a democracy. We are forming a group to effect positive changes to help protect our values. Contact us if you would like to join the group.

Also please contact us if you are experiencing problems such as water leakage, dampness, water spots on the ceiling, musty odors, cracks, rodents, etc.

We ask you to attend the upcoming annual meeting and vote your preferences. If you cannot attend, you would help by giving your signed proxy to someone in the group for positive changes. *If you send your proxy to the board or the management company, we will all get more of the same negligent maintenance, squanderous spending, and increases in the dues!*

Renters, keep your landlords informed about what is happening, as dues increase so will your rent. Encourage your landlords to care and to get involved by voting for positive change.

Positive changes have been made in other complexes and they can be made here too. It's up to us to take the responsibility of caring.

Bob, unfortunately BODs and management companies who have their heads in dark places rarely step aside in the interest of positive action. Your public plea to homeowners to handle their proxies wisely put the BOD and the management company on alert. They will act as quickly as bunnies to protect their positions by gathering up as many proxies as possible.

My last sentence would normally hold true. However, the BOD and/or management company *chose not to issue proxies* for their annual meeting! That indicates they sensed too many homeowners would comply with Bob's proxy request. Obviously they banked on apathy keeping unhappy homeowners from attending the meeting. *One of Bob's group was elected to the BOD.* Ha, ha, ha! Stop laughing. One good BOD member isn't enough.

Bob said, *"Two of our current board members are absentee landlords — they are rarely even seen in the complex. They don't care as much as those of us who live here."* Why would homeowners even consider electing an absentee to the board? Perhaps the fact that they were absentee owners wasn't even brought to light. Maybe someone collected a multitude of proxy votes from apathetic homeowners and absentee homeowners to swing the election. I can identify no other sane reasons.

Don't let all your hard work and research go to waste, Bob. Get your group to conduct a survey to ascertain how many unhappy homeowners there are in your complex. Then do a coup before it's too late to glue your community back together. It is falling apart.

Sometimes, as one problem ends the next one begins

Don, a sharp 87-year-old gentleman, has owned his home in Denver since 1985. The townhomes were built in the early 1970s.

Following are some of his comments and observations.

Don said, "The developer originally charged $37 monthly HOA dues. [Unrealistically low, even for the early '70s.]

"In 1996 the dues were $275 and I hear that they are about to be raised to $300. The fee covers outside building and ground maintenance, water and sewer, and patrolling by off-duty police. The dues also cover maintenance on a large pool, a small pool, and a clubhouse.

"Trash removal is not covered because that service is provided by the city. There is a blanket insurance policy, but the premiums are paid by the homeowners!

"The day after I moved in there was a severe rain storm. The inside of my home was like Niagara Falls . . ."

Don continued, "The shake shingle roofs were in dire need of replacement. They had been in need of repair since 1975. The HOA made an insurance claim. "A vote was taken to determine the type of roofing materials to use for replacement. The majority voted to use materials other than shake. The board ignored the vote and had shakes installed. Shake shingles aren't practical in Colorado. The climate is too dry. Fire spreads quickly in dry shakes, they are easily damaged by hail, and they deteriorate rapidly.

"The HOA received a large check from the insurance company for roof replacement. Then the insurance company refused to insure the shake shingle roofs or the buildings.

"The gutters leaked. The on-site maintenance man didn't make proper repairs.

"The board is run like a monarchy. They meet once a month and the minutes are supposed to be on display in a three-ring binder or mailed, if requested. When I requested to see recent minutes the representative of the management company said, 'They aren't available, they're being edited.'

"Everything was going downhill. A different maintenance man was hired every month or two. Even the management company was changed often."

Don said, "This spring we had a heavy snow storm that broke off a lot of tree branches. That caused an unexpected expense of $34,000 to clean up the mess. It almost depleted the HOA funds.

"The board has finally figured out we need a reserve fund of about 1.4 million dollars. They're trying to figure out how to do it.

"A review board would be helpful, like they have in the Bond Market, AA, B+, C, D ratings. I'm afraid our HOA would come up with a C or a D rating."

BODs cannot arbitrarily deny inspection of the records

BOARDROOM DISCUSSION
❖ Published by the LAW FIRM OF WINZENBURG, LEFF, PURVIS AND PAYNE, LLP ❖
● 1660 Lincoln Street, #1750 ● Denver, Colorado 80264 ● 303-863-1870

January 1993

RELEASING REPORTS, RECORDS, AND LISTS

A unit owner has the burden of showing a proper purpose for examining an Association's delinquency report, according to an Illinois appellate court decision. The court found that a "good faith" fear of mismanagement is a proper purpose and that once the purpose is established, an owner may examine all "necessary books and records."

Courts in Texas have also allowed access to records held by an Association's attorney and a Virginia Court allowed access to Association payroll records.

We are frequently asked if an owner has a right to a list of owners and their addresses. Colorado law states: "All books and records of a corporation may be inspected by any member or his agent or attorney for any proper purpose at any reasonable time." Since that information is in the county public records, it too should be released, if the Board determines the request is made for a proper purpose.

Tip: Establish procedures for when and how to release Association books and records.

[Further clarification and update]

OWNER'S RIGHT TO INSPECT ASSOCIATION BOOKS AND RECORDS

Colorado's law states that "All books and records . . ." The rights of inspection, however, are often limited by the right of privacy and confidentiality.

Minutes of all meetings should be available

BOARDROOM DISCUSSION
❖ Published by the LAW FIRM OF WINZENBURG, LEFF, PURVIS AND PAYNE, LLP ❖
• 1660 Lincoln Street, #1750 • Denver. Colorado 80264 • 303-863-1870
October 1992

IS SILVERADO A ROLE MODEL?

We have read how improperly several Board members of Silverado Savings and Loan acted during the 1980s. They had fiduciary duties similar to those that Associations Board members have. *Officers and Directors have a duty to act prudently and in the best interest of all members in conducting the business of the Association.*

Tip: Prepare and review minutes of all meetings. The signed minutes should prove that the Board fulfilled its duty of care, made reasonable decisions, and complied with the Business Judgment Rule. Each Board member should keep copies of the minutes in case an issue is raised years later.

Don, whose son lives in a CCC in California, further relayed the following information: California legislated to regulate the handling of all California community associations (Davis-Stirling Common Interest Development Act AB314). The Act became effective January 1, 1986. One of many points is that associations are required to prepare and distribute an annual budget to all homeowners before the end of each fiscal year. The association must provide a copy of the budget to every homeowner who requests it or encounter civil penalties or possible lawsuits.

That annual budget package is an immense help in determining an association's financial stability. The package must contain a statement of the current operating budget and an analysis of the long term reserve budget. Such reserve studies are endorsed by many industry groups and organizations.

It is definitely a prudent idea to keep a watchful eye on *all* HOA records. Most certainly, monitor the financial statements. If reading financial statements doesn't fall within your realm of aptitudes, get with someone who does readily understand them. It is extremely important to know what is taking place within your HOA. It is a wise move to squelch suspicious activities in the beginning, when they are usually relatively small. That is considerably easier to do than to wait until they become massive.

It takes less effort to flatten an anthill than to level a mountain. It's much less expensive, too.

CHAPTER 9

If You Feel Like Road Kill, You Have a Problem

Wednesday, May 8, 1991
Reprinted with permission of *The Denver Post*

Covenant pettiness peeves Parker couple

By Ginny McKibben
Denver Post Staff Writer

PARKER — This spring, nothing came up roses for one Parker couple. Bill and Judy McClarnon were sued by the Town and Country Homeowner Association for violating community covenants, starting with the artificial flowers they allegedly planted in their window box.

The window box was displayed outside the McClarnon's kitchen window all year when covenants specify it must be removed during winter months, the lawsuit said.

The suit, filed in Douglas County District Court, also seeks judgment against the McClarnons for displaying a non-conforming basketball hoop and garden hose holder, and for flying the American flag from an unapproved bracket on their townhome garage.

Neighbor Maryann Muldoon, who lives in one of the 500 Victorian-style townhomes in the development, is seething over association actions she called "silly and stupid."

"I think the homeowner association's board is trying to make Town and Country look like Army barracks," Muldoon said.

Judy McClarnon, a community resident since 1984, angrily blames the suit on the board's pettiness in covenant enforcement.

"You betcha I am going to fight them. I am so mad. That flag wouldn't be flying anymore except I am so torqued," McClarnon said. "I really have things I would rather do than hassle with my association."

Homeowner Association's President Dorothy Hajovsky and attorney Cheryl Torpy did not return telephone calls yesterday.

McClarnon, a former association board member, claims the window box, flag, and red-white-and blue basketball hoop were put up years ago and approved by an architectural control committee.

The fake flowers have been stored in the attic for more than a year, McClarnon said.

Friends of the McClarnons also claim they have been targeted by an unprecedented flurry of citations and fines.

Muldoon was cited for leaning her patio umbrella against her house and putting a "beware of dog" sign on the gate. Since then, she said, the association has outlawed her outdoor thermometer and told her to request new permission to display her wind chimes.

Fines can be hefty. They begin at $10 and increase until, after 20 days, an additional $100 can be levied every three days until the violation is corrected.

Some residents plan to march on the board's meeting next Monday. But they must petition for permission to speak.

Resident Gyl Condojani wrote other residents asking them to join her in demanding the board put homeowners' dues to better use than suing association members "for menial items."

Roar! Quick, throw some raw meat before all those homeowners become the HOA's lunch.

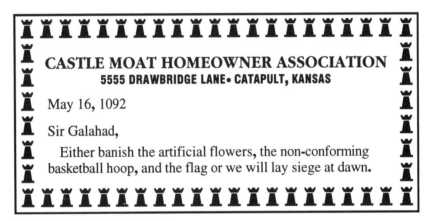

Gyl, have you noticed not all the *kookies* are in a jar? Some of them crawled out and are lurking in CCCs disguised as the BODs of the HOAs.

Every time I read that story I turn 18 shades of raging red. That BOD needs to get a life. Perchance they should seriously consider entering an institution to get a cure for their severe control-oholic problem. Without exception, the rank of importance for every one of the "lawsuit-worthy" issues is just below "On which side of the bed is it better to exit on Tuesday mornings when it's raining?"

It's astonishing how 500 residents will allow themselves to be terrorized by a handful of mean, Gestapo-like board members. Don't let your freedoms be violated. Everyone has the right to live each day as fully as it was intended to be lived.

Town and Country's charges marched the homeowners to court. It's my understanding that the judge's decision was *for* the HOA.

Shame on the developer for assembling such petty restrictions.

Shame on the BOD for enforcing the pettiness of the restrictions to the extreme.

Shame on the judge for not removing his ear plugs before *"hearing"* the case and voicing his or her decision.

Attila and his Huns marched again! Homeowners get so depressed and downtrodden they're ready to sell their homes for prices less than real market value, even in an up-market, just to get out quickly and regain their sanity.

Had the homeowners been more alert and active from the beginning, Attila and his Huns would have had less impact. Homeowners' involvement is critical.

▶ *RECOGNIZE THE REAL PROBLEM, IS IT THEM OR YOU?*

The homeowners were identified as the problem. The real problem was the BOD and probably the management company. The Court's decision makes the BOD feel extremely righteous and vindicated. The judge didn't change any of the BOD's wrongness. The judge simply compounded a bad decision with a worse one.

Town and Country's BOD adores restraining and dictating to the most trivial degree, exactly what everyone is allowed to do and not do. They squelch freedom and suppress enjoyment of living every chance they get. They keep their magnifying glass dusted off, in good working order. They don't let one little "problem" get past them.

Don't demoralize. Humanize and civilize.

Both the McClarnons and the Muldoons have moved. I certainly hope they experience more favorable circumstances. Wouldn't it be fun to tame Town and Country with a coup d'état?

Another road kill story

DIETER HANSHALL AND HIS WIFE MOVED FROM EAST GERMANY to remove themselves from the oppression of a society that was overly structured. He said, "We left Germany with the intention of enjoying our lives as free spirits. To us, this means our neighbors would have the same privileges.

"We searched from Los Angeles to Florida. We moved into a beautiful home in Parker, Colorado. It was the home and an area that seemed to be what we were looking for.

"We sent a letter to the developer October, 1989 regarding putting up a flag pole. We pressed for an answer several times. We took no reply as meaning yes.

"April, 1990 we moved in and were as happy as birds flying into their nest. Proudly we displayed the American flag. We were sued for that atrocity.

"The developer is a dictator and a professional vulture who has made this a prison. Compromise and easy going just doesn't work with him."

There was a brouhaha between the homeowners and the developer. Dieter said, "The developer banned Channel 2 News from the building. He had two policemen there as guards to keep them out.

"The representative of the management company drives around to selectively ticket cars that are parked on the street. One day I counted 21 cars that had *not* been ticketed. But, they managed to give one to me. Unfair treatment polarizes."

Dieter certainly didn't expect to jump out of oppression right into tyranny. *"We left Germany with the intention of enjoying our lives as free spirits."* How many letters do you think Dieter and his wife sent to friends and relatives proclaiming the "wonders" of living in the United States of America?

Learn to live together happily instead of flexing suing-power muscles. Reevaluate your rules, domesticate them, and render them civil. Lighten up. You may like it.

If a polarized posture of "them and us" exists, your community is in dire need of a cathartic overhaul. Or, perhaps, a double bypass may be in order. Transplant a new BOD and a new *service* company in place of the old *management* company.

Dieter continued, "Fight fire with fire. Hire the meanest dog attorney you can find and go for it! Once these jerks understand the real world, maybe they'll learn that life requires some give and take.

"Homeowners should band together, financially or otherwise, to demand reasonable representation and modify the rules to be livable in a covenants-controlled community.

"You move into a community to fly like a bird and discover you're not all singing the same caring song."

Dieter and his wife *lost in court!* As with many others, their suffering incited their move from that blitzkrieg area.

There are inherent hardships involved in making an otherwise undesired move. Why do human beings want to be the direct cause of a neighbor's moving? What joy do they get out of inflicting hardships? It's a tragedy!

Dilemmas arise when petty people determine it's their divine duty to place pointless, trivial rules superior to human comforts.

Take a look at the "exalted-controlling" purpose: the determination to enforce the "rightness" of ludicrous, unimportant rules. Do you wonder what they see when they look into a mirror?

Dieter probably received a Christmas card from the HOA something like . . .

> WITH CHRISTMAS COMES HOLLY
> AND SNOW ON THE EXTERIOR.
> REMOVE THE FLAG OR
> WE'LL SUE YOUR POSTERIOR.

Some BODs are from a friendly planet

BOARDROOM DISCUSSION
❖ Published by the LAW FIRM OF WINZENBURG, LEFF, PURVIS AND PAYNE, LLP ❖
• 1660 Lincoln Street, #1750 • Denver, Colorado 80264 • 303-863-1870

August 1992

• In Virginia, architectural covenants are being violated by a Navy veteran who wants to fly the American flag in front of his unit. The Association has offered to put up a community flag, and has sent its members a survey about the flag restrictions. If the majority of residents are in favor of dropping the restriction, the Board will do so.

We are all in the same universe. Look at that word closely. Think about it this way: uni-verse, uni (one) verse (song). There's only one song, one harmonious song.

A collage of wisdom learned from seminars, tapes, and books by the noted author, Dr. Wayne Dyer: Singing a song in discord with the one song is equivalent to being a cancerous cell. Recognize the absurdity of a cancerous cell. It reproduces and encourages healthy cells to become cancerous until all the other cells are devoured and die.

Everyone has the choice to sing the one harmonious song and be a healthy cell.

Edgar Mitchell, Apollo 14 Astronaut, is one of only 12 human beings in the entire history of humanity who have ever walked on the moon. His scientific perception of the universe came as he earned his Ph.D. in nuclear physics from MIT.

Dr. Dyer, a friend of Mitchell's shared this information at a seminar and on an audio tape. Mitchell told Dyer that as he walked on the moon he looked to his left and saw an infinity of heavenly bodies hurling through space at thousands of miles per hour. As he looked to the right, he saw a blue "quarter." That is what the earth looks like from the surface of the moon. Mitchell said at that moment he had an instant awakening. He realized that the universe, that we're all a part of, is an intelligent system. It's not some accidental fluke. Dyer said, "Edgar, I would think you would be aware of that before you got into the capsule." Mitchell said, "No. We had always been taught that we were to master it rather than to get into harmony with it." That space epiphany changed Edgar Mitchell's life forever.

When Mitchell walked on terra firma again, he left the Apollo Space program to pursue his harmonious philosophy.

We all deserve to sing the song we came to sing.

I hunger for the enforcers of barbaric deeds to read this book. Small chance. Nevertheless, if they do read it they might become enlightened to the anguish and suffering they, without concern, inflict on their neighbors.

I realize that is a lofty goal. In reality my book will probably only be read by the victims of the enforcers. However, if this book helps just one victim elevate his self-esteem and vitalize his incentives to take the necessary steps to humanize his community, I will deem my project worthwhile.

I'm not suggesting anyone has to tolerate such things as weird exterior colors, abandoned vehicles, a neighbor pouring old vehicle oil down the street and rebuilding his engine in the open, marathon barking or ferocious dogs, pipe fences, or grizzly bears.

I *am suggesting* laughing at the stupid, asinine, half-witted, injurious dictums by making provisions for *suitable living* conditions.

Ban the practice of ***not allowing*** homeowners to . . .

- display the American flag, British, Canadian, or any other non-militant flag,
- have tiny, clear Lucite holders to exhibit their holiday lights to express their joy,
- plant 15 purple pansies, ten marigolds, and five rose bushes, if they choose,

- fill flower boxes with attractive artificial flowers (that could brighten up snowy, wintry days),
- install a basketball hoop on their garage,
- have a retractable clothesline,
- have a swing set,
- have their garage door open while doing yard work or refinishing furniture, using the garage,
- welcome feathered friends with a birdhouse or a bird feeder, and
- have other than white backings on window coverings . . .

It seems as though the list of forbidden signs of life and enjoyment never ends.

We were put on this earth to derive joy and have regard for our neighbors. Where is it written that our purpose is to seek out means to be miserable and create significant sorrow for others?

If you find yourself in a road kill situation take time to organize other distressed residents to pull your community together in harmony. The Gestapo is not well known for its willingness to listen to reason and to institute compromises. A coup may be your only path to emancipation from the perpetrators of inhumane, savage acts.

❭ DUMB AND DUMBER MOMENTS

There are some really stupid moments in CCCs. Here are two that really irritate me.

No For-signs allowed

There are developments that won't allow one sign of *any kind*, such as For Rent or For Sale, to be put anyplace within the boundaries of their Home Sweet Home Community. The thought process goes something like this: If there are too many For-signs it will label our community as having problems and make us look like an undesirable area. Wrong!

Denying For-signs works against residents' accomplishing their objectives. HOAs should get in harmony to help homeowners meet their needs to sell or find renters for their vacant homes. No For-signs can cause homeowners to go into foreclosures if they are unable to sell or rent their homes. One of the worst blights on a neighborhood is an overabundance of Fore-closure signs. Try denying a lender or the government the right to display a Fore-closure sign.

The No For-sign policy paints a faulty picture for anyone intending to buy or rent in such a complex. If your community reeks, deodorize it and you'll lose your fear of For-signs. No matter where the restriction was originated, whether in an ancient, dubious set of Docs or in a recently modernized set (doubtful), find out how to modify it. If the restriction was set into place by the BOD, bury it and the BOD. To keep it as an active restriction only identifies that the signs aren't the culprits; the BOD is. Possibly there wouldn't be so many For-signs needed if the BOD shaped up their act to create a friendly community.

One enterprising homeowner in a No For-sign community parked his car close to his home with a For Sale sign on it and directional arrows pointing toward his house.

A condo rental unit that I owned was vacant. The complex disallowed For-signs in the common area. Every inch beyond the walls was common area. I put a For Rent sign behind the screen in the front window. When I returned to the property, the screen had been pried and the For-sign removed. Lee, a meager-minded board member, was the next door un-neighborly, neighbor. I replaced the For-sign along with a note that said, "Lee, keep your hands off my screen and my sign." The For-sign remained in place until the unit was rented.

Some communities candy-coat the "No For-signs" rule by allowing only uniform signs such as barracks-brown lettering on a banal beige background. They think that looks elite. It doesn't. It is boring and ineffective. Those signs could easily be mistaken for broadcasting, "Ralph's Roofing Company Is Proud To Install This Spectacular New Roof."

There's more than one way to spread the word

BOARDROOM DISCUSSION
❖ Published by the LAW FIRM OF WINZENBURG. LEFF AND MITCHELL. LLP ❖
• 1660 Lincoln Street, #1750 • Denver, Colorado 80264 • 303-863-1870

August 1992

• After hanging a "buyer beware" sign in the window of their condominium unit, a Florida couple was jailed, issued a permanent injunction and an order to pay the Association approximately $5,000 in attorney fees. Despite these punishments, unconfirmed reports state that the couple was seen driving their car on common ground with "buyer beware" signs!

Don't look at me. It's not my suggestion.

More about signs

BOARDROOM DISCUSSION
❖ Published by the LAW FIRM OF WINZENBURG, LEFF, PURVIS AND PAYNE, LLP ❖
• 1660 Lincoln Street, #1750 • Denver, Colorado 80264 • 303-863-1870

January 1993

REAL ESTATE SIGN ORDINANCE

A California District Judge found that an ordinance differentiating signs on the basis of whether they stated "for sale" or "for rent" violated the First Amendment. The community's aesthetic interest did not allow the Board to discriminate against "for rent" signs by setting a different standard.

Tip: The general rule is that Homeowner Associations cannot discriminate against renters in favor of owner-occupied units. For example: rules for all residents should be the same.

No backyards in sight

Another dumb practice is no backyards in most cluster home and townhome subdivisions. Some . . .

> . . . have condominium declarations. Every inch of land is common area. The homeowner doesn't even own the land directly under his home.
>
> . . . don't have condominium declarations, but the homeowner owns *only* the land directly under his home. The homes are completely surrounded by common area.

Why, why, why not give each homeowner a private, fenced yard when there are no units above or below? That practice would also diminish HOA expenses for common area upkeep.

My fractured crystal ball says when communities controlled by covenants emerged and the DABs were born, the thought process was, ***"Everyone*** who wants services to be covered in the HOA fee doesn't want one homeowner responsibility whatsoever, including not even a tiny yard." Wrong!

I don't know if there's any way an HOA can legally give yards to homeowners once the developer has recorded the plat and the Docs.

Developers need to rethink the yard premise. Homeowners in my complex enjoy the fact that they own their fenced backyards. Resale is a breeze because of the *uniqueness of having backyards.*

Backyards in townhomes and cluster homes should be a common feature. Backyards do not belong on the list of unique features.

Neither my neighbors nor I feel unique nor weird with our inclinations to have a small yard for grass, a flower garden, a vegetable garden, a private patio or deck with patio furniture, a grill at will, or any combination thereof in *our* backyards. It's a place for us, our children, grandchildren, and household critters to run as free as the buffalo run.

Sometimes homeowners aren't very reasonable either.

Overheard at a community holiday open house . . .

1 = *first Homeowner*   2 = *second Homeowner*   P = *HOA President*

1:   "Well, I want to know what child is writing with chalk on my driveway."

P: "I don't know, I can't see your driveway from my home and I don't do clairvoyance."

2:   "I wouldn't worry dear. Chalk does wash off."

1:   "Well, I don't like anyone on my driveway when I'm not home. Another thing I want to know is how a cigarette butt got in my garage. I don't smoke."

P: "Does your garage door fit absolutely tight?"

1:   "No."

P: "Then I would say it probably happened on trash pickup day. A cigarette butt or two spilled from someone's container and one blew into your garage."

1:   "Well, there were three of them right up by my house."

2:   "It probably happened on trash day. We have had some pretty stiff winds lately."

1:   "Well, what if a lit cigarette blew into my garage?"

P: "What if an airplane fell on your home?" By that time the president had become helplessly exasperated.

Perhaps the president's response was a little terse. But, how else does one answer impossible, go-nowhere, never-ending questions from one bent on just being irritating? I don't have any suggestions. Do you?

"Loving humanity is easy; it's loving your neighbor that is sometimes the big challenge!"
— Anonymous

Joe Thorwold worked for a management company, which will remain nameless because, frankly, they took a dim view of his being so candid with me. Joe represented the management company in several CCCs.

Joe explained, "There is no specific formula for management companies, but the job doesn't require a rocket scientist. Basically, you need to treat the board and the residents the way you would like to be treated.

"Some boards don't even read the contract with their management company and they hire on the basis of whether they *like* the person. There are boards that don't read anything or take any responsibilities. In those cases the management company should just be there for them and be fair with them.

"Sometimes a management company is hired merely to have someone to blame.

Joe said, "Briefly here are some of the things I witnessed.

- In one complex people would go around peering into neighbors' yards to see if they could find something wrong. In one case that caused $8,000 in legal fees.
- Another complex had one board president who unilaterally made all the decisions, no vote by the other members. The president hated renters and sued every chance he got until he finally broke the HOA.
- People with children or animals get more than their fair rash of complaints. Some of it they bring on themselves. Usually, they just want to live.

"When I get complaints from nosy neighbors I tell them, I'm not a cop. Talk to your neighbor.

"It floors me the way some of these people act with total disregard for their neighbors, the ones they should have real concern about."

Joe is more of a service person than a takeover management representative. Perhaps that's why he is no longer at that management company and why they took such a dim view of his forthright remarks.

"There are boards that don't read anything or take any responsibilities." Joe said that's when a management company just needs to be there for the board and be fair with them. Remember, Joe is service person. That's the very time a management person jumps in, takes the reins, the team of horses, the wagon, and everything in the wagon.

Joe didn't allow busybody complainers to lead him around by the nose. Take heed of his plea to convey concern for your neighbors.

Talk about nosy neighbors
"Learn to work together, not against each other."

Algird Pocius performs a variety of business surveys and census studies for several departments, including the U.S. Department of Commerce. Citizens' participation in such surveys and studies is on a voluntary basis.

Algird sent a letter to a homeowner in a Denver suburban complex. He then called to set an appointment. His purpose was to complete specific reports he had been assigned to accomplish.

Algird said, "I use a beat-up old car, a 1957 Chevy because, regardless of the neighborhood, no one bothers it."

He said, "I arrived at the appointment a little early so I parked on the public street and started reading while I waited for them to come home. A woman came up close to my car and looked at me as if to ask, 'Who are you?' Then two men came up to ask what I was doing in the neighborhood. Because of confidentiality I couldn't tell them anything other than I was there for the Department of Commerce waiting for the homeowners to come home. I had a Department of Commerce placard in the car window and a photo ID on a chain around my neck.

"When the homeowners arrived I went in their home with them (it was still broad daylight). About a half hour into the survey a knock came at the door. Now it was getting dusk and the only lights that were on were in the kitchen where we had been talking. In comes a hulk of a policeman acting overly officious. He had been called by one of the nosy neighbors. He said, 'I understand there's someone here claiming to be doing something for the government. I'm just checking to make sure everything is all right.'"

The homeowners answered, "Oh yes, he's with the Census Bureau."

Then the policeman asked, "Does he have an ID?"

Answer, "Oh, yes he does."

Policeman, "Well I want to see it."

Algird said, "At that point the policemen grabbed the ID chain and pulled me over by the window. He looked genuinely disappointed when I checked out okay. The couple complained to the policeman about what he was doing. The policeman replied, 'It's my job to check things out.'"

When Algird finished his survey, the husband asked him to stay a little longer. He wanted the prying neighbors who were infected with the nothing-to-do syndrome to receive the full treatment.

"When it was time for me to leave (now it was totally dark)," Algird said, "the couple very nicely said wait a second. They turned the porch light on and we chatted for about five minutes. That was for the benefit of the nosy neighbors so they could see I was okay and the couple was okay, in hopes they would leave them alone in the future. Then they watched me go to the car and waved at me."

Algird shared. "When I left I was followed by a vehicle until I was out of the area. The car then turned around and went back into the subdivision."

Algird added, "Learn to work together, not against each other. Neighborly concern is one thing. Nosy overreaction is entirely another."

"It is not meant that we should shoulder our problems alone. We are in the company of others by design. The growth that each of us needs to experience is tied closely to both the suffering and the celebrations that come to us all." — Anonymous

A friend, a neighbor

"Oh, the comfort, the inexpressible comfort, of feeling safe with a person, having neither to weigh thoughts nor measure words, but to put them all out just as they are, chaff and grain together, knowing that a faithful hand will take and sift them, keep what is worth keeping, and then, with the breath of kindness, blow the rest away." — George Eliot

I Address the Bench

When I first perceived the need for this book, I believed the responsibility for all the CCC problems were shared only by overzealous, power-hungry BODs, management companies, and profit-motivated developers/builders. They do all play shabby roles in the drama.

Since then, tales have unfolded that have exposed the part the legal arena plays in propagating homeowners' miseries.

Before I address the bench, I will emphasize the developers' responsibilities in the entire scenario. The developers and the legal profession have often joined hands in this whole saga.

Developers and the legal profession, fix the broken Docs!

It's the legal profession who created the regulations and who continue to make decisions based on the wording of those regulations. It's the developers who hired the legal profession to write the regulations. It's the developers who control the beginnings of every development. It's the developers who make the final decisions whether to spend their money to get updated Docs or just to haul the old moldy ones with them through decade after decade. It's like throwing a hand grenade right in the middle of new developments. It doesn't take much for power hungry BODs to pull the pins and wound a few homeowners.

Developers, after reading all the previous horror stories, can you sense that it's time to recognize the need for new sets of Docs to be written? Pay good attorneys to create modern, slender sets that are written in non-legalese. Sets that contain only humane rules that have passed the Significance Test (next page). Sets that have decent provisions for modification. Homeowners need to make changes to keep a steady pace with the rest of the progressive world. To create fresh sets of Docs would cost you only a *few dollars* and would only require the legal profession to put forth some caring effort.

Modern Docs would still qualify for approval from local agencies and lenders. Municipal agencies' and lenders' ***approvals do not require*** garbage rules and regulations.

❯ FROM DEVELOPER TO DISASTER

- The developer hired an attorney to form a set of documents.

- The attorney chose the ready-to-wear rules. "I'll take one of these, two of those, and one of . . ." He compiled the stack of documents for the new community.

- Worse yet, the developer may have just borrowed a set of musty Docs from a fellow developer or used a set that he got from an attorney three eons ago. The same dusty Docs he has been using in development after development. He may even have conjured up a few ratty restrictions of his own — the worst kind.

- The BOD and the management company rigidly enforced every rule in the Docs.

- A resident received a violation notice via a stern letter from the HOA.

- The attorney advised the BOD to stick to their guns. The attorney then filed a lawsuit.

- The set of canned Docs included the regular overdose of ambiguous legalese. Another attorney encouraged the BOD of Control-itis Townhomes to enforce the rules to the depths of suing. So sue they did. Without deviating from one printed aforesaid, pursuant thereto, militate, hereof, party of first, second, or third part, the judge adjudicated for the rules and Control-itis Townhomes' HOA. Have the legal eagles built job security into the Docs, or what? It's worth taking a minute to ponder. The circle of events started with a developer and an attorney and ended with a judge and an attorney.

- The resident and the HOA spent thousands of dollars. The HOA won. The resident moved.

From the inception of the Docs to the courthouse confrontation, the bulk of the legal profession seems to perceive living in a CCC to be as simple as: follow the rules, live with it, pay the fine, go to court, or move if you don't like it. Hardships? What hardships?

❯ FROM DEVELOPER TO DREAM

- The developer hired an attorney to form a modern, living, breathing set of Docs. The attorney was instructed to include only the bare-bones regulations that were actually needed to satisfy local governmental and lender requirements. Every rule passed the . . .

Significance test

A) Does the regulation/rule specifically address protection against
    threat or damage to lives?   ☐ Yes ☐ No

B) Does the regulation/rule specifically address protection against
    threat or damage to property values?   ☐ Yes ☐ No

- If the answer is *NO to either* of the above questions, a determination is to be made as to whether the regulation/rule is *really* necessary.
- If the answer is *NO to both* of the above questions, the rule is to be trashed. Quickly throw it into the un-recycle bin. It will serve no humane or reasonable purpose.

Only regulations/rules that pass the test of A) and/or B) are to be included in the declarations (recorded restrictions on the deeds of the properties) and require lender and HOA approval. Other rules are to require only approval of the members of the HOA.

- Language in all documents must be easily understandable, written for the benefit of those who don't quickly grasp legalese. No "unartful" ambiguity is allowed.

- The modification provision in the Declarations is to state, "Approval by 51 percent of the homeowners and the lenders is required to modify the Declarations." I believe anything over 51 percent is overkill. (CCIOA requires 67% to amend.)

- Additional rules (outside of the Declarations) may be added, modified, or removed as determined necessary by a majority of the homeowners. The majority vote is to be over 50 percent of *those homeowners voting,* not over 50 percent of *all* the homeowners. *All* homeowners must be notified of the proposed changes with *identical* written information. A provision must be given to offer the choice to vote at the meeting, by proxy, or by **mail** (absentee). The mail-your-vote-in method works just fine for federal, state, and municipal governments. Why should homeowners have the disadvantage of a process that is any less efficient?

- It is a fiduciary duty of the HOA to enforce the covenants with compassion and concern for the good of the whole community and to oversee that the service company does the same. The rules must be enforced uniformly, *never* arbitrarily or capriciously.

- When a resident is in violation, a representative of the HOA is to call the homeowner first for verification and/or the first notice of a valid violation. The second notice of a violation is to be a friendly, but firm, letter. When no emergency exists the Docs are to require negotiation between the violator and the board to reach a reasonable solution. Such consultation is to be initiated immediately before the problem gets moldy and out of hand.

- All legal petitions (not in conflict with the Docs) presented, signed by over 50 percent of the homeowners, are legally responded to by the officers of the board. The First Amendment gives the right to free speech and to petition.

- The developer's attorney focused on fostering tranquillity for the new community. Nonessential, wide open phrases such as "No attachments or modifications are allowed" did **not** appear.

- The residents of that development were permitted to have such signs of life and caring as birdhouses and essentially invisible, diminutive Lucite holders for festive holiday lights.

- The developer did his utmost to help create a functional community that glowed with pride of ownership from the front entrance throughout the entire development.

The above scenario is my dream. My dream doesn't always agree with state statutes, corporate law, or the legal profession — only with the U.S. Constitution. My dream also says that there will never be another set of Docs loaded with petty rules combined with no reasonable provision for modification of those petty rules.

Attorneys, make certain you don't put any of the litigating nitroglycerin rules and language into the *new sets of ready-made Docs.* Leave that stuff in the bunkers where it belongs. Remember to provide sufficient leeway for court decisions to be made that honor community harmony.

▶ *BENEFITS THE LEGAL PROFESSION OFFERS — ACCORDING TO RUMOR*

The purpose of the legal sister and brotherhood is rumored to be to promote equality and justice for all. Too often it turns out to be sub-equality and sub-justice for all.

Homeowners are not criminals. Yet, they are treated as such in the courtrooms when they are taken to task by their HOAs.

"The law is not a means to the end. It is not THE LAW because it is A LAW. Law is adaptable to establish and maintain reasonable order." — Anonymous

"The law itself is on trial quite as much as the cause which is to be decided."
— Harlan F. Stone, 12th Chief Justice U.S. Supreme Court

Laws and rules were not meant to be broken, but they need to be on trial to weed out the bad ones. There should be room for some bending. Bending requires a degree of flexibility.

Conforming to the old, dusty Docs causes conflict

Judges base their decrees on following the system's antagonistic rules verbatim. With a finger pointing at the homeowner they say, "Shame on you. Read the Docs and weep. It's written. You had a copy. If it's a rule, you're legally bound to remain forever faithful to it. Next case." It seems inconsequential to them that the rules often neglect allowing for enjoyment of living in one's own home.

Many judges strive to make fair decisions in momentous felony cases. Big-time criminal actions deserve thought-time decisions. Judges and juries usually take every precaution to make certain that they will not be judged as having made frivolous findings in big-time trials.

It seems that homeowners' problems are small-time to the legal elite. They are big-time hurts to homeowners. The fact that verdicts in favor of HOAs far outweigh those in favor of residents does not translate to HOAs being in the right more often.

Homeowners, don't overlook the advantages of trial by jury. It can be less expensive in the long run. Jury trials can offer a better chance for a fair decision. They can avoid the extra expense of taking the case to an appellate court to reverse an unfair decision by a judge.

Excerpt from "today's" legalese Decs

ARTICLE XII
GENERAL PROVISIONS

Section 1. Enforcement. Enforcement of the covenants, conditions, restrictions, easements, reservations, rights-of-way, liens, charges and other provisions contained in this Declaration, Articles of Incorporation, Bylaws or Rules and Regulations of the Association, as amended, may be by any proceeding at or in equity against any person or persons violating or attempting to violate any such provision. The Association and any aggrieved Owner shall have the right to institute, maintain and/or prosecute any such proceedings, and the Association shall further have the right to levy and collect fines for the violation of any provision of any of the aforesaid documents; in any action instituted or maintained under this Section, the prevailing party shall be entitled to recover its costs and reasonable attorneys' fees incurred pursuant thereto, as well as any and all other sums awarded by the Court. Failure by the Association or any Owner to enforce any covenant or restriction herein contained, or any other provision of any of the aforesaid documents, shall in no event be deemed a waiver of the right to do so thereafter.

There are only three sentences in that Enforcement Provision. My computer grammar check reports that the first and second sentences are . . . "too long to process for grammatical structure." I'm going to customize my grammar check to ferret out legalese and wave a flag of "Legalese can be difficult to comprehend. Consider softening and reconstructing the sentence."

Example of a ridiculous, ready-made rule

ARTICLE X
GENERAL PROVISIONS
Section 10. Vehicular Parking, Storage and Repairs.
    (a) Any house trailer, camping trailer, boat trailer, hauling trailer, running gear, boat, or accessories thereto, truck (larger than 3/4 ton), self-contained motorized equipment, *may be parked or stored on the Properties only if such parking or storage is done wholly within the enclosed garage, if any,* located on a Lot, or within any area which may, from time to time, be designated by the Association for the parking or storage of such vehicles, except that any such vehicle may be otherwise parked as a temporary expedience for loading, delivery, or emergency.

What is ridiculous about that rule? It's a restriction in a townhome complex that *doesn't have garages!* The *"if any"* is to cover any attorney's anatomy for covenants he's chosen that don't apply to the specific community.

A prefab rule that can be friendly or possibly open up a bag of worms

ARTICLE XIII
RESTRICTIONS
Section 18. <u>Rules and Regulations</u>. *Rules and regulations concerning and governing the Properties or any portion thereof may be adopted, amended or repealed, from time to time by the Board of Directors of the Association,* and the Board of Directors may establish and enforce penalties for the infraction thereof, including without limitation of the levying and collecting of fines for the violation of any of such rules and regulations.

That prefab rule can be an immense asset when a common-sense BOD uses it morally and reasonably for the betterment of the community. In the hands of a self-serving BOD it's an open invitation to get even more mischievous — a ticking time-bomb.

❯ *NOW CHOOSE THE RIGHT ATTORNEY*

Developers, please hire an attorney who specializes in CCCs and whose bent is to help avoid lawsuits. He may be more likely to lean in that direction if he lives, or has lived, in a community with an HOA. That attorney may diligently keep the time-bombs out of the Docs.

Too often the drafting of the documents is done by big-firm attorneys who have never represented HOAs or homeowners. They never see or feel the results of what they draft.

Attorneys and judges who have never lived in a CCC don't comprehend the congenial methods needed to maintain peace. They make TNT decisions with firecracker knowledge.

HOAs and homeowners, find an attorney whose honest desire is to solve problems in ways other than filing lawsuits, an attorney who cares and knows that lawsuits don't unite communities. Lawsuits irreparably polarize them.

If you do end up in court, unfortunately, you don't have the privilege of choosing the right judge. You just have to take your chances. If you're a homeowner just pray that you don't get a judge with the reputation of always finding *for* the HOA and the ancient, prefab rules.

Karen Abbott interviewed an attorney

February 8, 1994
Reprinted with permission of the *Rocky Mountain News*. The entire article is presented in four portions, ending on page 155.

Read the rules before moving in

"Trouble moves into a neighborhood when people don't read their covenants, when the rules aren't spelled out clearly and when governing boards try too hard to be kind," said Lynn Jordan, an attorney who often represents homeowner associations and developers.

"Communities try very hard to leave a lot of discretion in the rules so they can accommodate everybody," she said, "but I always advise them against that. Neighbors think, 'Oh, goodness, it will seem too harsh, too controlling.' Yet it's not. It lets everybody know what is and isn't acceptable."

Yes, yes, yes, *read the covenants*. Better yet, read the covenants before signing the contract to buy. Then find out if Albert Schweitzer or Attila the Hun is making the judgments on what is right, wrong, good, or bad.

". . . when rules aren't spelled out clearly . . ." Well, let's not forget who assembled those unclear rules. It's the same legal clique who continues to uphold every vague word of every rigid regulation.

Remember what Florida State Representative Steve Geller said, "Some associations' documents are completely incomprehensible, even to me, and I'm an attorney."

When is the last time anyone has seen covenants really created for a specific community or even updated restrictions that focused on producing happiness for the homeowners? However, if that were the case, what would happen to the "suit du jour?"

". . . governing boards try too hard to be kind . . ." I don't think so. If it's a BOD trying too hard to be kind, what are they doing in a lawyer's office? I'm not aware of many people who contact an attorney because they are practicing overt kindness and are asking for advice on the best method to pursue no action. That scene leaves room for doubt. The scenario I perceive is that any BOD in a lawyer's office is there to express a desire to enforce exact compliance to the rules. Possibly even to one of those unclear, hazy, nebulous rules.

"Communities try very hard to leave a lot of discretion in the rules so they can accommodate everybody," she said, "but I always advise them against that . . . It lets everybody know what is and isn't acceptable."

As Scarlet O'Hara said, "Thank God there's another day." Or was it, "I'll think about it tomorrow. After all, tomorrow is another day." Or maybe it was, "I think I'll get a second opinion?"

Reading some of the preceding and following articles with accounts from homeowners who were unjustly placed in distressing situations makes it clear that most problems arise when BODs or management companies get their jollies by exercising over control-itis. They *don't "try too hard to be kind."* They produce obstacles smack dab in the middle of the path of the intended benefits for homeowners.

February 8, 1994
Read the rules before moving in continued, an interview with attorney Lynn Jordan.

> Sometimes governing boards make bad exceptions for good reasons: In a neighborhood where swamp coolers are forbidden, a resident with an asthma problem may ask permission to have one anyway. Jordan said the board shouldn't give in because even the most well meaning exceptions make for resentments.

Sometimes convictions deserve reconsideration.

"...the board shouldn't give in because even the most well meaning exceptions make for resentments." Unbending BODs tend to close their minds to mediation and the true needs of the community.

WOW! DO NOT GIVE IN FOR ANY REASON WHATSOEVER! So much for making a community comfortable with livable conditions for the homeowners. Excuse me. Does it matter that a homeowner may be placed in an undeserved hardship to move because he was "inconsiderate" enough to have asthma?

Would it be a legal sin to make the rules more *clear?* BODs, please look for solutions to problems instead of provoking lawsuits. Modify the rule, or the interpretation of the rule, to accommodate a neighbor with a health problem. Allow that neighbor to have a swamp cooler or an air conditioner. Allow other homeowners the privilege to install the same in a specified, discreet location on each property. If the homes have neither backyards nor patios, allow the gadgets to be put on common area. Plant shrubbery around the eyesores.

Justifiably there are fair housing laws that protect minorities against discrimination.

It's an embarrassment to witness discrimination against people with medical problems. What happens when a current resident develops such a medical condition? Should the BOD merrily order the resident to, "Bite his tongue, grit his teeth, cry in his pillow, suffer in silence, or move?"

Might these decisions have a bearing?

BOARDROOM DISCUSSION
❖ Published by the LAW FIRM OF WINZENBURG, LEFF, PURVIS AND PAYNE, LLP ❖
• 1660 Lincoln Street, #1750 • Denver, Colorado 80264 • 303-863-1870

Reproduced with permission from *Lawyers Weekly USA*, (May 8, 1995) the National Newspaper for Practicing Lawyers. $125 per year. For subscription information, call 800-451-9998, or write Lawyers Weekly Publications, 41 West Street, Boston, MA 02111.

"DISABILITY" SUITS   August 1995

Associations are being sued by disabled residents who claim they must be "reasonably accommodated" under the Fair Housing Amendments Act. The Act provides for compensatory damages, punitive damages and attorney fees. According to a recent article in *Lawyers Weekly USA*, recent cases include

• An owner forced her Association to stop using pesticides because she had "multiple chemical sensitivity." She also collected $40,000.

• A resident was allowed to have a cat in spite of a "no pets" policy, because he claimed he was mentally ill and needed it for therapeutic reasons.

The Act says that disabled residents must be given such accommodations as "may be necessary to afford each person equal opportunity to use and enjoy a dwelling." An Association can be liable if it denies a reasonable request for an accommodation. The test is whether the accommodation would unduly burden the Association.

All it takes is a lawsuit and an Association has a major problem. What constitutes "reasonable accommodation" is highly fact-based. It is hard for an Association to know what the law requires. A ramp into a clubhouse is probably reasonable, but an elevator to reach roof-deck amenities probably isn't.

Could The Act be relevant? Isn't the disability from a health problem, such as asthma, equally as important as "multiple chemical sensitivity" or the need for a cat for therapeutic reasons? The Act says that disabled residents must be given such accommodations as "may be necessary to afford each person equal opportunity *to use and enjoy a dwelling.*"

February 8, 1994
Read the rules before moving in continued, an interview with attorney Lynn Jordan.

Covenants are created before neighborhoods are built, when developers get zoning. They vary widely; some are only a page or two long, and some are inches-thick documents full of legalese and technical jargon. Homeowner associations also enact rules and regulations that have the force of law, can impose fines for violations and can file liens against homes to collect the fines, attorney fees, or other costs.

Covenants-controlled neighborhoods are almost like little towns. The governing board, elected by the whole neighborhood, is the town council. The appointed enforcement committees — architectural control covenants enforcement is much like the zoning board and, well, the police.

You're thinking of painting your house bright blue? The architectural control committee must approve the shade first. You're certain your little-red-barn storage shed is so cute that getting advance approval would be just a waste of everybody's time? The architectural control committee can order you to tear it down. You prefer leaving your garage door open so the kids can get their bikes in and out easily? The covenants enforcement committee can order you to close it. And you say your garage is so full of the valuable antiques you're going to refinish pretty soon that you're forced to park your car on the street? Guess what?

"The appointed enforcement committees — architectural control covenants enforcement is much like the zoning board and, well, the police." Forbid we should lose sight of the covenants police waving an injunction to enforce the garage-doors-must-be-closed rule. That's just one rule on the interminable list of insane rules. I have never met anyone in his right mind who would leave his garage door open, day and night, for days or weeks at a time. What is so repulsive about a garage door open while one is doing, let's say, woodworking or yard work? Can anyone honestly say property values would decline because a prospective buyer might actually get a glimpse of the inside of a garage? The very thought of a garage door being open an hour or six absolutely horrifies me. Get real!

"The architectural control committee can order you to . . ." Do check with that committee before making any type of modification on the exterior of your home. If your community has a list of unreasonable, suppressed-breathing restrictions, get involved. Maybe you could help bring about some humanizing of the regulations.

February 8, 1994
The end of *Read the rules before moving in,* an interview with attorney Lynn Jordan.

"It's a very thankless job," Jordan said. "Many people object to having anybody tell them how they can or can't do things. There are certain things near and dear to their hearts they just feel there should be no control over."

Jordan's advice: Not only should you read the covenants and rules and regulations before moving in, but you should also drive through the neighborhood and carefully notice what is and what isn't there. If there are no television antennas, for instance, you probably won't be allowed to have one.

— Karen Abbott

How do you feel about bird feeders or watching the sunset in the winter on Wednesdays?

"It's a very thankless job . . ." Indeed and some bask in the misery of others.

". . . you should also drive through the neighborhood and carefully notice . . ." After you take careful notice as to what is and what is not gracing the scenery, check out the enforcers. They will inflict pain if they enforce with intimidating, prejudicial techniques based on the legal system's antique rules. If the enforcers demonstrate common sense and you choose to move in, make certain succeeding BODs have the same unselfish attitudes.

Let's say the drive through is satisfactory. Appearances indicate the neighborhood is a match to your preferred lifestyle. Buying a home and moving in would certainly seem to be in order. Then the enforcers suddenly change their interpretations of the rules, as in Jerry Beach's case (page 157). Even though he carefully read the covenants and drove through the neighborhood many times, it was no assurance of continued compatibility. The rules were arbitrarily and capriciously changed.

HOAs, urged on by an attorney, charge off to court destroying everything and everyone in their paths. *If the rules say it,* they judge it to be valid thinking. That breeds community agony to the point of homeowners moving to get out of the concentration camp.

Other injured homeowners just drop the whole subject. They acquiesce to the enforcers' demands. They crumble for fear of ending up in an expensive, emotionally damaging, no-win litigation. They silently try to stay out of the limelight and out of the path of the enforcers.

Some attorneys would suggest homeowners either sue or merely stroll on to another home to remove themselves from the tribulations. That course is not always economically feasible. Or they might propose, no matter how serious the problem is, that the homeowner resign himself to live with it — bite his tongue, grit his teeth, and cry in his pillow. That course is not always emotionally judicious.

Don't you wonder if Ms. Jordan has ever lived in a CCC? If not, she should try it. She might loathe it. Of course, that would depend on her expectations, the specific community she would choose, and the temperament of the enforcers. Perhaps she would select a community that strictly enforced every rule to the nth degree so that she would know, at all times, *"exactly what is and isn't acceptable."* Maybe she would happen into a caring community and never experience the symptoms of the HOA black plague disease.

Some attorneys advise mediation as the HOAs first step to negotiate *"what is and isn't acceptable."* That opens minds to truly hearing the other side's point of view and offers the potential of avoiding needless fractured feelings and costly litigation.

BOARDROOM DISCUSSION
❖ Published by the LAW FIRM OF WINZENBURG, LEFF, PURVIS AND PAYNE, LLP ❖
● 1660 Lincoln Street, #1750 ● Denver, Colorado 80264 ● 303-863-1870

USING MEDIATION TO RESOLVE DISPUTES   March 1994

Recently a Manager called requesting information on mediation. Most Associations have formal guidelines for controlling rule and covenant violations. However, many problems might be resolved through mediation rather than by lengthy, costly and divisive litigation.

Too many disputes cause more conflict than seems reasonable. Hostilities are often resolved only after substantial time and expense, or are settled superficially. Minor problems that are not quickly addressed often grow into major battles.

It is in the Association's best interest to resolve disputes in a way that minimizes cost and conflict and promotes community harmony.
INFORMAL MEDIATION MAY HELP TO RESOLVE SOME DISPUTES!

If you would like more information on this subject, call Kami at 303-863-1870 for a copy of Charles Bethel's "How Mediation Can Resolve Disputes in Your Association."

An outstanding way to avoid litigation and minimize conflict and shoddy community public relations is for the BOD to overhaul the Docs legally. ***The first step is to add a rule that mandates mediation before litigation.*** Homeowners, if your BOD is not inclined to adopt that policy, band together with a petition to force the issue. Do a coup, if needed.

BOARDROOM DISCUSSION
❖ Published by the LAW FIRM OF WINZENBURG, LEFF, PURVIS AND PAYNE, LLP ❖
● 1660 Lincoln Street, #1750 ● Denver, Colorado 80264 ● 303-863-1870

MEDIATION AND CONFLICT IN ASSOCIATIONS   July/August 1996

At a recent Community Associations Institute Membership Luncheon, Mary Avgerinos discussed mediation and conflict within Homeowner Associations, and addressed a study conducted by the Institute of Urban and Regional Planning in California that found

1. Boards often have an "oral tradition" of passing on policies so that past actions/decisions are unknown.
2. Assessment increases are the greatest sources of conflict.
3. Within a one year period, 44% of boards reported having a member harassed by another owner, 25% had been threatened by a lawsuit and 5% were sued.
4. Larger Associations have lower resident participation.
5. Self-managed Associations have higher levels of participation.
6. The greater the participation, the fewer covenant violations.

For a copy of the seminar material concerning mediation and conflict, please call us. Mary Avgerinos operates a private mediation company that specializes in Association matters. For more information, call her directly at 303-739-7280.

* * * * * * *

"If you try to please everybody, nobody will like it." — Murphy's Law

---

"If you please the majority, most will be happy." — Joni's Law of Democracy

Self-managed (item 5) doesn't necessarily mean there is no service company involved.

Self-managed can mean that the board makes all the final decisions and has hired a service company to take care of the busy stuff. Service companies wouldn't even entertain the thought of making a decision that is to made by the BOD.

Sometimes the rules change

Rules can be changed to make life miserable. Patricia Wigginton in Grosvenor Park, a CCC in Rockville, Maryland, said "They [the BOD] do things in secret. Last October they added a rule: NO ball playing, NO Frisbee throwing, NO flying kites is permitted anywhere on the common elements." (*Woman's Day* article "Trouble on the Home Front?" November 1, 1996, by John Grossmann.)

BOARDROOM DISCUSSION
❖ Published by the LAW FIRM OF WINZENBURG, LEFF, PURVIS AND PAYNE, LLP ❖
• 1660 Lincoln Street, #1750 • Denver, Colorado 80264 • 303-863-1870

REASONABLENESS TEST APPLIED   July 1992

An amendment to an Association's Declaration *prohibited Owners from leasing their units.* Is it enforceable against Owners who acquired their units *prior to* the adoption of the amendment? "Yes," said an Ohio court. A *reasonableness test was used* by the court to make its determination.

1. *Was the decision or rule arbitrary or capricious?* There *must be* some *rational relationship* of the decision or rule to the safety and enjoyment of the condominium.

2. *Was the decision or rule discriminatory or impartial?*

3. *Was the decision made in good faith for the common welfare* of the Owners and occupants?

Rule: *Carefully review all future Association actions. Do they meet the reasonableness test?*

When the intent is for the good of the majority of the residents, changing or adding rules that pass the reasonableness test can keep a community up-to-date and livable. Removal of archaic rules that don't pass the test has the same beneficial effect. All changes must be accomplished within the guidelines of the Docs. Conflicts can arise when an over-fervent BOD, like the one in Rockville, adds more and more *unreasonable,* stringent rules.

A case where mediation, instead of litigation, would have benefited both the HOA and the homeowner

---

Early in 1992, Jerry Beach bought a new single-family home in a covenants-controlled community in Littleton, Colorado. He and his children derive sheer enjoyment from traveling, boating, and general out-dooring. He carefully read the covenants which stated RV parking on the property is acceptable with proper screening, such as a six-foot privacy fence or redwood lattice shield. Jerry made arrangements to have his home placed a little differently on his lot to give over three feet more space to accommodate his proposed recreational ecstasies. Jerry said, "Things were fine with the builder, and reading the covenants, I saw no problem."

An excerpt from Jerry's Decs

7.3.17
No vehicles other than 4 (four) wheel automobiles shall be

permitted to be parked on streets adjoining lots and upon any lot within the property. this restriction shall apply to recreational vehicles, boats, motorcycles, campers, vans, hauling trucks, commercial type vehicles, trailers and mobile homes. *such prohibited vehicles may, however, be parked or stored on the side or in the rear yards of any lot so long as the same are completely surrounded by a sight barrier approved by the committee.*

The phrase "*. . . sight barrier approved by the committee*" offers the potential for arbitrary and capricious interpretation. That same wide open statement can give a caring committee the freedom and flexibility to further community harmony.

In midstream the BOD changed the advertised game plan . . .

Jerry said, "Before I had a chance to purchase my boat and motor home, the board sent out a newsletter, contrary to the covenants, stating, 'No more recreational vehicles allowed.' The vice president expounded, 'We don't want any more recreational vehicles. *We* represent the neighborhood and *we* make the decisions.' One board member has a boat, but his lot isn't big enough to accommodate his parking it, so he has to store it. It's occurred to me he might be a little cranky because others *do* have sufficient space.

"As homeowners requested permission to install their six-foot fences (per the covenants) each received a verbal from the board, 'No more six-foot fences. Only five-foot fences will be allowed.' The two new edicts were made by the board without the endorsement of vote to modify the rules. No change was recorded. The covenants weren't changed. The only things that changed were the board members' minds."

Another excerpt from Jerry's Decs

No fence or......... *not to exceed 72 inches in height,* or as allowed by applicable law, whichever is lesser.
This declaration may be amended by an instrument approved in writing by not less than 51% of the owners.

The board sent a copy of the specific rule to Jerry. They crossed off *72 inches in height* and *penciled in five feet!*

The BOD completely ignored "*This declaration may be amended by an instrument approved in writing by not less than 51% of the owners.*"

The covenants I've read from Jerry's subdivision make it apparent that the developer really tried to offer sufficient latitude for homeowner-friendly covenants. Bad covenants can strangle a good BOD. Good covenants cannot discipline a bad BOD. Remove the bad BOD.

The Judge judges. Who judges the Judge?

"The builder, who was still involved in the HOA, intervened and resisted the efforts of the board to ban RVs," Jerry said. "I sent a letter requesting official approval for a boat and a motor home. I then went to the head of the Architectural Committee and she helped fill out the authorized form. I received RV approval.

"First I bought my boat, then my motor home. I parked the boat on the street for a few days while I completed the driveway to my RV parking. Promptly, I received a letter from the HOA's attorney telling me to get the boat off the street and move it to the back. I immediately put the boat in the back and sent a letter of apology. A second letter from the attorney arrived saying to get the boat entirely out of the community because they had only given permission for a motor home, *not* a boat." [A phone call or a friendly, but firm, letter from the HOA doesn't diminish finances and causes less community animosity. A letter from an attorney to a homeowner should be a last resort, not the first move.]

Jerry continued, "The president rides around in a golf cart to check on the happenings in the neighborhood. When my kids accidentally leave the gate open, I get a letter from the HOA's attorney.

"I misunderstood and assumed the RV approval included the requested boat. It turned out the Architectural Committee person had only listed a small motor home and neglected my request for a boat.

"By the time the boat incident occurred, the builder was out of the area and the HOA. No more help from that corner. The board makes arbitrary decisions and doesn't spell them out clearly.

"They brought suit against me early in March 1992 to force me to remove my boat and the case is still pending."

Jerry said, "I hired an attorney to handle my case against the HOA. I explained to him that I could only pay him $100 a month for his services. He agreed to the arrangement and he came to my home to survey the situation. The discussion of my problem took about half an hour. Then we chatted idly. I received a bill for $500 for two and a half hours of counseling and research in the law library. I could see this was not going to be a good working arrangement. He had told me he understood HOA cases, so *I thought he already knew what he should know.* I had no intention of paying for his education. By the way, *never* give an attorney your original documents.

"In my pursuit to find another attorney to handle my case, the next one charged $78 for a half-hour consultation, the next two offered free half-hour counseling. *All three of these attorneys flat turned me down. The reason given by each attorney was identical: The courts always rule for the HOA. The odds are against the homeowner.*

"After two years of conflict, I was about to give up and just move when I located a new young attorney. He worked very hard for me.

"I called the first attorney and said I would no longer need his services and gave him the name of my new attorney. He, the first attorney, sent me a second bill for an additional $200. He noted the name of my new attorney on his bill. Other than the two-and-a-half-hour consultation charge, all other charges were for his research in the law library. For $700 I received not one bit of useful information. I fired him. He still kept on researching and billing me anyway.

"In court the Judge ruled I had to pay an *additional* $800 to the attorney. *The ruling was because I hadn't fired the attorney in writing!*"

"I thought he already knew what he should know." To present a well-prepared case *some* law library research is understandable. Hours and hours and hundreds or thousands of dollars worth of study is absurd. Attorneys, don't charge your clients for your continuing education. Clients rightfully assume you are erudite on their specific subject when you accept the case. Either don't take the case or get another student loan to pay for your own education if you don't have adequate training and expertise. You pay for it, sweet pea.

"All three of these attorneys flat turned me down. The reason given by each attorney

was identical: The courts always rule for the HOA. The odds are against the homeowner." Three honest attorneys! A good question to ask an attorney who has expressed a willingness to take your case is, "How many cases that are relative to mine have you won recently? Keeping client confidentiality, tell me about a little bit about them."

"The ruling was because I hadn't fired the attorney in writing!"

Silly me, I used to have the Pollyanna notion that the court system's goal was to administer justice judiciously. Jerry's story smacks of overt miscarriage of justice. Capricious and arbitrary decisions should not be allowed by judges either.

An opinion by an attorney or a court decision does not automatically translate to right, fair, just, principled, conscientious, ethical, impartial, equitable, humane, or judicious.

Attorneys who specialize in cases *for* HOAs know that rigid HOAs, with their deep pockets overflowing with homeowners' money, have the ability to fight to the end. Almost any attorney feels he can do a wheely on any case for an HOA with his hands flying off the handlebars. He knows if he presents any kind of case at all the judge will likely rule in favor of his client. It takes a very special type of judge to put an HOA case into proper perspective.

Only hire a specialist

To hire an attorney whose talents have not been directed in the area of your case is tantamount to going to a podiatrist when you're in need of brain surgery! Only employ an attorney who specializes in CCCs *for homeowners and HOAs, not just HOAs.*

Interview the attorney. Ask carefully constructed questions. Make certain he isn't just another hungry attorney who will claim any and all topics to be his forte. If you find an attorney who has been educated firsthand with the street-smart experience of having lived in a CCC, put him on the top of your list.

Barry Sharoff, a marketing consultant to the legal field, composed a list of questions you must ask before hiring an attorney.

1) *Do you handle matters like mine, or will you be learning along with me?* A competent attorney can learn a new area of law, but I don't believe that you should have to pay him for his education. The full rate should never be charged in such a situation.

2) *Who will actually be doing the work?* Find out what elements of the work the lawyer will actually do. Don't pay high lawyer's fees for work performed by para-professionals or non-professionals.

3) *What are your billing practices?* Does the attorney bill by the tenth or quarter of an hour? Get a detailed description about this and other costs you will be charged.

4) *About how long will it take to complete this matter?* Find out what all the steps are, what happens with each one, and how long each one takes. Get a time-table in writing, and signed by the attorney. At the very least, this estimate should include a possible range of costs and a maximum allowable fee.

After three and a half years, the suit and the dust finally settled

August 1995, I called Jerry to get an update. He said, "Last month we went to court again and made an out-of-court settlement. Part of that settlement is that I am not allowed to discuss the agreement. Who would ever have thought it would take three and a half years to settle such trivial matters? But, then why would any attorney *want* to settle fast. Long litigation puts more money in their pockets."

Jerry added a few more details, "I *will* tell you that before this whole mess went to court I kept trying to offer solutions.

Jerry: "What about redwood lattice?"
Board: "We don't like redwood lattice anymore."
Jerry: "How about my enlarging my storage shed?"
Board: "No, that's too much like a garage."
Jerry: "I'll plant trees."
Board: "Plan rejected."
Jerry: "I'll extend my fence."
Board: "No, get the boat off the premises."

The Court's decision in the County Public Records indicates that, as part of the settlement, Jerry has agreed to put new four-by-four, seven-foot posts for his five-foot fence. The fence has to accommodate seven-foot *redwood lattice* panels attached to extend two feet above his existing five-foot fence. He must plant and maintain two vines growing up each lattice panel for further screening. He agreed to plant five evergreen trees (seven-to-eight-foot, upright junipers) and two shade trees (broad leaf variety, at least 15 feet tall). Jerry was given 45 days to complete those tasks.

Jerry is to keep his wood gate closed at all times except when removing or parking his motor home or pontoon boat. The stipulations for storing his vehicles are extensive; they read like a whole new set of Decs. He is only allowed to purchase new recreational vehicles that are the same size or smaller than the ones he already owns. No upgrades.

When Jerry sells his home he is not allowed to represent to any prospective buyer that they would have the same privileges for having recreational vehicles stored in the same manner on the property. He can only say his name, rank, and "This is a covenants-controlled community." Upon sale he is to remove, at his expense, the lattice work, except for the four-by-four, seven-foot posts supporting the lattice work. However, the posts have to be cut to a maximum of five feet, *if required in writing by the association.*

Jerry said, "It's cost me $8,000 to $10,000. It certainly hasn't been a very recreational experience. The board must have spent at least $16,000 to $20,000 in legal fees. I don't know for sure. I find no mention of legal fees in the financial statements. They *spent homeowners' funds for frivolous purposes.*"

Jerry said, "The board really knows how to spend homeowners' money. Why do the new shade trees have to be more than twice the height of the lattice screen?

"The board compounded the problem when they lowered the allowable fence height to five feet. That reduced the fence barrier by one foot. A further irritant is that one pays by the linear foot for fencing that comes in six-foot lengths. The five-foot rule causes paying for one foot of waste for every strip of wood.

Jerry continued, "I have no problem with the covenants. I know what was intended when the covenants were written, although some are antiquated, like the one about no satellite dishes. The problem is the board's interpretations. They're abusing their positions and causing misery.

"Everything I do I weigh as to whether or not I'm going to stay here and try to make a life. All I want is to live in a nice community. I love my neighbors. They're terrific. You can't put a value on that.

"The HOA is a poor loser. They watch me like a hawk to see if they can find a new infraction of the rules to harass me about. For instance, they constantly monitor whether my gate is left open too long. I would **never** move into another CCC. Moving now would cause a hardship."

Jerry ended with a quote from American orator, Wendell Phillips, "What is defeat? Nothing but education, nothing but the first step to something better."

That is a prime case of the lawsuit process only succeeding in depleting the emotions and the finances of the opposing parties.

CAI spokeswoman, Debra Bass admits, ". . . all the litigation is only benefiting the lawyers." (*Woman's Day* article "Trouble on the Home Front?" November 1, 1996.)

Attorney Lynn Jordan advised not only to read the covenants and the Regs before moving in, but also to drive through the neighborhood and to notice carefully what is and what isn't there. That's good advice. But, driving around a complex is only the first step.

There's a BOD waiting to happen in *new* communities. They have not yet established all of the procedures that will ultimately be set into place. It takes time for the true character of the board and the impact of the covenants to come into full view.

Jerry Beach drove through his development many times. He talked to the developer. Unfortunately, the newness of the community worked against Jerry's best efforts. His subsequent problems still ended up costing him approximately $10,000 in legal fees! Don't feel bad, Jerry, there are homeowners who have paid a quarter of a million in legal fees and still lost their clearly valid cases.

▶ *IS THE FOX IN CHARGE OF GUARDING THE CHICKEN COOP?*

What is the legal profession's bonafide agenda? At times it seems as though the legal beagles got their on-the-job training at the law firm of Scrooge, Simon, and Legree.

What if we didn't have attorneys and judges to *solve* our problems? That's a happy fairy tale to tell your kids and grandkids.

Attorneys encourage HOA little Caesars and Caesarettes to harass citizens by strictly following and enforcing all the rules to the point of focusing on the unmitigated minutiae of life. That stance inflicts sheer torture on homeowners.

Rigorously following rules that weren't intended for the benefit of humanity worked only for a while for Hitler, Attila the Hun, and the Spanish Inquisitions. I don't sense the Christians were too happy with their bouts with the lions for any length of time either. Fortunately, that vein of thinking has not been extended to today's society. Or has it?

From my vantage point, I detect a lack of dedication of the entire legal community to identify the underlying reasons why there are so many HOA cases heard throughout the nation's courts. Court time could be used more productively hearing true culprit-creature cases, rather than frivolous, "It's the written rule. Read the rules and abide. The birdhouse has to be demolished, foundation and all. I find for the HOA. Next case."

Attorneys and judges pay dearly for their education and definitely deserve to make an above average income, but not at the expense of innocent homeowners who pay dearly for the privilege of owning a home.

Unfair lawsuits are filed against homeowners who have diligently worked to accumulate enough money to invest in a home with the anticipation of living in a reasonably benevolent style. In most cases a home is the largest asset the homeowner will ever have.

After achieving their goal, their dreams of enjoying the fruits of their labors can rapidly be dissolved in a courtroom fracas over some trivial issue.

There is a gigantic line between what is qualitatively, monumentally significant and what is unequivocally unimportant. Monumental issues are those that *cause authentic threats to residents and property values.* Insignificant issues allow some individuality and *do NOT generate any threat to residents and property values.*

Recall some trivial issues: There shall be no security doors (a safety measure for residents), no tiny, clear Lucite Christmas holiday light holders (a festive declaration), no RVs (even when the covenants declare it's permissible with proper screening), and no displaying of the American flag (well, sometimes with a conforming bracket).

You probably know many more of the immaterial topics that have summoned material sorrows. Do you perceive they are a danger to homeowners or property values? Do you feel they are suit-provoking issues? The legal profession did!

It is the legal profession and rigid HOAs that *cause threats to residents and property values* over unimportant issues. Far too often HOAs and the legal clique make monumental mountains out of insignificant mole hills.

Consider Pearl Harbor, the burning of Joan of Arc, "Let them eat cake," the Salem witch hunts, the Alamo, and the massacre at Wounded Knee. Those are perilous events.

Learn to weigh perilous against paltry and pointless.

The judge perpetuates a homeowner's anguish as he delivers the final insult with the usual verdict for the HOA. There needs to be a more equitable balance of the scales of justice. HOAs need to soften their attitudes about ridiculous, trifling issues. For a case to reach the court, the painful process is usually initiated by a representative of the HOA. Eliminate grievous situations. Mediate. Stay out of court. Conserve funds. No one wins in a lawsuit except the lawyers!

As a homeowner, if you do find yourself being siphoned into court, thorough preparation is your best defense. That provides you with, at least, some chance of winning, especially *if you're current with your dues.* Don't ever stop paying your HOA dues to prove a point.

Attorneys, judges, developers, and BODs, make room for compassion. Make leeway for residents to enjoy life. Be cognizant of what is good for the majority of the residents. You will all still survive.

The legal profession may even gain the prestige of being removed from the top of the public's list of "those I most distrust." They may never hear another, "Did you hear the one about the attorney who . . . ?" They might have to forgo an occasional golf game or two and maybe they will have to put off buying that Lexus for a year or more. It is highly doubtful though that any will ever be forced to take residency in the poor farm because they embraced empathy.

In the meantime, some recommended reading . . .

● *Problems of Long-Standing Homeowner Associations,* by Jim Winzenburg, published by Matthew Bender, one of the country's leading lawbook publishers. This treatise, which deals with legal issues facing associations, expands the Matthew Bender series of real estate books for attorneys who practice Community Associations and Real Estate law.

● *The Complete and Easy Guide to All the Law Every Home Owner Should Know,* by The American Bar Association. Chapter two is "Sharing Ownership" *Condos, Co-ops, and Other Common-Interest Communities.* Another very interesting chapter is "How to Keep Petty Annoyances from Turning into Major Headaches." This easy to read book could help keep you out of court. It's available in some bookstores or by calling 800-733-3000.

● *Finding the Key to Your Castle: A Guide to Cooperative Living in Your Condominium, Townhouse or Planned Development Home,* by Beth Grimm, Esq. and Jim R. Lane. It is a cleverly written and entertaining book that is full of practical advice. To purchase a copy call 510-674-1500.

● A booklet, *Caveat Emptor: Before You Buy That California Condo,* by Frederick L. Pilot, Common Interest Consumer Project (CICP). Write to CICP, 915 L Street, C-281, Sacramento, CA 95814 or e-mail at fpilot@directcon.net.

A *wee pause for a moment of attorney levity*

Back to "Did you hear the one about the . . . ?" The only problem with attorney jokes is that attorneys don't think they're funny and nobody else thinks they're a joke.

Why does California have the most attorneys and New Jersey the most waste dumps? New Jersey had first choice.

As *we creep back to the serious side* . . .

My number two son, David, at age 14, directed parking cars at a ski area. The driver of one car resisted David's parking directions. Instead, the driver rolled his window down and said, "Do you know who I am? I'm Judge . . . I don't want to park there. I want to park closer to the ski run." David replied, "Do you know who I am? I'm David Greenwalt and I'm in charge of parking cars. Park there, judge!"

Too many attorneys and judges come from that same, "Do you know who I am?" ego-trip attitude. They act as though it's a privilege for you even to be allowed to step into their *fine* office. Remember when you *hire* an attorney he is supposed to be working *for* you. **You pay him.** You call the shots. If your lawyer uses intimidating tactics, keep looking for a good one.

A lawyer who sincerely wants to serve your needs will not talk down to you. He will communicate with you as an equal human being. Those wonderful lawyers are out there. If you can't find a good attorney, drop the case. No attorney is better than a bad attorney.

The HOA *doesn't always win, even when it should*

Betty Procter lives in Pleasant Meadows Townhomes. It's a small complex with cedar siding.

The HOA hired a painter to stain the siding for $3,500. In the middle of the job, he quit. Disappeared. A second painter was hired to complete the project.

The first painter sent a bill for the whole $3,500. Fairly steep for an incomplete job. When the HOA didn't rush a check off to him, he sued!

An attorney who *specializes* in HOA cases was hired.

There were many depositions and witnesses available for testimony for the HOA's case. The attorney offered not one of the depositions nor did he call one witness! He presented a *"no case"* case for the HOA. Does it surprise you that the HOA lost?

Naturally, the HOA wanted to appeal. *Only the original evidence presented* can be used in Appellate Court. No original evidence, no appeal allowed.

Betty said, "We ended up paying about $5,000 including court fees, *plus* paying the second painter who deserved payment."

Is something missing or is something amiss? The scales of justice seem to be askew.

It takes pure gall to bill for services not rendered. The painter had a double dose of gall to have the nerve to sue after he walked off the job. Don't you wonder if that's his regular business plan? Slap a little paint or stain on, leave, bill, and sue.

I'm not an attorney, but I think I could have slam dunked that case with my feet in quick sand and my hands tied behind my back!

Then the attorney conjured up a half dose of gall. He *threatened* to sue Pleasant Meadow Townhomes' HOA for $15,000 for his *services,* or *non-services* in this situation.

Painters and attorneys, as in every profession, come in categories of good, bad, and varying degrees in between. Remember the 80/20 rule? Pleasant Meadows HOA found both a painter and an attorney who were at the very bottom of the 80 percent group. They hooked up with two incompetent, village idiots! Where is Perry Mason when we need him?

Betty sent a letter to that attorney and explicitly inventoried his negligent court preparation and presentation. It's been over three years since the BOD of Pleasant Meadows Townhomes has received another pay-the-bill letter.

> Betty is nimble,
> Betty is quick,
> She smacked that attorney
> with a reality stick.

Betty said, "Even though we certainly had a few hurdles to jump, with determination and hard work, everything is running smoothly for the homeowners now." Betty gets involved. She never shirks her responsibility to help keep HOA affairs on the right track.

Developers, I beseech you to stop recording deed restrictions that deny congenial living.

Legal profession, I beg you to go to a new, friendly, caring drawing board. Draw up new off-the-rack rules that *allow* congenial living styles. While you're at it, remember to add a reasonable provision for modification. Homeowners need flexibility to keep up with the times.

Say it again and then sing it, Sam. Now listen to the rest of the melody.

Systematic procedures and classifications are formed from the left side of the brain. Those who think predominately from the left brain want everything exactly in a straight line with no deviations. They are oriented to precise routines. It is easy for them to make strict, rule-following decisions because they aren't straying from their interpretation of the rule.

Daydreaming, imagination, and creativity, thinking "out of the box," are molded from the right side of the brain. Those who function predominantly from the right brain prefer curves and squiggles in their lines. They constantly change their routines.

Monumental feats are accomplished by those who use both the methodical left-brain and the creative right-brain functions. Think of the achievements of Henry Ford, Orville and Wilbur Wright, Thomas Edison, Alexander Graham Bell, Madame Curie, and Jonas Salk.

New, imaginative people pleasures are produced daily. Original accomplishments have been expanded to give us radio, television, jet planes, computers, advanced software, fax machines, voice mail, cordless and cellular phones, Internet, lifesaving drugs, and lifesaving alternatives to drugs. Who knows what is next to come?

Let's be innovative and put both sides of our brains to use. Let's think outside of the restrictions of "the box." Just because the same musty, dusty HOA Docs have hung around the necks of homeowners for over 30 years does not mean we have to continue with them.

Let's not die at a stuck stoplight, or a stuck Doc-light. Let's prepare for the next century by getting some Docs that are suitable for this decade. Let's introduce a fresh, modern set of Docs that is void of job security for the legal profession.

Your Decs may need amending, but it isn't easy

BOARDROOM DISCUSSION
❖ Published by the LAW FIRM OF WINZENBURG, LEFF, PURVIS AND PAYNE, LLP ❖
● 1660 Lincoln Street, #1750 ● Denver, Colorado 80264 ● 303-863-1870

THE DECLARATION SAYS WHAT???   May/June 1996

Many Associations must comply with documents that are outdated and impractical. Most Association documents require high quorums of the votes of most owners <u>and</u> *all* mortgagees (lenders) in order to amend the Declaration. When an Association discovers a serious difficulty with its documents, many Boards examine the alternatives:

1. Learn to live with the problem.

2. Determine whether automatic provisions of the Colorado Common Interest Community Act (CCIOA) address the issue. [There are similar acts in other states.]

3. See if the problem is caused by a lack of clarity that can be reasonably "interpreted" by a Board Resolution or by a vote of the owners.

4. File a Declatory Judgment action to ask a court to interpret what the documents mean or require.

5. Request a court to "reform" the problem document — not practical in most instances.

6. Amend the document.

In many cases, the owners and mortgagees must be consulted if the Declaration is to be amended. Associations wishing to amend their documents should give timely notice to the parties involved. Use terms that the owners and lenders will understand so they will appreciate the need for the amendment. Clear communication, in a positive tone, and timely follow up will increase your chances of successfully amending the documents. After amendment, send another notice to the owners and lenders that the documents have, in fact, been amended. Thank them for their cooperation.

Imagine my pure delight when I received *that* newsletter! Check your Docs to see if you can legally amend problem rules to solve homeowners' dilemmas.

Some states have passed acts that contain statutes that can take precedence over recorded association declarations. Developments built in Colorado since CCIOA passed July 1, 1992, are required to be under CCIOA regulations. Communities built prior to that time have a choice whether to accept the entire terms of that Act. Filing a lien on a property for up to six months delinquent dues (no late fees or attorney costs) is one CCIOA regulation that automatically applies to all associations. The HOA's lien goes into first position, senior to the mortgage company's lien if the loan was originated after the Act was passed.

Lois and Sam Pratt from New Jersey have studied the proposed UCIOA (Uniform Common Interest Ownership Act). UCIOA is intended as a plan for adoption state by state. The Pratts say, "It is no panacea for homeowners and associations. Homeowners should carefully compare provisions in their current law that are important to them with the specific language of comparable UCIOA provisions. In New Jersey, for example, the proposed UCIOA would weaken existing provisions for transparent governance; grant significantly more open-ended authority to boards than is granted in existing law, while weakening provisions for accountability and enforcement by a state agency; and grant boards increased powers to define what furthers "general welfare" than exist in present law.

"Since the original 1960s laws were enacted there have been valuable legislative improvements designed to meet associations' and homeowners' contemporary needs. Indiscriminate adoption of retrogressive features of UCIOA imperils that progress."

Other states which have enacted improved legislative provisions could similarly lose them under UCIOA. For example, California and Colorado associations, which have stronger open meeting laws than New Jersey would lose such protections.

An urgent need

It's time the awkward, ready-made Docs take on a new look to facilitate amicable communities suitable for today's living. That is most likely a familiar song by now. It's the first verse to the CCC Anthem. The second verse is empathy for residents' comfort level.

Take a close look at this

OVERT DISCRIMINATION is a SIN of COMMISSION.
It is UNJUST and ILLEGAL.

It's been only a few years since property values were "protected" by overt discriminatory restrictions. Such restrictions proudly and legally adorned the covenants of many subdivisions.

A buyer of a wrong race, unpopular religious beliefs, inappropriate political affiliation, and so on was not allowed to purchase a home in one of those secure little colonies.

The legal profession assembled those prejudicial rules and regulations just as they have assembled the rules and regulations for CCCs.

For years those covenants were legally upheld by the courts. *The legal profession staunchly supported every one of those regulations to the finest letter of every written rule.* Does that have a familiar sound?

Overt sin of commission is like shouting to Wyatt Earp to gun someone down in full view of the townspeople.

COVERT DISCRIMINATION is a SIN of OMISSION.
It is UNJUST, but STILL LEGAL!

The parallel is obvious between the narrow-minded, biased covenants of yesterday and the unclear, inhumane, and over restrictive rules found in CCC covenants of today.

There are *no overt discriminatory* regulations in CCC covenants. The federal government will not allow that any more. However, there are many regulations that can effectively conceal the true intention of those who enforce the rules. The wording doesn't disclose the possibility of "legal" discriminatory actions.

First Right of Refusal is a prime example of a discriminatory cover-up. That covenant stipulates that the HOA and/or homeowners have a specific time period to decide whether they will buy the property or allow the buyer's contract to prevail.

Recognize the masked discrimination for that covenant to prevent "undesirables" from moving into their little colony. *"If we don't want that buyer in our community, for whatever reason, we will buy the home to keep him out!"*

Disguised sin of omission is like whispering to Wyatt Earp that it's okay to gun someone down, just don't do it where anyone will see it.

Overt discriminatory covenants were sentenced to the guillotine. That may give a flicker of hope for the demise of *covert discriminatory* HOA rules, regulations, and hostile covenants.

▶ *ANOTHER CULPRIT AT THE BASE OF HOA PROBLEMS IS EXPOSED*

There is a problem that goes beyond the antiquity of the Docs. (The birth of the Docs that put the *control* in the covenants is in chapter 3, *Thirty-year old whiskers are growing on today's Docs.*) HOAs are mini-governments, under the handicap of corporate law procedures. Consider the chaos that would be created if federal, state, and municipal governments were forced to change to corporate law procedures. Only 49 percent of those of eligible voting age voted in the 1996 presidential election. If the constitution required a quorum, it's unlikely this would qualify. Under corporate law we could be left with no president and Congress could slowly dissolve. It's time to recognize corporate law isn't working well for HOA governments either. Corporate law often places insurmountable obstacles in the path of democracy. New, practical, constitutional processes of governing need to be introduced. (Detailed suggestions are presented in the Summary on page II.)

In 1994 I heard Dr. Evan McKenzie on the radio discussing the book he had just written about CCCs, *Privatopia: Homeowner Associations and the Rise of Residential Private Government.* Dr. McKenzie, an attorney and an assistant political science professor at the University of Illinois, used to represent HOAs. He said CCCs were a threat to state and municipal governments because associations would, basically, eventually secede from the "Union" by enforcing HOA rules *above* governmental rules. I thought, "Chubby chance."

That was then. This is now. Dr. McKenzie told me that some states are considering lowering property taxes for those who live in CCCs. Homeowners feel they are being double dipped with HOA fees and property taxes. According to David Diamond (*USA Weekend* "Behind Closed Gates" January 31-February 2, 1997), residents in New Jersey have already won the right to receive rebates on property taxes because their HOA dues pay for such services as street repairs and lighting.

It's unlikely that the HOA governmental conundrum will be solved until homeowners are given back their rights of freedom to enjoy their lives and their homes. CCCs are putting a large hole in the dike of the United States and, perhaps, in the dike of the world.

I suggest everyone in a CCC read Dr. McKenzie's book *Privatopia,* a comprehensive history of CCCs and the original sources of today's extensive problems.

Dr. Evan McKenzie's *Privatopia* © 1994 by Yale University, page 106

The Community Associations Institute is the nation's voice on community associations issues. — CAI Statement of Core Purpose, 1992

CAI was in part a social experiment to see if disparate interest groups could work together for the common good....CAI quickly became dominated by those in the business, principally managers and colleagues....I sense that the Institute is headed even more surely toward a manager and colleague trade association. While this is the easiest way to continue, it disturbs me.
— Lincoln C. Cummings, cofounder of CAI, 1992

Woman's Day "Trouble on the Home Front?" by John Grossmann (November 1, 1996) was a marvelously informative article. I learned that in many states there are *huge* CCCs that provide almost everything. Some even include such amenities as auditoriums, theaters, and libraries. They become a self contained city within a city. I also learned that there are many states that *disallow homeowners to speak at association meetings!* Sieg heil. Buying a home in a CCC in one of those states is like saying, "Lock me in the cage. Just tell me which of my legs you are going to shoot first."

In that same article, Jackie Speier (a former California assemblywoman) explained that homeowners' rights get defeated by lobbyists. Speier noted, "I think what's happened here in California is that the *special interest representing the attorneys that specialize in this kind of property management law have helped craft the laws to their benefit.*"

John Grossmann quoted some comments from Dr. McKenzie. Dr. McKenzie noted that residents are fast losing their liberties. He stated, "It's worse than trying to fight City Hall. At least City Hall must pay attention to the U.S. Constitution [and the Bill of Rights]. Homeowner associations are essentially private corporations and about as democratic as most corporations. They will fight you to the last dollar, using your money, all the while saying, 'Why can't you just go along?' It's like *The Stepford Wives.*"

I found a court case from Pennsylvania that will curl your toes: *Midlake Condominium Association vs. Cappucio* addressed the validity of U.S. Constitutional rights in a community controlled with covenants.

In violation of a covenant, the Cappucios put two For Sale signs in their windows. When the association ordered them to remove the signs, the Cappucios took it to court. The court ruled for the Cappucios as a violation of their First Amendment right of free speech.

Beware of the enemy at one o'clock. An appellate court overruled the decision. They said that *contractually homeowners give up their constitutional rights* when they buy a home in a covenant-controlled community! Decisions like that continue to fan the flames.

"All laws which are repugnant to the Constitution are null and void." *Marbury vs. Madision,* 5 US (2Cranch) 137, 174, 176, (1803)

"Where rights secured by the Constitution are involved, there can be no rule making or legislation which would abrogate them." *Miranda vs. Arizona,* 384 US 436

"An unconstitutional act is not law; it confers no rights; it imposes no duties; affords no protection; it is in legal contemplation, as inoperative as though it had never been passed." *Norton vs. Shelby County* 118 US 425 p. 442

"No one is bound to obey an unconstitutional law and no courts are bound to enforce it." *16 Am Jur 2nd, Sec 177 late 2nd, Sec 256*

There is a movement to form a nationwide network to institute CCC homeowners' rights. Michael Van Dyk is president of Miami based SHORN (Secure Homeowner Rights Now). In New Jersey, Lois Pratt is vice president of C-IHC (Common-Interest Homeowners Coalition). Patricia Wigginton is president of Maryland Homeowners' Association (MHA). All fight for legislation to lessen the power of BODs and give more rights to homeowners.

Patricia Wigginton said, "MHA wrote an association Bill of Rights that shaped SB 769. Maryland State Senator Jean W. Roesser introduced the bill. It passed unanimously in the senate. However, there is a faction that strives to stymie every attempt to give constitutional rights back to homeowners. In his article on June 5, 1997 in *The Washington Post,* columnist Steve Twomey said, 'But, the bill failed,' said Roesser, 'when some legislators bowed to that notion of associations as private clubs where decency need not prevail.'" Patricia continued, "A couple years ago Senator John Glenn was considering hearings on associations and their problems. Unfortunately, he was somehow dissuaded."

It's time for us to take action

I can assure you if *we* don't press the issue, developers and builders will not do it under their own unmotivated steam. They'll remain in their status quo, I-won't-spend-money-for-new-Docs, coast mode.

The legal fleet would rather damn the torpedoes and full speed ahead. Homeowners are the dispensable enemy. Let the hardships fall where they may. HOA skirmishes are just too lucrative to let drift away. That could spill all the gravy right out of their boat.

The court system has the scales of The Lady of Justice way off balance when it comes to cases between homeowner associations and homeowners.

Legislators will continue to be swayed by pressure from the lobbyists who work for those who find it more profitable to keep homeowners controlled and in their "right" place.

On which side of the aisle are you?

CHAPTER 11

You're on the Board.
Now What Do You Do?

▶ *USE ETHICS, EMPATHY, AND COMPASSION*

Wouldn't it be a delight if our maxi-government used ethics, empathy, and compassion rather than blind compliance to the rules? Of course, blind compliance is only when the rules apply to others. Somehow, they have an altered outlook when it comes to applying those same rules to themselves. Instantly, they acquire the knack of selective recall with absolutely no memory of the content of the rules.

If you don't have a heart chock-full of fondness for the way our government (the big one) currently operates, then don't emulate them in your HOA mini-government.

The rules that historically may have been followed to the nth degree were written by an attorney whom not one homeowner has *ever* met. That attorney has never once gazed into your eyes nor even talked to you on the phone. Why then would anyone want to turn the comfort and living style of the homeowners over to the dictates of a person who doesn't know you and doesn't care about anyone in your community?

I'm not suggesting you throw the rules in the river and wing it. You need guidelines. You need some kind of teeth to have the authority to solve *real* problems. Focus only on genuine problems rather than seizing an opportunity to flex your rules-enforcer muscles.

From the 1940s to the early 1960s, Burma Shave had an extremely popular, progressive road sign advertising campaign. Rejected for being in bad taste in the 1950s was

> Listen you birds
> these signs cost money.
> Roost a while,
> but don't get funny.

That seems quite tame in today's world. Life advances. When will HOAs and HOA rules advance in pace with life?

Del Kurtz, a homeowner in San Dimas, California said, "Our board enforces rules as though they're afraid the world would end tomorrow if they even dared consider the human elements involved. But, get this, they meet in secret, take no minutes, and blatantly state that they are not obligated to follow the rules because they are volunteers." Wrong!

Now what do you do? — part one of two

● Inaugurate common sense and moral principles into your HOA. That combination can accomplish gargantuan feats. The gray-matter effort and time it takes to strive for community harmony are well worth it.

● Target your efforts to achieve desirable results rather than starting a rebellion against the rules. Don't focus your energy on what you don't want. I don't even believe in the *War* on Drugs. Say what? Are you for drugs, Joni? Nope, I give credence to working *for* a drug-free nation rather than *against* drugs. Work *for* a happy community.

● Allow homeowners to audio or video tape all meetings. That's an accurate method of recording what actually occurred at a meeting.

● If parking is a problem because your streets are private and narrow, don't ban all street parking. Limit parking by painting the curbing yellow on one side of the street.

● Use ethics, empathy, and compassion. That doesn't mean you have to allow a neighbor to paint his home chartreuse with passionate purple pinstripes and rosy-red trim.

● Neither harmony nor order is produced by exerting total control or buckling under with unconditional surrender. One extreme or the other will cause chaos.

● You'll get some off-the-wall requests from residents. Bowing to every request will bring about the very turmoil you want to avoid. Be above board. Scrutinize your reasoning to make absolutely certain you don't label a request as off-the-wall simply because it isn't burning in your heart as a fond, personal desire. If the appeal is *truly* not detrimental to your neighborhood, your neighbor's need will very likely benefit many others in your community. Often modification only requires *modifying the interpretation* of an existing mandate. Never let your BOD powers overshadow your moral obligations.

● Explore practical, legal ways to make the rules and regulations fit the true needs of your community. Soften harsh rules and clarify vague regulations. Ignore silly rules. Focus on meaningful issues. Study the rules carefully. Interpret them with compassion in your heart for your neighbors. Don't compound obnoxious rules. Remain as adaptable as the law allows to leave yourself enough latitude to look for reasonable approaches to *solve problems*. Don't make interpretations that will cause problems. Publish your interpretations in a set of rules and regulations.

● Make certain your enforcement of all rules is consistent with your interpretations. Never be selective about which neighbors you're going to clamp down on and with whom you'll be more lenient. Never be arbitrary and capricious. All board and committee members are equally as obligated to the same adherence to the rules as all the other homeowners.

● Be extremely cautious defining how you will handle that rule that is in so many HOA Docs. You know, the one that goes something like "There shall be no appendages attached to the exterior of any home." Don't let that rule lead you to any scenario that might sound like "Sam, we'll fine you and ultimately sue you if you don't immediately remove those horrible, 5/8-inch, clear Lucite holiday light holders. They're terribly unsightly." "Betty, we removed the birdhouse and the hanging plant from your patio. They were sullying our community, running our values down, and you know it's the *rule*. We must maintain uniformity."

What a boring picture flawless uniformity paints. Denying plants, birdhouses, and holiday light holders most likely is from interpretation rather than the original intent of the rule.

● If you're uncomfortable unraveling the legalese, you may want to hire an attorney in the 20 percent group. An even better choice is for the BOD to translate the regulations and have their interpretations verified by the attorney. That conserves funds and gives the board more control over the interpretations. In any case, make certain the terminology is in *real people, simplified, understandable* language. *Don't let the attorney slip one bit of legalese or one lawsuit-provoking word* into your rules and regulations.

It's also helpful to the BOD to have a brief explanation of important issues, such as
  ● the number of members required to constitute a quorum in various situations,
  ● the percentage of votes needed to pass specific issues (usually, there are three or more variations, depending on the particular topic and the specific document),
  ● the number of days required to give notice for regular and special meetings,
  ● the number of days required to give a resident to correct a covenant violation,
  ● when it is acceptable for decisions to be made by a majority vote of the BOD, and
  ● when a vote of the homeowners is required.

When the Docs state the BOD has full power to make decisions, BODs who care to maintain or create a sense of community pride will initiate the community voting process on major issues to make certain the BOD is serving the needs of the majority.

A tale from my complex: We had several cottonwood trees that were guilty of dumping extensive cottonwood "snow" onto our complex. That snow was not an aesthetic asset to the community and it was an aggravation to those with allergies. Even though the BOD had the authority to order the trees chopped, we felt it was a major decision and chose to ask for a vote of the homeowners. We mailed the information along with a ballot for them to mark their vote and mail it back. A much higher percentage voted using that method. It was the decision of the majority to remove the trees and replace them with a friendlier species.

We got bids, but then the cottonwoods didn't cotton that year. Chop The Trees Company said, "We can still chop. We can identify which trees are the culprits even when they are not blooming or throwing cotton." I recalled going to a dentist who pulled the wrong tooth. The BOD didn't buy Chop The Trees Company's story. We knew they just wanted to collect money now. We told them, "Not one tree will be cut until it exposes itself as an offender. We will not be guilty of unintentionally eliminating one friendly tree."

The following is an extremely reasonable regulation lurking in the Decs of some associations. You may gain new congenial freedoms from similar wording in your Decs.

Helpful off-the-rack rule

Article V
ARCHITECTURAL CONTROL COMMITTEE

Section 7. Variance. The Architectural Control Committee may grant reasonable variances or adjustments from any conditions and restrictions imposed by this Article or Article X [REGULATIONS] hereof, in order to overcome practical difficulties or prevent unnecessary hardships arising by reason of the application of the conditions and restrictions contained in this Article or Article X hereof. Such variances or adjustments shall be granted only in case of the granting thereof shall not be materially detrimental or injurious to the other property or improvements in the neighborhood and shall not militate against the general intent and purpose hereof.

Section 8. Waivers. The approval or consent of the Architectural Control Committee, any representative thereof, or the Board of Directors of the Association, to any application for architectural approval shall not be deemed to constitute a waiver of any right to withhold or deny approval or consent by the Committee, any representative thereof, or said Board of Directors, as to any application or other matters whatsoever as to which approval or consent may subsequently or additionally be required.

That regulation offers some flexibility to bend a rule a little if the bending doesn't cause harm. Granted, the point could have been made with fewer words. However, legalese or not, it allows the right to soften some restrictions. Maybe like the *no clothesline* rule?

Now what do you do? — part two of two

If you've lived in your complex for any length of time, you're familiar with the beat of the drum that the enforcers have been playing. If it's been a friendly peace drum, keep the rhythm moving without skipping a beat.

If it's been a war drum, immediately write a new song with a beat that sends a message of unity. Drop the trivia and go for the Reasonableness Rule Enforcement approach. That is a dependable way to mold a contented community. (The Reasonableness Test is on page 181.)

● Rarely does a BOD get any monetary compensation for their tour of board duty. Often BODs get cranky when too many items fall in their hands or on their heads. It's essential to prevent BOD burnout and preserve BOD sanity. Bookkeeping, paying bills, developing and keeping track of the budget is too much to expect any homeowner to do as a freebie. Service companies make a good buffer. They are fully equipped with buoys and lifesavers to protect and rescue those on board. (***Basic services performed by service/management companies*** is in chapter 7.)

● Protect HOA funds by having a caring service company write the checks and two board members sign the checks. Depletion of the treasury is more likely to happen when the funds are controlled only by the BOD or a self-serving management company.

The experience your representative at the service company gains from handling the happenings of other associations provides him with knowledge to present qualified guidelines to you. Remember, this is his career. It certainly isn't yours unless you're retired and choose to devote a major part of your life to overseeing the daily duties. That is not an invitation to hand over the BOD's elected powers. Keep those in the boardroom. Make it clear to all homeowners that the BOD is still running the show.

Every HOA has its fair share of coaster-dwellers. Their presence is another prize reason for the BOD to enlist the aid of a service company. Coaster-dwellers never lift one little pinkie to do one microscopic task. They seldom sign proxies or read HOA newsletters and announcements. They put HOA meetings on the top of their off-limits list. The only time coaster-dwellers are heard from is when they have a complaint. Coaster-dwellers freely ride on the kite tails of those who give their time and efforts gratis.

Paying a service company to assist the BOD obligates the coaster-dwellers to share, at least monetarily, in *some* HOA responsibilities. BODs volunteer their time and knowledge to support their community. "Personal elf" to coaster-dwellers is not in their job description.

• Unless you're bent on taking a masochistic approach, stick to significant tasks. Let the service company representative handle the minutiae.

The relationship between the service company and the BOD is the BOD . . .

• makes the final decisions,
• approves the budgets,
• approves the final draft of newsletters,
• signs checks that have been written by the service company representative, and
• authorizes phone calls and letters to homeowners.

• Make certain there is always a friendly overtone in newsletters, phone calls, and letters to residents. Unless you have developed a friendly, but firm, form letter method, proofread the specific contents of every letter sent for violations. All letters can be cordial. Let's take a letter that gives a resident a specific length of time to replace a dead tree. He is advised that it has to be done within that time frame or the HOA will do it, bill him, and that could eventually result in a lien on his property. Even that letter can have a polite overtone.

Residents rarely take the responsibility for being the cause of a violation notice. They prefer to get angry at the BOD. Following are some phrases that you can incorporate in your citation letters to put the responsibility where it belongs: This is not a position the board enjoys taking. We are sorry you have not corrected this violation. The Board of Directors of Happy Homes does not enjoy issuing violation notices.

• Keep a high profile with your community. Maintain the truth of being self-managed. As stated in *Boardroom Discussion,* self-managed associations have higher levels of participation. Having a service company does *not* remove you from that category.

• Maintain good public relations with your community. Example: Don't fire off a late charge notice to a homeowner the first time he is late with his HOA fees. Make it a policy to inform all homeowners that there is a valid late charge due, but that the HOA will waive it for any homeowner with an excellent payment history.

Barbara, a homeowner with an outstanding record of paying her dues, called me to explain why she was late that month. This case set the precedent for the BOD to waive the late fee and do the same for any homeowner who is late only one time in a 12-month period (not a calendar year). Collecting the $10 late charge would not be worth the bad public relations it would cause. Late charges are not what any HOA's count on to receive their money.

Case in point: A year later Barbara's lawn suddenly started looking as though it was in need of Federal Disaster Aid. Her lawn had always been so well manicured. Some of the sod had been removed, presumably with the intention of replacing it. The rest of the lawn had turned a dark shade of brown. When I called her she graciously thanked me and said that she had been pressed for time and that her lawn was suffering from lack of care.

Barbara said my call encouraged her to get back on track with her original goal. Within days she contracted for a sprinkler system, professional landscaping, and new sod.

Enforcing that $10 late fee would have labeled us as an uncaring, rigid board with total lack of compassion. That stance would have produced a defensive, irritated reply from Barbara instead of her amiable response and rapid action.

Good public relations with your community are imperative

BOARDROOM DISCUSSION

❖ Published by the LAW FIRM OF WINZENBURG, LEFF, PURVIS AND PAYNE, LLP ❖
• 1660 Lincoln Street, #1750 • Denver, Colorado 80264 • 303-863-1870

May/June 1996

Reprinted with permission of Dartnell, 4660 North Ravenswood Ave., Chicago, IL 60640, 800-621-5463. From *The Customer Service Rep's Emergency Survival Guide*.

TEN WAYS TO MAKE UNHAPPY PEOPLE HAPPY

1. *Hear the person out.* In addition to getting a problem resolved, the person wants a sympathetic ear.
2. *Don't argue.* They may be angry or saying things that simply are not true. Don't fight back; let the person sound off.
3. *Show you are sorry.* Let the person know you are sorry there is a problem but that you're glad to hear about it. You are not admitting error, but simply letting the person know you regret the situation, no matter what the reason is or where the fault lies.
4. *Win them over with understanding.* Let them know you understand how they feel: "That must have been frustrating for you. I can see how disappointing it must have been."
5. *Start the investigation.* Once the person has settled down you should be able to ask questions and get answers that can help you accurately determine the scope and nature of the problem. After you ask a few questions repeat the information conveyed to you to make sure you understand exactly what the person perceives as the problem.
6. *Find out what the person wants.* Do they simply need to blow off steam, without expecting anything to be done? If they want something more, be sure you understand exactly what he or she is asking for. Get all the information that might be needed.
7. *Explain what you can and cannot do.* If the person wants you to do something that is within your power, do so at once. If it's not that simple, explain why.
8. *Set up a plan.* Set up an action plan that is agreeable to the person. Be specific: "I will meet with the Board tomorrow. You should expect to hear from us next week."
9. *Take action.* Carry out your promises. Act promptly.
10. *Check back with the person.* Afterwards, check to see that the implementation has been satisfactory. Let them know you appreciate the opportunity to make things right.

HOAs need to be reasonable

BOARDROOM DISCUSSION

❖ Published by the LAW FIRM OF WINZENBURG, LEFF, PURVIS AND PAYNE, LLP ❖
• 1660 Lincoln Street, #1750 • Denver, Colorado 80264 • 303-863-1870

July 1995

ASSOCIATIONS SHOULD ACT REASONABLY

The following letter is, unfortunately, typical of many that have been received.

I was out of work last year. Money was tight. All my creditors worked with me, including my doctors. I tried to pay something every month and *did not have a problem until it came to my community association*.

When my assessment came due, I explained my situation to the managers. They did not seem to have a problem with that. However, I received letters threatening foreclosure on my home if I did not pay my dues. I sent a check for $5 toward my account, acknowledging that although it did not seem like much, I was making an effort to pay. Once I was able to work again, I promised to pay the balance. They returned my check, saying that $5 was not enough and that I needed to send at least $25.

Then I received a letter informing me that a lien would be placed on my home and demanding a payment of $318, which included attorney fees because the "lawyers were already involved."

I hope what has happened to me does not happen to others.

Recommendation: There are times to be firm and business-like and times to be understanding. A wise Board will understand the difference. For example, a long-time resident who has *never* missed a payment might be given a little more time to pay than a habitual delinquent owner. Be reasonable and consistent in your distinction, so you are not selectively enforcing policies.

Our service company representative called me to say that a homeowner was $465 in arrears with her HOA fees and that the attorney said it would cost $150 to file suit. The board unanimously determined that would be an anti-productive course. If it ended in the courtroom, we felt it presented the potential of not only depleting thousands of dollars of our HOA funds, but also presented the possibility of our forcing the homeowner to sell her home or, even worse, causing her to lose her home through foreclosure. Instead we chose to file a lien on the property, an inexpensive process, if it became necessary. It turned out that the homeowner had lost her job, but had just started on a new one. She made arrangements with us to get caught up on her fees. You won't read that story in the newspapers.

An even more preferable scenario would have been for that resident to have called the HOA when she lost her job. Up front communication is a marvelous tool.

• Have your financial records reviewed every year by an independent accounting firm, *no matter who is doing the bookkeeping*. Some documents specify a full audit. That is a more much expensive process.

• In most states, with a valid reason, homeowners may look at the financial records by making an appointment with the holder of the books.

• If your Docs are sufficiently flexible, opt for no more than three to five board members.

You know all the clichés: A camel is a horse designed by a committee and too many cooks spoil the broth. Any more than five is definitely overkill and becomes a horse designed by a committee spoiling the broth. Oh, sure, let's spread the responsibilities around. Since we're not getting paid, let's have seven on the board. Seven does not always mean that each member will take one-seventh of the responsibilities and perform one-seventh of the work. Instead, it tends to be that each thinks, "I don't have to work that hard because there are six more to take care of it." In reality, either one or two will do the work or no one will do any work. Too often one or two will take over just to handle their personal agendas.

The only time over five board members are acceptable is in "anthill" communities of hundreds or thousands of homes. In that case, divide the homes into several groups and have a separate BOD of three to five members for each group. Those BOD members should live in the group of homes that they represent and be elected by the homeowners in that group.

Have the Master BOD coordinate the group of BODs. The Master BOD sits at the head of the table as the final decision makers. Either the entire community elects that BOD or they may be elected by the members of the other BODs.

With a BOD of three, it's preferable to replace only one board member each year to maintain a smooth operation. Three-year terms work well.

No matter how many members there are on the board, it's a problem if the majority is for inflexible enforcement on infringements of every paltry rule rather than for governing ethically for the enjoyment of the residents. "Residents" refers to renters as well as homeowners. Renters make monthly rent payments the same as homeowners make monthly mortgage payments. All want to live peacefully. All deserve to enjoy their homes.

● When the majority of the BOD is new, the tendency is to get all new contract labor such as lawn care service, general maintenance service, new service company, and so on. That causes problems. It's preferable to determine, with time, if it's broken before you fix it.

● When homeowners get sideways on issues they sometimes dispatch veiled threats to sue the BOD. Don't be intimidated if you're following proper procedures. They are just trying to control you. Keep making fair decisions and ignore the idle threats. Make certain the BOD's liability is limited in the Articles of Incorporation to protect them against frivolous law suits.

Boardroom Discussion agrees

BOARDROOM DISCUSSION
❖ Published by the LAW FIRM OF WINZENBURG, LEFF, PURVIS AND PAYNE, LLP ❖
● 1660 Lincoln Street, #1750 ● Denver, Colorado 80264 ● 303-863-1870

LIMIT THE BOARD'S LIABILITY   **July 1992**

Our previous Newsletters have addressed the 1986 legislation on directors and officers' liability. *Board members can decrease their liability by amending the Association's Articles of Incorporation,* which is usually a fairly simple procedure. *Do you know if your Association has protected the board from liability?*

We amended our Articles of Incorporation under the authority of the provisions of the Colorado Nonprofit Corporation Act and provisions given in our Articles. The one-page amendment was drawn up by an attorney. The amendment was adopted with the required vote of the homeowners, a quorum being present.

Our amendment states in part

---

1) The Articles of Incorporation are amended to add a new Article XIII, as follows:
The Corporation shall indemnify its Directors to the full extent permitted by Colorado law.

2) The Articles of Incorporation are amended to add a new Article XIV, as follows:
The personal liability of a Director to the Corporation or its members for monetary damages for breach of fiduciary duty is eliminated; except that this shall not eliminate or limit the liability of a Director to the Corporation or its members for monetary damages for: Any breach of the Director's duty of loyalty

to the Corporation or its members; acts or omissions not in good faith or which involve intentional misconduct or a knowing violation of law; acts specified in C.R.S., Section 7-22-101.5; or any transaction from which the Director derived an improper personal benefit; or any act or omission occurring prior to the date when this provision becomes effective.

• It is also imperative, and inexpensive, to have a Directors and Officers liability insurance policy to limit the BOD's liability further.

Boardroom Discussion and "Managers Report" agree

BOARDROOM DISCUSSION
❖ Published by the LAW FIRM OF WINZENBURG, LEFF, PURVIS AND PAYNE, LLP ❖
• 1660 Lincoln Street, #1750 • Denver, Colorado 80264 • 303-863-1870

DIRECTORS AND OFFICERS LIABILITY   November/December 1996
INSURANCE IS A BOARD MEMBER'S LAST LINE OF DEFENSE

Reprinted with permission from *Managers Report* in the March 1996 issue. The following is a condensation of that article by Michael Johnson.

If you serve on the Board of your Community Association, your Directors and Officers (D&O) Liability insurance policy may be the most important insurance coverage you can purchase.

The majority of the D&O policies are designed to defend and indemnify directors and officers for lawsuits seeking only *monetary* awards. However, *most D&O claims go beyond the scope of what is covered under these policies. Under many of the policies currently on the market,* **non-monetary** *claims (such as lawsuits seeking an injunction against the Board) would be excluded. There is a good chance they would* **not** *be covered.*

Associations can be liable for many thousands of dollars in defense costs. Assets of directors and officers could also be at risk. *Comprehensive D&O protection is a must.*

When evaluating your D&O insurance, have your agent provide written answers to these issues. Does the policy . . .
- Name the correct entity and insure the Association named in the definition of who is insured?
- Insure past and present directors, officers, committee members, volunteers, trustees, and employees?
- Cover prior acts?
- Insure the developer/builder while serving on the Board?
- Defend non-monetary claims?
- Cover libel and slander and copyright infringement?
- Provide a duty to defend?
- Carry an A.M. Best rating of at least an "A"?

The more comprehensive policies will cover each of the above areas. *If you find that your D&O policy falls short on these items, speak with your insurance agent about getting a quote for a more comprehensive policy. These policies can usually be purchased on a stand-alone basis, so it most likely doesn't matter where you've placed the rest of the Association's insurance,* subject to the exact terms and conditions of the policy.

I suggest subscribing to *Managers Report*. It's an inexpensive, extremely helpful magazine for HOAs. Contact them in West Palm Beach, Florida at 800-425-1314.

Homeowners can also protect themselves from certain wrongful acts by the BOD. I have an endorsement (a rider) with my own content insurance policy that protects me against special assessments due to some wrongful acts of the BOD. That coverage paid my assessment when our secretary/treasurer "borrowed" our bank account.

- As a new board member you can expect one of the following scenarios.

Scenario 1

You've been very happy with the board's decisions and their caring attitude toward residents. You want to do your part to help keep things going in the same contented direction and to help enrich the HOA's achievements. You anticipate the assignment will be fairly easy since there's nothing to fix. Neither *easy* nor *fairly easy* translates to *no work*.

Scenario 2

You've been less than happy with the board's decisions and their lack of caring attitude toward residents. You want to do your part to change things for the good of your community. Your anticipation is that, with your common sense approach, you will easily modify the thinking of the other board members. It will be neither *easy* nor even *fairly easy*. You're doomed to be defeated if the rigid-thinking good old boys, male or female, on the BOD outnumber the thinking "boys and girls." They will out-vote you every time. Don't give up. Organize a coup, if necessary. Offer an early retirement to the good old boys.

Work is relevant in any scenario

The amount of work will depend on which position you hold on the board. As president, you have the most responsibilities. If a special duty or need arises you can request delegation of that duty be given to another board member or to the service company. You can also ask for a volunteer committee to perform the duty. Some homeowners are more dedicated than others to donating time to perform drudgery chores. At least, give it a try.

Being a board member does not qualify as a no-brainer. There's an abundance of work. Don't expect the president to handle everything. Be a board member in the 20 percent group.

▶ TURNING BADS BACK INTO DABS

The acronym DAB for Declarations, Articles, and Bylaws seemed an excellent way to put the Docs in the proper perspective.

***DAB* vt., vi. dabbed, dab'bing 1.** to touch or stroke lightly and quickly **2.** to pat with something soft **3.** to put on with light, quick strokes — **n.** a light, quick stroke; tap; pat **3.** a small or soft bit of something.

Mr. Webster comes through again.

There's an appropriate phrase from a 1950s TV and radio Brylcreem commercial, "A Little Dab'll Do Ya." Freely translated, "A little bit will work."

DABs get twisted around to BADs in some complexes to rob residents of their freedom. They are BADs when *power* is used *incorrectly* to enforce every trivial rule rigidly without caring thought. The perception is "it must be true, it's written in the Docs." Surely the Docs have importance equal to that of the Bhagavad-gita, the Torah, and the Bible all put together.

To those who covet the opportunity to control others and to everyone with a framed law degree, I request you please carefully read the definitions of **BAD** and *power*.

> ***BAD adj.* worse, worst 1.** a) not good; not as it should be *[a bad* attitude, a *bad* deal*]* b) defective in quality **3.** below standard; inadequate **2.** unfit; unskilled; unfavorable; disagreeable *[bad* news*]* **4.** rotten; spoiled *[a bad* apple*]* **5.** incorrect **6.** a) wicked; immoral b) not behaving properly; mischievous **7.** causing injury; harmful *[bad* for one's health*]* **8.** severe **9.** sorry; distressed *[he feels bad* about it*]* **10.** offensive; disgusting **11.** *Law* defective; not valid; void *[a bad* title*]*

Power is like a big stick. You can choose to use it to hit, merely throw it into the water to float slowly downstream and decay, or use it as a walking stick to help.

> ***POWER* n. 1.** ability to do, act, or produce **2.** a specific ability or faculty **3.** great ability to do, act or affect strongly; vigor; force; strength **4.** a) the ability to control others; authority; sway; influence b) [pl.] special authority assigned to or exercised by a person or group holding office c) legal ability or authority; also, a document giving it **5.** a source of physical force or energy; force or energy that is at, or can be put to, work **6.** the capacity to exert physical force or energy **7.** a person or thing having great influence, force, or authority **8.** a nation, especially one having influence or domination over other nations [the great powers] **SYN. — power** denotes the inherent ability or the admitted right to rule, govern, determine, etc.; **jurisdiction** refers to the power to rule or decide within certain defined limits [the jurisdiction of the courts]

Thank you again, Mr. Webster. He had more to say, but I think the point is well made.

In this analogy, think community in place of child and HOA and BOD in place of parents. Any reliable doctor or psychologist will advise parents to nurture a child with love, compassion, kindness, and integrity. That will encourage the child to be physically and mentally healthy. Not one will ever advise being either heavy-handed or overindulgent.

A consistent, kindhearted attitude offers the most favorable environment for a child to grow into a happy, responsible, mature adult with high self-esteem. The trick is in balancing the firm and the tender aspects of nurturing.

Put the Docs in their proper perspective. Make the Docs a little DAB of your lives. Nurture your community to the DAB's way of living. See if you can pass the . . .

Reasonableness test

SECTION ONE. When there's a *problem* between a rule and a resident ask yourself . . .

1) Is what I perceive as the *problem* really creating disharmony for the majority of the residents or is it primarily a personal issue with other board members and me?

2) Will the current plan to solve the *problem* create harmony for the majority of the residents or is it merely a plan geared to satisfy other board members and me?

SECTION TWO. On a scale of 1 to 4: **1** = *always,* **2** = *usually,* **3** = *sometimes,* **4** = *never*

● If your Docs are unclear and do not specifically forbid certain homeowner pleasures, would you interpret the rules and make provisions in your Regs to allow . . .

1) a plant hanging by a front door?   1 2 3 4

2) a birdhouse and a bird feeder on a resident's patio or balcony?   1 2 3 4

3) a flag pole bracket to be mounted to a home or garage?   1 2 3 4

4) tiny, clear, 5/8-inch Lucite holiday light holders and allow them to remain attached to homes?   1 2 3 4

5) window flower boxes or flower pots to be adorned with attractive artificial flowers in the winter?   1 2 3 4

6) screen, storm, or security doors to be installed?   1 2 3 4

7) a trash enclosure, matching the theme of the complex to be constructed?   1 2 3 4

8) residents to change a tire or battery in their driveway or on the street?   1 2 3 4

9) vegetables to be grown in backyards or in containers on the patios?   1 2 3 4

10) toys in the front yards or on common areas during play time?   1 2 3 4

11) children to play freely on the well groomed common areas?   1 2 3 4

12) a couple of purple pansies and some marigolds in a five-white-petunia regimented community?   1 2 3 4

• If your Docs state certain homeowner pleasures are prohibited, would you be to willing promote community harmony by pursuing legal means to modify the Docs to allow ...

13) retractable clotheslines to be used?   1 2 3 4

14) a basketball hoop to be installed?   1 2 3 4

15) a garden hose holder to be attached?   1 2 3 4

16) mini-vans or pickup trucks?   1 2 3 4

17) individual garage sales?   1 2 3 4

18) residents to have window air conditioners because one resident has requested one due to health problems?   1 2 3 4

19) satellite dishes up to 18 inches in diameter or a community satellite dish if your complex has only common area with no private yards?   1 2 3 4

20) residents to have home businesses (with no additional traffic generated to the home over normal residential traffic) that involved a corporation being operated using a computer and a modem, selling Avon, having a paper route, or occasional baby-sitting?   1 2 3 4

21) a garage door to be open while a resident is doing yard work?   1 2 3 4

• Would you ...

22) investigate into the validity of a complaint before issuing a citation or violation letter?   1 2 3 4

23) avoid nastiness and mediate with a homeowner, against your attorney's advice to stick to your guns and sue?   1 2 3 4

24) ask residents to vote on significant issues even when the Docs give the BOD full power to make the decision without a vote?   1 2 3 4

Your reasonableness test score

• Total your score for section two   _____

SECTION ONE

 • Give yourself *one point for each question* you answered with *the majority of residents*.

_____

 • Give yourself *four points for each question* you answered with *other board members and me*.

_____

If you are a resident and recognize the answers given by your BOD would obviously end with "other board members and me," remember the five choices given in chapter 6: bite your tongue, grit your teeth, cry in your pillow, move, or consider a coup.

SECTION TWO

 • Be careful with your answers to 10) and 11) in section two. You are *not* to discriminate against children. Residents' equal access to common areas means children, too. If you answered anything but one *(always)* on either question, go back and give yourself a four.

Your score from section two _____

 • Your GRAND TOTAL _____

26 to 34 — Stay on the board. You and the residents are on the same page.

35 to 53 — Stay on the board, but take BOD 102 again. You need to loosen up a little.

54 to 78 — Take a leave of absence from the board until you pass at the top of the BOD 101 and BOD 102 class.

Over 79 — Resign from the BOD and go get a life. It's the kind and humane thing to do. YOU DO NOT BELONG ON THE BOARD.

 • Every time you're in a position of enforcing a mandate, put the regulation in question to the ultimate guiding **REASONABLENESS RULE TEST.**

1) Would infraction of the rule *really* damage or threaten lives? ☐ Yes ☐ No

2) Would infraction of the rule *really* damage or threaten property values? ☐ Yes ☐ No

3) Could the rule be interpreted differently to make the majority of homeowners happier and better the community? ☐ Yes ☐ No

4) Would legal modification of the rule make the majority of homeowners happier and better the community? ☐ Yes ☐ No

 • If your answers were *NO* to both 1) and 2) and *YES* to either 3) or 4), for the love of humanity, open your mind up to *find a real solution to the problem*. Either modify your interpretation of the rule, legally modify the rule, or vacate your position on the board to make room for someone more reasonable who can pass the Reasonableness Test. Someone who will allow the residents to get on with living their lives. Following the rules too strictly is a point of view that is chaotic and precisely choreographed to oppose comfortable living conditions. The flip side allows the natural flow of living to prevail.

Covenants can be abandoned

BOARDROOM DISCUSSION

❖ Published by the LAW FIRM OF WINZENBURG, LEFF, PURVIS AND PAYNE, LLP ❖

 • 1660 Lincoln Street, #1750 • Denver, Colorado 80264 • 303-863-1870

September/October 1996

HAVE YOUR COVENANTS BEEN ABANDONED?

Most Homeowner Associations are empowered to enforce restrictive covenants. However, the Association may lose the right to enforce a specific covenant if it hasn't been enforced in a timely and consistent manner.

A Utah Association tried to enforce a covenant that required use of wood shingles. However, out of 81 homes completed in the subdivision, *58 homes had wood shingles* and *23 had non-wood shingles*.

The Association sued an owner who installed fiberglass shingles. The court held that the Association could not enforce its wood-only shingle covenant. Since over one quarter of the homes did not comply, the court found that the covenant had been *abandoned*.

In a Louisiana case, a covenant required buildings to be constructed of brick or wood and prohibited metal buildings and roofs. When an owner built a building with a metal roof and constructed a metal building, a suit was filed. The violating owner contended that the developer-controlled Architectural Control Committee never required him to obtain its approval and that there were several other violations throughout the subdivision. The trial court ruled that the metal roof restriction had been abandoned. However, it found that the "development scheme" had not been entirely abandoned and concluded that the metal building was a violation that could be enforced. An appellate court later ruled that neither restriction had been abandoned and determined that both restrictions had been violated.

A covenant and an ACC that should be abandoned

A homeowner who has his home listed for sale needs a new roof on his single-family CCC home. The covenants essentially state: shake shingles or other materials, as approved by the ACC. That's a friendly covenant in the hands of an ACC that possesses common sense. It's an atomic bomb if the ACC is vindictive and overbearing. I'll call the homeowner John since he is still doing legal battle with his kindergarten-mentality ACC.

The former ACC interpreted the roof covenant to mean shake shingles or *more expensive* roofing materials. Two of the current ACC members were forced by a previous ACC to replace their roofs with tile. So, of course, they interpret that covenant in the same unthinking, stupid, asinine way as the preceding ACC. Would you expect them to allow anyone else to get by with anything other than shake or tile? Hey, gang, have you ever heard, "Two wrongs don't make a right."? Two fools don't make a wise man either.

John discovered that most insurance companies will no longer insure shake shingle roofs or, at best, they charge an exorbitant premium. John wants to use a composition shingle that looks like shake. Those shingles are installed on many very expensive homes. They are very attractive and much more durable than shake. John could make his life much easier by just agreeing to use shake shingles. He feels that would not only place his future buyer in jeopardy, he would lose any buyer whose insurance company will *not* insure a shake roof for *any* premium. He doesn't want the extra cost of a tile roof. He can not add enough to the sales price of his home to recoup the added expense. Often it's also necessary to make expensive repairs to reinforce the home's structure due to the excess weight of tile.

It doesn't matter that there are homes in the community with composition look-like shake shingles. Even though all of several phases are governed by the same HOA and ACC, to muddy up the murky waters, *each phase has a different set of covenants!* The developer obviously had his head in a very dark place when he came up with that idea. The problem could be resolved by an ACC who had their heads where they could see one ray of light.

I suggested that John petition the BOD to add the issue to the agenda of the next HOA meeting or to call a special meeting, if necessary. I proposed he take samples of the shingles to show his neighbors. John agreed that was a sound idea. But, he said that others who had tried approaching neighbors on several other issues had received anonymous threats of reprisal. He detected that some of the real enforcers, those who influenced the ACC's decisions, were underground. He feared that he might inadvertently approach an enemy.

That scenario points out why specifics, such as shake shingles, should never be in the recorded covenants that run as a restriction on the property. The place for specific items that do not pass the Significance Test is in the Rules and Regulations. Those items need to be agreed upon by over 50 percent of the homeowners as being important enough to be included for the purpose of aiding community harmony. Rules and Regs can easily be updated to allow homeowners to adjust to modern living styles. (A set of Rules and Regs is reproduced on pages IX to XII. They were assembled by our BOD to offer freedom and harmony within our community. You may find them helpful to use as a guideline.)

Another analogy

Paraphrased from more good stuff by Dr. Wayne Dyer: There is a story of a Holy Man who saw a scorpion that was drowning. The Holy Man reached down to lift the scorpion from the water and the scorpion stung him. The Holy Man tried once again and a second time was stung. An observer said, "Holy Man, why do you keep trying to pick up the scorpion? It is evil and will only sting you." The Holy Man said, "It is the dharma (destiny, pronounced dar'ma) of a scorpion to sting and the dharma of a Holy Man to protect life."

It is the dharma of a tulip bulb to emerge as a tulip. The dharma of a butterfly is to fly. It should be the dharma of BODs and ACCs to represent the homeowners and promote harmony.

If you're a board member who persists in pursuing hostile behavior merely because you have the power to do so, may an obese elephant step on your foot and stay there until you put love for your neighbors in your pursuit of enforcement of rules. I can hear you from here, "We enforce the rules to protect property values." Bat dung!

You've heard of love thy neighbor *as* thy self. Note that it says, *"as,"* not, *"less than,"* or, *"better than."* You cannot regard anyone *more than* you regard yourself. Obviously you don't think very highly of yourself or you wouldn't even consider belligerent, uncivilized behavior toward your neighbors. Before you issue the next *petty edict*, stop and visualize yourself in your neighbors' moccasins. How do you think your antagonistic attitude affects their frame of mind? Can you see yourself smiling if you were on the receiving end of the same badgering, narrow-minded procedures?

So the rule is there. It's been there since the attorney pulled the store-bought phrases off the wall and threw them into your Docs to be tied tightly around the necks of unsuspecting homeowners. The Docs satisfied the legal aspects. Why don't you now start weighing what rules are *actually meaningful* to satisfy your neighbors' comforts? Stop being on such a short fuse to control or, worse yet, to sue.

If all traffic laws were adhered to and enforced as stringently as HOA rules, there wouldn't be one car on the streets. We'd all have our licenses revoked or we'd be in jail.

You who have taken your neighbors to task in court, how many times have you committed one, or more, of the following traffic violations without being ticketed, fined, sued, or arrested?

Have you ever . . .

    . . . driven over the speed limit?

    . . . held traffic up by going way under the speed limit?

    . . . changed lanes in an intersection?

    . . . run a red light?

    . . . not turned your turn signal on soon enough before turning?

    . . . not turned your turn signal on before changing lanes?

    . . . turned onto the street and caused another driver to put on his brakes?

    . . . crossed a double yellow line?

    . . . not stopped at a stop sign?

    . . . made a rolling stop at the stop sign?

There are endless other possible infractions that you have likely committed.

The BOD in Control-itis Townhomes has the *privileged* opportunity to maintain constant vigilance on homeowners for every trivial transgression of the rules. Police officers don't have the same "see all" advantage. There just didn't happen to be a police officer around as you faux pas'd down the street. You weren't abiding by the fine letter of the law and you were endangering lives! If you really believed in the rules for yourself as strongly as you do in punishing your neighbors, you would have issued a citizen's arrest, turned yourself in, and asked for a court date. Got the picture?

The ultimate result of constant conflict is that nobody really wins. You can't remain monarch of the hill forever. Fulfill your dharma now. It will provide the most desirable peaceful possibilities for both a happy BOD and a happy community. Imagine how tranquil your life will be when you no longer have to look over your shoulder as you walk down the street. ♦

❯ *YOU'LL NEVER REACH THE PEAK GOING DOWNHILL*

> *DOWNHILL* **adv. 1.** toward the bottom of a hill; downward **2.** to a poorer condition, status, etc. — **adj.** sloping or going downward

❯ *IF YOU'RE AT THE PEAK, STAY THERE*

> *PEAK* **n. 1.** the crest or summit of a hill or mountain **2.** the highest or utmost point of anything; height; maximum *[the peak of production]* **3.** *Elec.* the maximum value of a varying quantity during a specified period **adj. 1.** maximum *[peak performance]* **2.** to come or cause to come to a peak; reach or bring to a high, or the highest point.

If your BOD has a caring attitude, your community will remain at the peak of the hill and you don't have to worry about the following BOD types A or B other than to guard against their sneaking onto your board.

Board type A . . .

. . . with lack of compassion, they follow the rules to the letter, as if they were all of major importance. They take so many trifling things so seriously. Type A BODs are made up of vehement, power-hungry zealots. They constantly swing their *power sticks to hit* their neighbors. They *know* their entrenched convictions are *right*. It's exceptionally difficult to reason with a BOD who suffers from terminal correctness and staunchly believes in its royal rightness. To admit that there may be another way that would work better is a dreadfully, *painful* process. How does one gracefully back down after having made so many *strong* proclamations? The members believe stern convictions come from a point of strength. They can't comprehend that real strength is portrayed when one is confident enough to mouth the words, "I don't know," or admit they could be, or even are, wr — wr — wr — wrong. The slightest hint of being able and willing to keep a fair and open mind will gain respect from their neighbors beyond their utmost dreams. Don't be afraid of new ideas. No one knows everything. There is always your way and their way. There is no *one* right way.

"We are all ignorant, just about different things." — Mark Twain

"We are all intelligent, just about different things." — Anonymo-Joni

Board type B . . .

. . . has the lax approach. It inches its way along and sort of slouches toward taking care of HOA business. With the same lack of compassion and kindness as BOD A, a lax BOD offers little or no guiding structure. That also encourages defiant, rebellious residents and a run down neighborhood. The community will deteriorate and present a shabby appearance. As shabby takes hold the neighborhood is fated for a trip to the bottom of property values.

Type B is a little less threatening than type A. While nonproductive, sometimes it can be easier to guide toward a concerned and caring position. This BOD, deep down, probably knows they're out of control and running amuck. It feels inadequate, maybe even wrong. That's a difficult thing to admit, even to oneself. If it refuses to shape up its lackadaisical attitude, it takes less time and effort to perform an overthrow.

If the inherent element of pride of ownership was firmly in place before board type B arrived, the good, clean guys and gals will prevail. Board B is destined to be as gone as the mythical goose, left without one golden egg.

If pride of ownership was lacking before BOD B came on board and the rest of the residents are also lax, the neighborhood is probably already at the bottom of property values.

Both BOD types A and B are spiraling downhill 100 miles an hour over the speed limit. Notice, in either situation, out of control exists in one form or another.

Your choices

• You can choose to cause the revolution, the coup, by continuing to swing your BOD stick-powers to hit. That will hasten your trip downhill. You're mean.

• You can choose to cause the revolution, the coup, by continuing to allow your BOD stick-powers to float slowly downstream. Your stick will never make a wave. It will just slowly deteriorate and eventually rot away. You're lax.

LAX **adj.** [to be loose, lax, whence slack] **1.** loose, emptying easily **2.** slack; of a loose texture; not rigid or tight **3.** not strict or exact; careless **4.** *Bot.* loose; open; said of a flower cluster

---

● You can choose to use your BOD stick-powers like a walking stick to support your entire community. A happy, tidy, neighborly community will continue to offer the highest probability for pride of ownership and protection of property values. You and your community will reach and stay at the peak.

Following are excerpts from nine *Boardroom Discussion* newsletters. They contain valuable information on such subjects as rule enforcement, amending restrictions, updating restrictions, ambiguous language, and duties of the BOD. The *Boardroom Discussion* masthead will appear only on the first newsletter.

Don't be guilty of breaching your responsibilities

BOARDROOM DISCUSSION
❖ Published by the LAW FIRM OF WINZENBURG, LEFF, PURVIS AND PAYNE, LLP ❖
● 1660 Lincoln Street, #1750 ● Denver, Colorado 80264 ● 303-863-1870

FOR SUCCESS, EXAMINE THE ADVICE OF OTHERS   October 1992

Experts were asked: *"What responsibilities are most often breached by Board members?"* Here are some of their answers:
- **Conflict of interest.**
- **Failure to properly insure the property.**
- **Failure to fund a reserve account.**
- **Failure to supervise the management company.**
- **Not acting to collect delinquent accounts.**
- **Failure to enforce the covenants; being too zealous in enforcement; or showing favoritism.**
- **Taking action before consulting professional advisors.**

That is one powerful list of what *not to do*. I will expand briefly on three issues . . .

   ● **Failure to supervise the management company.** To supervise the management company translates to ***the company is never to be in a position of managing the BOD or the complex!*** The BOD must always retain their elected powers.

   ● **Failure to enforce the covenants; being too zealous in enforcement; or showing favoritism.** Back off and don't be capricious and arbitrary, either.

   ● **Taking action before consulting professional advisors.** Caveat: Make certain the professional advisor is in the 20 percent group, not money-hungry and sue-happy.

The BOD has responsibilities and duties to the association

FIDUCIARY DUTY   March 1995

Each Association Board member has a "fiduciary duty." But what does that duty really cover? Courts define two duties:
1. *Duty of Care.* The duty of care requires a Director to (a) participate in decisions by the Board, (b) exercise independent judgment, (c) rely on trustworthy sources, (d) set policies, (e) oversee the Association's agents, and (f) be informed as to data relevant to all corporate decisions.

If business is conducted in this manner and if Directors act in good faith, in the Association's best interest, then courts usually rule that Directors are not liable since it is inappropriate to "second guess" the Board's decision or action. This is known as the Business Judgment Rule.

2. *Duty of Loyalty.* This duty requires Directors to exercise their powers in the interest of the Association, and not in the interest of themselves or another person.

A. *Conflicts of interest:* Be aware of the potential for conflicts where they may be affected by personal interests or obligations to some other person or entity. A Director should make full disclosure of his or her interest and allow a disinterested majority of Board members to decide if they want to approve the Director's conflict. Also, include the disclosure of the conflict in the minutes.

B. *Confidentiality:* Under no circumstances should a Director or Officer disclose information about the Association's affairs unless done in the regular course of business, or unless they are already of public record.

Confidentiality is the reason I use a fictitious name in this book for my complex and pseudonyms for the residents.

Conflict of interest procedures and a code of ethics for Board members

January/February 1997

Ken Caryl Ranch Master Association, Littleton, Colorado, authorized *Boardroom Discussion* to share their Conflict of Interest Policy, Conflict of Interest Procedures, and Code of Ethics. Each of these is signed and dated by each Board member upon election or appointment. These documents can be revised to suit your Association. (*The Conflict of Interest Policy is three pages long.* For a copy write to or call Kami at *Boardroom Discussion.*)

Reprinted with permission of Ken Caryl Ranch Master Association

CONFLICT OF INTEREST PROCEDURES

The following shall be followed by all members of the Board of Directors.

- The Board shall annually review the Conflict of Interest Policy.
- Each Board member will sign and comply with the Conflict of Interest Policy and Board Member Code of Ethics.
- Each Director shall annually, and as circumstances dictate, file a Notice of Conflict of Interest, with an explanation of how the Board member intends to address any Conflicts of Interest.
- The Board will review all Conflict of Interest Notices and discuss any problem with each member's proposed action.
- At each Board meeting, the President will ask if any Board member has any Conflicts of Interest pertaining to items on the meeting agenda.

CODE OF ETHICS

Board members are expected to meet moral standards of conduct as well as legal standards. The Association has adopted the following code of ethics for Board members. AS A MEMBER OF THE BOARD, I WILL

- Represent the interests of all people served by this Association and not favor special interests inside or outside of this Association.
- Not use my position on this Board for my personal advantage or for the advantage of my friends or supporters.
- Maintain confidentiality.

- Approach all Board issues with an open mind, prepared to make the best decisions I can for everyone involved.
- Do nothing to violate the trust of those we serve.
- Focus my efforts on the Association's mission, not on personal goals.
- Never exercise authority as a Board member except when acting in a meeting with the full Board or as delegated by the Board.
- Disclose all potential conflicts of interest and how I intend to resolve these conflicts.

There would no longer be stories published relaying homeowners' miseries if every board member in every association would sign and adhere to a good Code of Ethics.

There is an excellent *Code of Conduct for Association Board Members* by Lois Pratt, Ph.D. and Samuel Pratt, Ph.D. For a free copy write to Cassie Publications, Inc. • P.O. Box 261368 • Denver, CO 80226.

It would be wonderful if all homeowners were required to sign a similar code of ethics at the same time they sign the closing or escrow papers to purchase their home. I WILL

- Take an interest and keep aware of what is happening in the community.
- Attend meetings.
- Focus my attention for the betterment of all, not just on my personal desires.
- Not harass the BOD with complaints about issues that are only self-serving to me. The list could easily be expanded. All others involved with HOAs should also be obligated to sign such a code of ethics — service/management companies, attorneys, etc.

Let's sing the "Amend the Rules" song

Reprinted with permission of *CondoManagement Magazine*.
DEALING WITH TWO-LEGGED PESTS   **September 1995**

Attorney Stephen Marcus discussed unreasonable enforcement of *rules* in a recent article in *CondoManagement Magazine*. He stated that new trends are evolving which regulate the manner in which rules and regulations are enforced. In the past, *all* restrictions had to be enforced in *all* cases without regard to circumstances. However, there are now certain circumstances where enforcement of restrictions as written would create more problems (example: enforcing a no-pet policy against an association owner who has goldfish).

There are some restrictions that simply do not make sense today. Associations may want to evaluate the *purpose* of the restriction. *To enforce a restriction simply because it appears in the documents may not be reasonable if the owners and the Board no longer see the purpose of the restriction.*

Many Association documents have waiver language that state that failure to enforce a restriction in a particular case will not institute a waiver of the restriction in all cases. This language gives Association Boards some flexibility in determining when to enforce a restriction.

Marcus stated that many restrictions have a sound basis in terms of protecting and enhancing the quality of the community; these restrictions should be maintained and enforced. However, Boards must act reasonably and consistently when enforcing them.

<u>Legal Tip</u>: *Associations may wish to review and possibly amend their current rules and regulations.*

Homeowners and BODs, when you need an attorney, find one like Stephen Marcus.

Another verse of the "Amend the Rules" song

AMENDING YOUR DOCUMENTS

October 1992

Before an Association amends its documents, the Board must identify the procedures to be followed. The procedures are based upon three sources:
- The express terms of the documents.
- State statutes.
- Cases which have interpreted prior amendments.

Tip: As Associations age, some requirements of governing documents don't work. Rather than enforce unworkable documents, think about amending them.

Take that tip to heart and add one more beat. Your Association's documents were probably well aged and had long beards way before your Association was even born!

"State-of-the-ark" hasn't been reached, let alone "state-of-the-art"

September 1992

AMBIGUOUS LANGUAGE CONSTRUED AGAINST ASSOCIATION

An Ohio Association sued an owner for attaching a satellite dish to his residence (in violation of the Declaration). The court held the Declaration set forth specific guidelines and limitations, but did not grant the Association the right to ban certain types of antennae based on their "look." *The court determined that the wording in the Declaration was ambiguous, and could not be enforced.*

Warning: Even though Associations usually have no input into the original drafts of their documents, they must be reviewed occasionally to assure *"state-of-the-art," enforceable language.* Some Associations can and should adopt rules and regulations or architectural guidelines that further define what is not allowed.

Legally modify your rules and bring them up to today's *"state-of-the-art."*

Some rules don't hold water

ARE YOUR ARCHITECTURAL GUIDELINES UNCLEAR? March 1995

The architectural review committee of a Florida Association approved construction plans submitted by Owner A. Owner B sued Owner A for not complying with the Association's covenants.

The court found in favor of Owner A. It held that covenants must be construed in favor of the unrestricted use of property. If the terms of the covenants are not ambiguous, the courts will enforce such restrictions according to the intent of the parties, in the clear and ordinary meaning of the terms used. However, *a covenant that is ambiguous will be resolved against the party claiming the right to enforce the restriction. In light of this and other cases, you might consider having your architectural guidelines reviewed.*

That deserves reading several times. It's an invitation to update and drop kick those ambiguous rules!

Can pets be banned?

PET RESTRICTIONS

October 1992

A recent California case held that *a total ban on pets* (except for birds and fish) for unit owners *could be found unreasonable.* Just because pets may cause a problem is not a good enough reason for an Association to ban them. If so, the same conclusion could be made to ban stereo equipment, social gatherings and visitors between the ages of two and 18, which could be argued pose more of a threat to the peace and quiet of the community.

Tip: Before enforcing pet restrictions, determine
1. if the Declaration prohibits pets,
2. whether there has been consistent enforcement,
3. whether enforcement is practical, and
4. what benefits will result from the enforcement.

Legal Tip: The Declaration is superior to the Rules and Regulations, so the Board cannot adopt a Rule that *conflicts* with the Declaration.

That Tip applies to more than just pet restrictions, it applies to *all* rules. ***Before enforcing restrictions, test them against all four Tip items above.***

Sizing up board members

Reprinted with the permission of *Common Ground* ©1992 Community Associations Institute
August 1992

Common Ground reported the results of a survey of 250 Board members.

20% were retired; 70% said they serve on the Board to protect property values; 65% cited Board service as a civic duty; 80% thought their professions had prepared them for Board service; 65% described themselves as organizers/facilitators; 25% considered themselves as "consensus builders" while a small percentage said they were confrontational or were pursuing a cause. Other questions asked:

Has any Board member ever been the subject of legal action related to Board affairs?

Yes	13%
No	87%

How many hours a month do you devote to Board activities?

1 to 10 hours	56%
36 to 45	30%
46 to 55	10%
55 and up	4%

Do you intend to run or serve on the Board again?

Yes	68%
No	26%
Undecided	6%

How old are you?

26 to 35	14%
36 to 45	16%
46 to 55	22%
55 and up	48%

Thank you for strolling along the trail with me of some very enlightening advice from the *Boardroom Discussion* newsletters.

Dull-witted moments continue

Sunday, July 28, 1996
Reprinted with permission of the *Rocky Mountain News*

Covenants rankle residents

By Shelley Gonzales
Rocky Mountain News Staff Writer

When Paul Emmert moved into his new condo in Aurora last spring with fiancée Nichole Werthaiser, he thought he was doing the right thing.

As required by the Deerpointe Village Condominiums' covenants, the couple called to register Emmert's truck.

Emmert described the 3/4-ton white Chevy pickup with a utility box. He uses the truck in his technician job at Amoco to respond to emergencies in case of a natural gas pipeline leak. He was issued a parking sticker after assuring the homeowner association that the vehicle had no commercial markings on it.

A month went by. Late one Friday, the couple found a warning ticket on the truck saying it was a "commercial vehicle" and needed to be removed.

Werthaiser was unable to reach the manager. The next night, the truck was towed.

It cost Emmert and Werthaiser $175 to get it back. The couple said they have run into a brick wall trying to get the homeowner association to reconsider banning the vehicle from their lot.

The property manager could not be reached for comment.

Emmert, who is on 24-hour call, faces losing his job of six years if he doesn't have immediate access to the truck.

"I had heard of covenants," said the 27-year old Texas native. "But I thought it was more about not keeping your grass eight feet high — not what vehicle you can drive."

His fiancee has a harsher view. "I think covenants were intended to better the community but more often than not end up being abused by people who want a little power in their lives."

New home buyers may be surprised to find that some subdivisions don't allow permanent clotheslines (Highlands Ranch) or backyard tents (Ken Caryl Ranch).

Less than two weeks ago, more than 250 homeowners in the Rock Creek subdivision near Boulder packed an association meeting to oppose tighter rules that would limit parking in driveways to 72 hours and give association representatives the authority to enter homes "at reasonable hours."

The rules also would bar people from shaking rugs out on decks.

"Outrageous," said Carl Alessi, president of the architectural committee at The Meadows in Castle Rock.

The response to infractions is usually a warning and a "very generous" amount of time to correct the problem before a fine is imposed, said Douglas County Commissioner Michelle Cooke, who has lived in Highlands Ranch since its early years. She spent four years on a tribunal and the community association board that oversees the covenants.

Still, Cooke admits her feelings were a bit hurt a few weeks back when she received a letter from the covenants police that her grass wasn't "green" enough.

"I thought it looked pretty good," she said. "But I know they were just doing their job. But we seeded and fertilized some areas and, you know, it does look a lot better."

"The property manager could not be reached for comment." Hide when your comments might be held against you.

Don't forget that managing companies and BODs are *representatives of the homeowners, not managers of the homeowners.*

BOD members are not the crowned rulers of the community throne either.

Many choose a three-quarter ton pickup for their family vehicle. Paul Emmert's pickup isn't a commercial vehicle just because he also uses it at work. Usually there are no restrictions on any car that is licensed and operable. So another resident could drive a beat-up, multicolored car and nothing could be done. Ugly cars are okay. Pretty pickups aren't.

Nichole told me that the board claimed three notices had been issued. The only notice they ever saw was the one they found on their pickup late one Friday. That notice stated that the violation was for the lack of a parking validation sticker. There *was* a parking validation sticker on the truck! There was no mention of a citation for a commercial vehicle. The instructions were to contact the management company or the truck would be towed. The management company was closed on Saturday. Saturday night the president of the board had the pickup towed away! That doesn't exactly qualify as a neighborly procedure.

The board took every conceivable step to create problems and community havoc. A good service company would have advised the BOD against such malicious behavior. It's the players who make the music work, not the conductor who makes the music play. The homeowners are the real players. Perhaps the baton should be put into the hands of a more caring set of board members.

The HOA won the court case! It cost Paul and Nichole over $4,000. Another hole-in-one, unfair decision dispatched by a judge. Did that judge even look at the facts of the case?

Paul and Nichole said they absolutely loved their home, but they felt forced to move. They found a friendly covenants-controlled community where the pickup has full privileges.

The BOD of Rock Creek proposed some very homeowner-hostile rules. Limiting parking in driveways to 72 hours opens up the executive job position of meter maid.

Quick action!

Well, it didn't last long. Homeowners got involved. The BOD reversed those silly decisions only nine days after the preceding article ran in the *Rocky Mountain News*.

Wednesday, August 7, 1996
Reprinted with permission of the *Rocky Mountain News*

Subdivision gives up fussy rules

By Tillie Fong
Rocky Mountain News Staff Writer

SUPERIOR — Rock Creek residents can continue to shake out their throw rugs any way they like.

Changes in the covenants to prohibit such activity have been abandoned by the homeowner association at Rock Creek, a subdivision northwest of Denver between Louisville and Boulder.

The board of directors backed off, representatives said Tuesday.

"There will be no changes in the covenant," said Nichole Johansmeier of Choice Management, Inc.

The proposed changes included a rule against parking in one's driveway for more than 72 hours, as well as the prohibition on beating rugs from decks. And there was a proposal to allow representatives of the homeowner association to enter people's houses during "reasonable hours."

Johansmeier said that, after an emotional July 16 meeting of homeowners, the five members of the board decided not to pursue the proposed changes.

A notice dated July 22 was sent to the 900 homeowners announcing the decision.

Homeowners said they were pleased about the board's action, or lack thereof, on the rules.

"I was glad that the board is responsive to the feelings of the homeowners," said Jan Stokes, 42. "I felt they had over-stepped their bounds."

Ten gold stars for Rock Creek homeowners. In such a large complex it's usually very difficult to get homeowners to pull together in joint action. I imagine no matter how disturbed they were about limited parking and no rug shaking, the one that really pulled them together was the proposal to *"allow representatives of the homeowner association to enter people's houses during 'reasonable hours!'"*

Rock Creek homeowners, keep a constant vigil. Don't get complacent as you breathe a deep sigh of relief. Take heed in what tales further reveal. After homeowners win a point the bad guys systematically gather proxies in preparation for the next time they ask for a vote on the same unpopular subject. Recall what happened in LovingWay Condos.

The next tidbit will convince residents of Rock Creek never to be tempted to move to Carolina Condos. Restrictions of particular interest are in bold, italics. You may want to skip the Decs and go directly to page 196 and just read the interpretations.

A few popular, old, canned rules

DECLARATION OF
COVENANTS, CONDITIONS AND RESTRICTIONS OF
CAROLINA CONDOS

13. <u>Use and Occupancy of Condominium Apartments</u>. Each owner shall be entitled to the exclusive ownership and possession of his Condominium Apartment. Each Condominium Apartment shall be used for residential purposes only. *No Condominium Apartment shall be used at any time for any business or commercial activity, except as follows*:

A. The Owner thereof may lease or rent such Condominium Apartment for private, residential, living or sleeping purposes;

B. Declarant [developer] or its nominee may use any Condominium Apartment(s) as a model or sales unit until all Units owned by Declarant are sold; and,

C. Declarant, its employers or agents, may lease or rent any Condominium Apartment owned by it for private, residential, living or sleeping purposes.

D. The Association shall have the right but not the obligation to purchase and own any Condominium Unit for storage, recreation, or conference area or any other uses which the Association determines is consistent with the operation of the Project and the Association may also maintain offices within the General Common Elements.

15. <u>Various Rights and Easements</u>.

B. *<u>Association Rights</u>: The Association, the Board and the Managing Agent shall have a non-exclusive right and easement to make such use of and to enter into or upon the General Common Elements, the Limited Common Elements and the Condominium Apartments as may be necessary or appropriate for the performance of the duties and functions which they are obligated or permitted to perform under the Declaration, including providing fire and police protection.*

28. <u>Restrictive Covenants and Obligations</u>.

F. <u>Restrictions on Signs</u>: *No signs or advertising devices of any nature shall be erected or maintained on any part of the Project without the prior written consent of the Association.* The Association shall permit the placing of at least one (1) sign of reasonable size and dignified form to identify the Project and the Units therein and the Declarant may erect signs of a number and shape deemed necessary by the Declarant to effectively market the Units.

31. <u>Miscellaneous</u>

B. ***Amendment and Termination***: Any provision contained in this Declaration may be amended or additional provisions may be added to this Declaration, or this Declaration and Condominium Apartment ownership of the Project may be terminated or revoked, by the recording of a written instrument or instruments specifying the amendment or addition or the fact of termination and revocation, executed by the Owners, as shown by the record in the office of the Clerk and Recorder of the County of Arapahoe, Colorado, of Units *representing an aggregate ownership interest of 75% (seventy-five percent), or more, of the General Common Elements and not less than 100% (one hundred percent) of the Mortgagees;* provided, however, that, subject to the provisions of Paragraph 33 of this Declaration, in no event shall the undivided interest of an Owner be decreased without the unanimous consent of each Owner and each Mortgagee. [Forget paragraph 33, it's of no help] The consent(s) of any junior Mortgagees shall not be required under the provisions of this Paragraph. Prior to the sale of all Units, Declarant retains the unrestricted right to amend this Declaration to enable it to comply with rules and regulations of the Federal Home Loan Mortgage Corporation (FHLMC) [Freddie Mac], Federal National Mortgage Association (FNMA) [Fannie May], Federal Housing Administrations (FHA) [also known as HUD] or the Veterans Administration (VA).

Those old rules were plucked from 99 legal-size pages of Docs for a new condominium development in Aurora, Colorado. Included are nine amendments that were filed in 1984. The year 1984 doesn't mean that's the first time those hostile Docs surfaced. I'll bet they have a long, interesting history. They definitely have the smell of a musty basement.

An added wallop: The copies of some of the amended rules are totally illegible! That's what happens after the umpteenth time of copying and recopying. Oh yes, read the rules before moving in, *if you can*. If you can't, don't move in.

Very few will have the stamina to read every word on all 99 pages. I can hear the legal society and HOA zealots shouting, "The rules are recorded. You should read them before moving in or if you don't like them move out." Developers shouldn't be allowed to dump such a volume of Doc-dung on homeowners.

Of those who are fortunate enough to have the endurance to stay awake long enough to find out whodunit, how many will thoroughly comprehend what they have just read? Will they understand the impact the rules can ultimately have on their lives and their financial investment? The plot is exceptionally dull. I'll tell you whodunit. The developer and the legal profession, that's who!

Item 13: My lay person's interpretation of A, B, C, and D says the ***homeowners shall never be allowed to conduct any type of business whatsoever from their homes.*** However, the HOA and especially the developer retain special rights and privileges!

Item 15: B is a prime example of an ambiguous rule that allows abusive interpretation. It ***gives the BOD or any representative of the HOA the right to enter homes, "as may be necessary or appropriate." "Necessary or appropriate"*** as determined by whom?

That rule *implies* entry for emergency situations. Why doesn't it specifically state *to enter homes in cases of emergency situations?* It stomps on the protection of the Fourth Amendment against improper search. In the hands of a BOD, management company, or a maintenance crew with tendencies toward invasiveness, it can be an open invitation to ???

If you went to court because there was an undesirable entry into your home, how do you feel about the roll of the dice on the decision that would be handed down by a judge? Who knows? Entry by many is clearly sanctioned in these crummy, written rules.

Item 28: F negates owners placing a For Sale or For Rent sign. *No For-signs allowed.* At the same time, the developer can do whatever he needs to advertise and promote the complex until he sells the last unit. It gets curiouser and curiouser why the developer deems signs necessary for him to sell units and absolutely unnecessary for homeowners to sell or to rent their units. If you're wise, you'll rapidly run away from such a complex. Start the process of teaching developers that even signs won't sell units saddled with such rotten restrictions.

Those who haven't read this book can innocently get trapped into buying such a non-home. When they decide to sell or rent their units: "Sorry, Charlie, no For-signs allowed."

All of those provisions will remain as restrictions on those properties forever because of item 31: B the caustic little item that dictates the required *procedures to modify* the Decs. Forget it! The Decs call for an affirmative vote of a minimum of 75 percent of the homeowners — that's the first problem. The real problem is the required approval by affirmative vote of *not less than 100 percent of the lenders. That provision is a no provision to modify the Decs.* It's equivalent to saying, "Sit on it!" Getting 100 percent of the lenders to agree on anything is beyond the realm of possibility on this planet.

Modification of the Decs would have been equally as effective if that entire paragraph didn't even appear. The results would still be "We wrote the rules. You read the rules. You live with them or move out!" Move out if you can figure out a way to rent or sell your unit.

Exclude all complexes that sport such voluminous, antiquated, antagonistic, legalese-language Decs. To buy into such a community is comparable to voluntarily locking yourself in a jail cell after committing *no* crime!

Ignoring one rule doesn't dump the rest. However . . .

Ignoring *a rule* for years can weaken the legs on which it's standing.

Monday, October 21, 1996
Reprinted with permission of the *Rocky Mountain News*

Covenants: altering the landscape
A horse too many spurs legal battle in Douglas

By Marlys Duran
Rocky Mountain News Staff Writer

DOUGLAS COUNTY — Jan and Allen Burris love all four of their horses. So much so that the couple is waging a court fight in hopes of avoiding a painful decision: which three Arabians to keep and which one to send away.

"It's like picking out which one of your kids you want to send to the orphanage," Allen Burris said, his voice choking.

The Indian Creek Ranch Improvement Association sued the Burrises in July in District Court to enforce a covenant that limits horses to three per lot. No trial date is set.

The covenant says "no more than three horses and three dogs" may be kept on any lot. Association president Ed Fox says the wording is clear. Burris says it is vague.

Burris argues the association waived its right to enforce the covenant because the couple has had all four horses since moving into the subdivision near Sedalia six years ago. He said several other families also have kept more than three horses over the years.

"It's just totally unconscionable and outrageous that this is happening," Burris said.

Fox acknowledges that covenant enforcement once "was not as pristine as it could be. We're a very low-pressure community." The laxity encouraged some residents to break covenants on grounds that others aren't being enforced, Fox said.

Burris said his neighbors have never complained to him about the horses. "They have told us repeatedly that our place is immaculate," he said.

Fox said, however, that several families have complained to the board about numerous covenant violations in the subdivision, including the Burrises' extra horse.

Lawyers advised the board to act on all complaints, Fox said. "The board doesn't have the authority to enforce this covenant and not that one."

Fox said two other residents moved extra horses after receiving warnings from the board. "The only ones who have refused to take action are the Burrises," he said.

Burris, a former board member, said he's being portrayed as trying to destroy the covenants. "That's not my motivation at all," he said. "It's just not fair to ask me to remove a horse."

"Lawyers advised the board to act on all complaints." Is that a shock or a surprise to your system? Let's keep those legal fees rolling in!

Allen and Jan Burris were mentioned in another article by Marlys Duran in the *Rocky Mountain News* headlined ***Proposal would trim power of subdivisions over their homeowners*** (chapter 4). From that article: "He [Allen] says more than three horses have been allowed on lots since the subdivision was created more than 20 years ago." That and the fact that they have had four horses for six years should have put that rule to bed a long time ago. *Boardroom Discussion* (pages 183 to 184) said, "The Association may lose the right to enforce a specific covenant if it hasn't been enforced in a timely and consistent manner." But, some Decs have a provision such as shown in the General Provisions (page 150), Section 1. Enforcement. "Failure by the Association or any Owner to enforce any covenant or restriction herein contained, or any other provision of any of the aforesaid documents, shall in no event be deemed a waiver of the right to do so thereafter." Judges can use such a provision to reactivate the enforcement of abandoned covenants and restrictions.

As with many other homeowners, when I read about their plight, I gave Allen and Jan a copy of the pre-press manuscript of this book. I had a twofold purpose, one to offer help to them and the other to get their honest critique of the book.

Allen said, "If you had given this book to me a year and a half ago I would have said, Problems? What problems? Things had always been run in a very livable manner. Then there was a changing of the guard. New enforcers of the rules were elected. Wow, what a difference attitudes make! We assumed everything would always continue in the same congenial fashion regardless of who was on the board. We were negligent in not thoroughly checking the attitude credentials of those running for election. And there are too many others who apathetically never go to the meetings and don't even vote by proxy. We allowed the Pearl Harbor of Indian Creek Ranch to make history in our lives." Allen noted, "Having *the right* doesn't make *it right* [rigid enforcement]."

When Allen was on the board in 1991 and 1992, the agenda of the meetings was always how to help improve the neighborhood. After so many years of living happily, it's easy to get lulled into a false sense of the security of the continuation of happiness.

The Burrises hired a good attorney and they felt very confident that they would be allowed to keep their four horses because since 1971, there are 35 of the 165 homes that have had more than three horses on their property. There have been as many as eight horses on one property, but four and five is a more common number. The BOD did not issue a violation notice to every homeowner with four or more horses.

A drive through Indian Creek Ranch is no assurance that what you see will be allowed.

After approximately $30,000 legal expenses, the court ruled against them. Is it possible that the courts make arbitrary and capricious decisions in favor of a BOD enforcing covenants arbitrarily and capriciously?

Now, *"It's like picking out which one of your kids you want to send to the orphanage,"* Allen Burris said, his voice choking.

When will it end?

Sunday, October 6, 1996
Reprinted with permission of the *Rocky Mountain News*

Association neighborhood bully?

Battle over pickup costs homeowner thousands in legal fees

By Marlys Duran
Rocky Mountain News Staff Writer

ARAPAHOE COUNTY — Neil Larsen says the Willow Creek III Homeowners Association picked on the wrong guy this time.

Larsen has dug in his heels in a covenant dispute that might be sparking a wider rebellion in the 550-home neighborhood near South Quebec Street and East Mineral Avenue.

And Larsen's lawyer, Daniel Schendzielos, says there's an even broader issue: whether homeowner groups are trampling on constitutional rights in their zeal to enforce esthetic harmony.

"These boards have almost become fascist in the way they arbitrarily and capriciously enforce these rules and regulations," he said.

"When it becomes so personal that the full force and weight of a homeowners board can be singled out to cause an emotional distress, something needs to be done," he said.

Last November, Larsen bought a 1996 Ford extended-cab pickup that is too long to fit in his garage. So he parks it in his driveway. The homeowners association's architectural control committee says that violates Willow Creek III covenants, which prohibit "boats, trailers, trucks, campers, or commercial vehicles."

The committee issued several warnings, but Larsen has refused to move his pickup. He says pickups have become such popular family vehicles that it is ridiculous to ban them from neighborhoods.

"I could understand if I had a wheelbarrow or a welding torch in there, the 41-year old businessman said. "But I just drive it around. I go to meetings. I pick my kid up, just like normal people do."

Larsen said he talked to neighbors before buying the pickup and none objected.

The homeowner association sued Larsen in Arapahoe County Court. Larsen tried unsuccessfully to get the case transferred to U.S. District Court. Now, he is trying to move it to Arapahoe County District Court.

To date, Larsen's legal bill totals more than $11,000. The association has a $5,007 lien against his home for attorney fees, and he has spent over $6,000 on his defense. The tab likely will continue to mount.

Still, Larsen insists he won't back down. "I have never liked bullies. This is what happens when you give small-minded people a little power," he said.

The battle goes on even though Larsen and his wife, Leslie, put their house up for sale in April. The couple is building a home in Littleton's Polo Reserve where, Larsen said, their pickup is welcome.

"Life in Willow Creek has become a constant hassle, Larsen said. "I don't want to live like this."

Larsen contends the association illegally diverted his monthly dues to pay legal fees, then dunned him for unpaid dues. He has canceled checks showing that his dues are paid through next month.

Larsen said he plans to sue association president Bill Thompson and board member Steve Bocher, who formerly headed the architectural control committee. He contends Bocher trespassed when he showed up unannounced in the Larsens' backyard to inspect the property.

Larsen said Thompson walked into his home during a real-estate open house, announced the home was overpriced and couldn't be sold because there was a lien against it. A neighbor confirmed Larsen's account of the incident.

Bocher and the association's attorney, Carolyn Pontius, declined to comment, citing the unresolved litigation. Thompson didn't return calls from the *Rocky Mountain News*.

As word has spread about Larsen's dispute, allies have begun appearing. Several residents told the *News* that they share Larsen's concern that some association officials are being too zealous in their roles as covenant watchdogs. All requested anonymity, citing a fear of retaliation by the association.

Donna Analovitch has no such qualms. "It's gotten so extreme that I think it is feeling oppressive," said Analovitch, who lives in Willow Creek's townhome complex and has been active in the association.

"I'm watching what's happening to people around me. It just annoys me to watch the dictatorship," she said.

Analovitch is putting out the word that the board meets at 7 p.m. Thursday in the clubhouse. Two board seats will be filled by election. She hopes a large number of residents will attend in support of moderating the covenant patrol.

"We hope to get the board to sit down and examine who's been interpreting what, how loosely has it been played with and is there a happy medium for a lot of this," she said.

Analovitch blames the discontent on a few board members trying to create a perfect community. "I don't know if there's one out there," she said.

That restriction needs a shot in the arm of today's living serum. The fermenting Docs aren't safe. They have an outdated label. Willow Creek's (Craggy Creek could be more fitting) BOD translates the no-truck rule about the same as Deerpointe Village's BOD. "A truck, is a truck, is a truck." Not so, there are semi-trucks and there are family vehicle trucks.

When Larsen refused to back down, the HOA decided to settle by stipulation; they opted to leave Neil's truck alone. Generous of the HOA? No. From past experience of numerous other legal confrontations they realized they could spend tens of thousands more money in legal fees that they quite possibly would not recover if they pursued the issue.

Larsen's lawyer, Daniel Schendzielos said, " *. . . there's an even broader issue: whether homeowner groups are trampling on constitutional rights in their zeal to enforce esthetic harmony. These boards have almost become fascist in the way they arbitrarily and capriciously enforce these rules and regulations . . . something needs to be done.*"

It is time to give human rights back to the people

The Constitution and the Bill of Rights were designed to protect the rights of the citizens of the United States of America. A conspicuous exception materializes within communities controlled by an association. There should be a huge sign at the entrance of every community with an HOA: "**YOU ARE NOW LEAVING THE AMERICAN ZONE.**"

Sadly, forfeiture of rights is not only allowed, it is *propagated* and *encouraged.* It is *propagated* by developers and builders (eager to sell their *new* homes, apathetic about the continuing comfort of the homeowner, and no desire to spend money for modern governing Docs), real estate brokers (eager to make *a sale*), and homeowners themselves (eager to pursue the *myth of "carefree" living*). It is *encouraged* by self-serving attorneys (eager to *make money*), management companies (eager to *make money*), and officers of the board and architectural control committees (*eager to control the lives of others*). It is *further propagated, encouraged,* and *upheld* by court decisions.

There is an urgency for homeowners to regain their customary and constitutional rights. Associations need to be made accountable for their inhumane actions. It should be a felony to steal another's freedom and happiness. Across the nation there are more covenants stories every day. They all have the same putrid odor. Actually, there is no reason for single-family, detached homes with little or no common areas even to have an association.

Developers and attorneys need to live in what they perpetrate on the public. Consider the Confucian curse. "May you live in interesting times."

Let it be known, let it be said, let it be written

As a homeowner, insist on livability. Everyone deserves to live with dignity and their Constitutional rights in tact. Don't accept counterfeit enjoyment and counterfeit freedom from a synthetic board or management company that is focused on controlling everyone and everything down to the tiniest birdhouse. Don't accept it from a self-serving, greedy developer or builder either.

Set aside the first Saturday of each month to visit a new Development! Look at new homes. Pretend to be a prospective buyer. Ask to see a copy of all the recorded and unrecorded governing documents for the community. If the rules and regulations are rotten and musty tell the sales representative that he can tell the builder that he builds a lovely home, but you wouldn't even consider buying one of his homes until he either learns to create lovely documents that allow comfortable living in today's world or just plain eliminate the HOA and the documents all together. That will help the world progress.

Only the public's involvement will effect reform. Hey, there are no agencies, state or federal, that have the authority to enforce state HOA statutes, let alone HOA governing documents. There is no way to force an HOA board or management company to follow the ambiguous rules and state statutes. They merely get away with ruling by intimidation with their own self-serving interpretations. However, if you, the homeowner, ends up in court, an expensive process, 99 times out of 100 you will lose your case and maybe even your home.

It's time the outmoded, ready-made Docs take on a new look, in human-race language, and to put HOA documents on a strict diet until they shrink down to bite size or even disappear.

It's time to defuse ballistic boards and architectural control committees and make them accountable for their deeds.

It's time to regulate HOA boards and management companies and their activities.

It's time to facilitate amicable communities suitable for today's living.

Essentially 100 percent of all communities being built today are CCCs. There will soon be little choice whether or not to move to a CCC. It will require many of us taking the responsibility now to influence the necessary powers to make all communities as friendly and inviting as they are advertised to be.

A common presumption is that CCCs are run in a democratic manner. They are not. Don't expect your voice and the voices of your neighbors to be automatically heard. It will never happen unless you all get involved and stay involved in the governance of your community. CCCs are not automatic "carefree" living.

I state again: Whether the stories reported came from the 1980s or 1990s, the same stories will continue in the 2000s and 3000s if the public doesn't take positive action now to improve living in community associations.

Paraphrased from Dr. Wayne Dyer's sixth tape in his series *Freedom Through Higher Awareness:* Peaceful, harmonious thinking creates a peaceful, harmonious environment. Guess what toxic thinking creates.

Creating harmonious community living is bringing into the positions of power those leaders who are not motivated and driven by lower instincts, primal intelligence, and self-centered decisions. Rather, empower those who see good as their objective and who govern with cooperation, love, and tolerance. When this happens all communities will be peaceful, fulfilled, and true pride of ownership will manifest.

When will there be a Constitution for Covenants-controlled Communities? Of the people, by the people, and for the people.

"A government for the people must depend for its success on the intelligence, the morality, the justice, and the interest of the people themselves." — Grover Cleveland

"He who accepts evil without protesting against it is really cooperating with it."

— Martin Luther King, Jr.

I hand the torch to you and ask you to help make an impact toward humanizing or eliminating CCCs. If you don't take part in the solution, *you* are part of the problem.

GENERAL SUMMARY

Living in a community governed by an association can be pleasant and rewarding — all deserve to live happily in their homes.

- Carefully investigate before you buy.
- Don't buy in a complex if the regulations don't pass the significance test.
- Pressure developers/builders to update, humanize, and slim the documents that run as restrictions on the deeds of properties to make them contain only significant rules. Tell the developer you'll be back when he offers decent documents or no association at all.
- If your Docs are hostile, legally update and humanize them.
- Ask essay questions of contenders to a position on the BOD.
- Either attend the meetings or give your proxy to a friend who will attend and vote for you as you would vote.
- Never allow a puppet board to stay in power— a BOD that has become personal marionettes of the management company.
- Board members are not the royal heirs to the HOA throne. Don't allow a sub-happy situation to continue. Remove the BOD. Do a coup, if necessary.
- Make certain the management company is not managing the HOA and the homeowners.
- If the management company is the problem, remove the BOD. Do a coup. Then replace the management company with a good service company.
- If the BOD refuses to replace a hostile architectural committee, remove the BOD. Do a coup. Then appoint a new architectural committee.
- *Never* allow a service/management company to be the signer of HOA checks.
- The keeper of the checkbook, the one who writes the checks, should *never* be the entity that signs the checks. Require *two board member signatures* on *all* checks. That procedure will help prevent the HOA funds from taking a trip to another country.
- Make certain the guardians of the HOA funds are bonded.
- Stay out of court. Before penalizing, offer mediation between the homeowner and the BOD. Negotiate instead of litigate and truly listen to the homeowners' concerns.
- Volunteer BODs are not exempt from proper procedures. They are duty bound to inform homeowners of meetings, take accurate minutes of the meetings, and make the minutes available to all homeowners.
- Get involved and remain ever vigilant. Attend the meetings. HOAs are not carefree living.
- Be neighborly, not nosy.
- Don't permit power-hungry people to beat you down and dissipate your energies. Quality living is worth the effort.
- Read all the documents. Then make certain the enforcers are and remain a friendly entity.
- Especially check the provision for modification in the document that contains the restrictions that are recorded on the property.
- If your board is corrupt, distribute a newsletter to keep your neighbors informed.
- Board members are not volunteer neighborhood secretaries, landlords, or flunkies.
- Make certain the HOA's corporation is registered with the state.
- Only pride raises property values. Pride of ownership cannot be legislated. Rigid enforcement diminishes pride.

SUMMARY and ADDITIONAL SUGGESTIONS for DEVELOPERS, the LEGAL PROFESSION, DOCUMENT MODIFICATION, and LEGISLATION . . .

- Homeowner associations are mini-governments, encumbered with corporate law procedures. (For more details see page 169 and read *Privatopia* by Dr. Evan McKenzie.)

- Consider the chaos that would be created if federal, state, and municipal governments were forced to operate under corporate law. Only 49 percent of those of eligible voting age voted in the 1996 presidential election. If the constitution required a quorum, it's unlikely this would qualify. Under corporate law we could be left with no President and Congress could slowly dissolve.

- The Docs specify the exact percentage of the members that constitute a quorum. That percentage varies from corporation to corporation, from HOA to HOA, and from issue to issue. Some HOA Decs specify no less than 100 percent of all members. That basically negates action. Corporate law allows little or no deviation from the stated quorum. Quorum requirements are met only by representation of attendance at the meeting or by proxy. The quorum procedure must be followed before any action can take place. The choice of homeowners voting by absentee, mail-in ballots is rarely permitted.

- It's time to recognize corporate law isn't working for HOA governments any more than it would work for any other governmental body.

- Legislation is necessary to bring about practical, democratic, and constitutional methods of governing HOA mini-governments.

- Further legislation is needed to prohibit the current practice by developers and the legal profession of throwing rules together that become impossible, strangling restrictions. Such restrictions the communities' hands behind their backs and prohibit homeowners' rights of enjoyment. That custom has caused the existing grief of homeowners nationwide.

- It's been suggested why the legal profession does it, but other than saving a couple of dollars, what pleasure does a developer gain from this folly? When the developer completes building and selling his homes, he leaves the area, never to be seen again and never to be involved in the misery he has created.

- The number of homeowners residing in CCCs, CICs, or CIDs increases every day as the majority of new communities are developed to be *ruled* by an association. Dr. Evan McKenzie said that in 1970 about one percent of housing was in covenants-controlled communities, in 1994 around 12 percent, and he estimated that by the year 2000 that would grow to about 25 to 30 percent! (From the *Hi-Riser*, a Florida paper, November 3, 1994.)

Change the system, or the grim stories will continue.

- Include only *absolutely significant rules* in the recorded document that ransoms the properties with restrictions.

- Publish additional regulations — specific to the needs of homeowners — in the Rules and Regulations. Follow procedures to determine which rules fit the needs of homeowners.
  - Make the determination of adding, modifying, or deleting rules by vote of the entire membership, not just the BOD.
  - Before the meeting mail identical ballots to every homeowner. Clearly state the issues.

II

- Allow ballots to be returned by mail from the homeowners (absentee vote). It works for the government. Why should CCC homeowners accept less?
- Each separate rule must pass with *over 50 percent of those voting, not over 50 percent of all homeowners.*
  - Allow all homeowners the freedom to vote even if they are in arrears in their HOA dues. The government doesn't require property taxes be current to exercise the freedom and the right to vote.
- Allow modification of the recorded restrictions anytime the homeowners deem it necessary to adjust their living to modern lifestyles or if they determine a rule is not working properly for their community. That would be accomplished in the same manner as the above information for adding rules.
- Minimize the volume of the total pages of documents.
- Use only ***non-legalese, easily understandable language*** in all documents.
- Eliminate all ambiguous language in all documents.
- Reenact the freedom of speech in all HOAs. Allow speaking time in all meetings for homeowners to voice their suggestions and concerns. Allow constitutional rights in CCCs!
- Make all financial records available to all homeowners by their making an appointment, within ten days of their contact with the keeper of the books.
- Require that minutes to be taken at all meetings and to be made available to all homeowners for inspection within ten days after the meeting. That is one instance where corporate law usually does work well.
- Minutes of all meetings are to be kept in a book in chronological order and open to homeowners.
- Homeowners are to be allowed to audio or video tape all meetings.
- Executive sessions are to be allowed only for discussing matters of a private and personal nature of a homeowner. Such a session is never to be used to create or modify rules. All rules and modification of rules are null and void unless presented in the method described above.
- Allow HOAs to contract only with a *service company* that is licensed under the regulatory umbrella of the Real Estate Commission (or another regulatory agency) and whose representatives have a real estate license (or are licensed by another regulatory agency). Disallow contracting with a *management company.*
- Disallow service company representatives, developers, and their representatives to sign checks from the HOA bank account.
- Require two signatures of pre-approved board members on all checks.
- Allow a proxy to be valid only when it has a time limit and the homeowner has designated a person of his choice.
- Allow true involvement in the HOA by the homeowners while the developer is still in charge. Too often developers hold the actual control of the HOA. They only give pretend powers to the homeowners. You may want to review pages 69 to 73.
- For large communities that require several HOAs, with a master HOA at the top, disallow the practice of using the same service company for the master HOA as is used by one or all of the subsidiary HOAs. That avoids problems when conflict arises between the subsidiary and the master HOA. Require that each subsidiary HOA have equal representation on the board of the master HOA.

Appendix

SAMPLE HOMEOWNERS' QUESTIONNAIRE

Find out how the residents really feel. Modify this form to meet your HOA's needs. It can be given at the beginning of a meeting or mailed with the announcement of the meeting.

- On a scale of one to four in what order do you perceive the chain of command (the pecking order) of the homeowner association (one being first place)?
  _____ the homeowners
  _____ the officers of the association (board of directors)
  _____ the service company [you'll get a lot of ones if it's a management company]
  _____ the architectural protection committee

- What do you like about this community? _____
  _____
  _____

- What do you dislike about this community? _____
  _____
  _____

- What do you perceive as your position and responsibilities as a homeowner? _____
  _____
  _____

- What do you like about how the complex is being governed? _____
  _____
  _____

- What do you dislike about how the complex is being governed? _____
  _____
  _____

- Would you be willing to serve on the board?   ☐ Yes ☐ No
- Would you be willing to serve on a committee?   ☐ Yes ☐ No
- What are some of your specific interests and talents that could be of help to the HOA? _____
  _____
  _____

- What services would you remove or add to be covered by the HOA? _____
  Remove _____
  _____

  Add_____
  _____

- Additional comments and suggestions _____
  _____
  _____

Please write additional comments on the back of this page.

Name   *(optional but preferred)*   Address

A Brief Guide to Parliamentary Procedure

Based on *Robert's Rules of Order Newly Revised (RONR)*, 1990 edition.
When there is a conflict between organizational bylaws and RONR, the bylaws take precedence.

- **The principles of Parliamentary Procedure are based on**
  - Rights of the majority
  - Rights of the minority
  - Rights of the individual members
  - Rights of the absentees
  - Rights of all of these together
- **The objectives of Parliamentary Procedure are**
  - To expedite business
  - To maintain order
  - To insure justice and equality for all
  - To accomplish the purpose for which the group was organized

KNOW YOUR ORGANIZATION

- Any organized society, from the local level though the national level, requires certain rules to establish its basic structure and manner of operation. The real function of parliamentary procedure is to assist individuals in taking orderly action as a group, and so rules are needed to accomplish this.

- Before the president and other officers, chairmen of committees, and members participate in any meeting or activity, they should have a copy of those rules pertinent to their individual group. These should include one or more of the following:
  - Corporate Charter (Articles of Incorporation)
  - Constitution and/or Bylaws
  - Rules of Order (the Parliamentary Authority) and any Special Rules of Order as adopted by the membership
  - Standing Rules

- The **Bylaws** are the most important since they are the legal document for the organization and are therefore the fundamental rules of the group and more permanent. It should require previous notice and a two-thirds vote to amend these rules.

- The term **Rules of Order** refers to the written rules of parliamentary procedure that are formally adopted by the organization. These rules relate to the transaction of business in meetings and to the duties of officers, boards, and committees.

- The term **Standing Rules** relates to the details of the administration of a society rather than to parliamentary procedure and these rules can be adopted by majority vote according to the needs of the society.

PREPARE FOR PARTICIPATION

- If you are an officer, you should have a copy of your Bylaws.
- You should have a copy of any Policies, Procedural Manual, or instructions.
- The President should prepare, in advance, an agenda listing items of business to be dealt with at the meeting. The Secretary may prepare the agenda or assist the President with it.

- All officers and chairmen of committees should be contacted before the meeting to make certain of attendance and any reports to be given.
- Official notification of any meeting is mandatory and should be in accordance with the rules of the organization.

ORDER OF BUSINESS (AGENDA)

- **Call to Order**
- **Opening Exercises** (optional)
- **Welcome and Introductions** (optional)
- **Roll Call** (optional)
- **Reading and Approval of Minutes**
- **Reports of**
  - *Officers*
    President
    Vice president(s)
    Treasurer — Financial report
    Secretary — Correspondence
  - *Boards — Executive Committee*
    Recommendations to be acted on by the membership
    Report of any action taken
  - *Standing Committees*
    Usually the Chairman reports
    The chair calls only on those who have reports to make
- **Reports of Special Committees**
- **Special Orders**
  - Items of business that are mandatory, according to the Bylaws, or items of business that were made a special order by vote of the assembly.
- **Unfinished business and General Orders**
  - Business (motion on the floor) that was pending when the last meeting adjourned is unfinished business and would be taken up under this heading.
  - A question (motion) that was postponed to the present meeting is designated as a general order.
  - An item of business that was laid on the table can be taken from the table under unfinished business if the time has not expired.
- **New Business**
  - Any new business may come from the floor in the form of a main motion.
  - Any item of business that was laid on the table may also be taken up under new business.
  - Correspondence requiring action can be presented under this heading.
- **Announcements** (optional, but should be made before program or Adjournment in case action is necessary by the assembly)
- **Program** (optional)
- **Adjournment**

TIPS FOR THE CHAIRMAN

". . . no rules can take the place of tact and common sense on the part of the chairman.

"The application of parliamentary of any size, with due regard for every member's opinion, to arrive at the general will on a maximum number of questions of varying complexity in a minimum time and under all kinds of internal climate ranging from total harmony to hardened or impassioned division of opinion." — Henry M. Robert

- **Before the Meeting**
  - Plan the agenda. Review items of the previous minutes, mandatory items in the bylaws for a parliamentary meeting, and input from committee chairs.
  - Know of reports from Officers and Committees.
  - Assign responsibilities — those who will give specific information, timers, etc.
- **At the Meeting**
  - Promote free debate but don't let the meeting lag.
  - Keep the tone of the meeting impersonal.
  - Don't let the meeting get out of hand.
  - Insist that all members address the chair.
  - Refer to yourself as the Chair, not as "I."
  - Leave the chair if you wish to debate.
  - If in doubt on any issue, ask for a vote from the assembly.
  - Keep the members clearly informed on all matters.
  - Be sure of the correct voting procedure.
  - Even **when it is absolutely evident** that the affirmative votes carry, *take a negative vote also.*
  - *Always announce the results.*

TIPS FOR MEMBERS

- Attend the meetings.
- Participate.
- Always be recognized by the chair before speaking.
- Avoid personalities when speaking.
- Be courteous even when disagreeing.
- Be responsible as a member to help achieve the goal of your group.
- Do the work necessary by volunteering.
- Be a contributing member and serve on committees when requested.

A PARTICIPATING MEMBER IS A VITAL ASSET TO ANY ORGANIZATION!

- For a more complete guide to parliamentary procedure, *A GUIDE FOR EFFECTIVE MEETINGS,* published by the Professional Parliamentary Research Unit of Colorado . . .

Write to: PPR Pamphlet • P.O. Box 1295 • Colorado Springs, CO 80901
or call: 719-635-0217 (Ask for current price information, approximately $1.)

Among other items the pamphlet contains suggested dialogue, motions and voting, a chart showing the 13 ranking motions, sample minutes and what should be contained in the minutes, sample budget, sample financial statement, sample tellers' report, the eight steps of a motion, and the three processes of amending. Also included is information about committees, bylaws and other rules, nominations, and elections.

Pleasant Valley Townhomes Rules and Regulations
A summary of the recorded Restrictions

Pride of ownership is the only ingredient that will maintain and bolster property values! No one can have pride without respect for themselves and others. Pride is an attitude. Attitudes cannot be legislated. Therefore, pride of ownership cannot be legislated.

From the Board of Directors: With respect for all, our focus and goals are for the good and happiness of the majority of the homeowners. We strive to support neighborhood pride, caring, and harmony with a community atmosphere of appreciation for the rights of others. We encourage all residents to care and be considerate of your neighbors.

We present the following:
- Owners and tenants are encouraged to follow the spirit of a caring philosophy and the governing documents to ensure amicable and safe living for all.
- It is always necessary to have consideration *for* our neighbors, whether we live in a *single-family* home, a *townhome*, a *condominium*, or *an apartment*.
- The following Rules and Regulations have been developed by the Board of Directors under the authority of the Association's governing documents to help assure cooperative, *harmonious* living. These are a clarification of items taken from the governing documents. Refer to the governing documents for complete details of all procedures, rules, and regulations — the Declarations, Articles of Incorporation, and Bylaws.

ASSOCIATION ADMINISTRATION

- The HOA is governed by the Declarations, Articles of Incorporation, Bylaws, and Rules and Regulations as administered by the Board of Directors. A Service Agent is contracted by the Association to assist in the day-to-day affairs of the Association. Owners are assessed a monthly maintenance fee to cover the following costs paid by the Association.

  SERVICES PAID BY THE HOA FEES . . .

  . . . SPECIFICALLY FOR EACH RESIDENT
  - Exterior painting and roof repair or replacement.
  - Blanket insurance policy (each homeowner needs a content insurance policy).
  - Front lawn care (from the home to the street curb): edging and weekly mowing; aerating and fertilizing (two times per year).
  - Trash removal.
  - Water and sewer.

  . . . FOR THE WHOLE COMMUNITY
  - Streets and parking areas: snow removal, maintenance, and repair of curbs, asphalt, cement pans.
  - Common areas: electricity, lawn care, care of bushes and trees, sprinkler system maintenance, fence repair and maintenance.
  - All other related Association bills.

- *All other repairs and maintenance of homeowners'* properties are the responsibility of the individual homeowners.
- Property from the street curb to the fenced backyard is owned by the homeowner.
- The interior of the homes is the responsibility of the homeowner, as are the windows, *gutters*, siding, driveway, fences, weeding, additional fertilizing, trees, shrubs, and general *maintenance except as stated* above.
- The Servicing Agent receives the bills and writes the checks. The distribution of funds is at the direction and final approval of the Board of Directors. A minimum of two Directors review the bills and two Directors sign all checks.
- *Requests or questions regarding maintenance or services provided* should be directed *in writing* to the Servicing Agent.

- If you plan any modification to the exterior of your home, you must submit your plans and written request to the Architectural Protection Committee.

RULES AND REGULATIONS

- The homes are intended to be used only for residential purposes. Occupancy will be in accordance with local zoning laws. It is intended that units will be maintained in a clean and sanitary condition with no unsightly objects or nuisances to interrupt the peaceful enjoyment by occupants of the complex.
- *Owners shall notify the Servicing Agent of their residential and business phone numbers.* If you rent your property, notify the Servicing Agent immediately of your new mailing address and phone number(s) Send a copy of the lease agreement and your tenant's phone number(s) to the Servicing Agent.

    At your option, you may list your phone number(s) in *Pleasant Valley Homeowners' Directory*. Contact the Service Representative.
- For insurance purposes: If your mortgage lender changes, immediately notify our Servicing Agent with the name of the new lender, their address, and phone number.

HOMEOWNER'S INSURANCE AND SMOKE ALARMS

- Owners are strongly encouraged to obtain content insurance to cover personal liability and personal property protection. Contact your insurance agent (or the agent who has the blanket coverage policy on Pleasant Valley) to make certain you are covered under all circumstances for all contents and liability.

    Blanket policies vary from company to company. Some policies cover many items such as, carpet, built-in cupboards, interior walls. Some policies specify that the walls are covered if the walls are of original structure Check with the Servicing Agent for a copy of the blanket policy.
- Everyone is encouraged to have at least one smoke alarm installed on each floor. Our insurance policy calls for a working fire extinguisher in all homes.

INTERIOR ROADWAYS AND VEHICLE PARKING

- To maintain adequate ingress and egress for emergency access by the fire department, police, public utility, and other emergency and service personnel within the confines of Pleasant Valley Townhomes:
    - No vehicles are to be parked by the yellow painted curbing.
    - RVs and some other types of vehicles, by the governing documents, are not permitted to be parked within Pleasant Valley other than out of sight within a garage (see Article X, Section 10 for further clarification).
    - Vehicles parked in violation are subject to ticketing, towing, impounding, or other means as deemed appropriate.
    - No oil, antifreeze, or other toxic materials shall be allowed to drain onto the street.
    - The speed limit is fifteen (15) miles per hour for the safety of all residents.

DRIVEWAY USE

- Driveways are intended for vehicle parking. They are not to be used as storage areas for such items as camper covers, inoperable or unlicensed vehicles, etc. Vehicle repair must not extend past a 48-hour period or create an unsightly situation or damage to the concrete.

PROPERTY DAMAGE

- Results of damage to common area property due to negligence of an owner, tenant, their agents or guests may be repaired by the association. The cost of such repairs will be an assessment to the owner. (See fines and late fees.)
- Owners will be notified to put back to standards any damage or deferred maintenance on the owner's property (fences, driveway, trees, shrubbery, lawn, weeds, gutters, down spouts, windows, screens, etc.). If the owner does not make the required repairs or maintenance within 30 days, the Association will have the work completed and will place an assessment on the homeowner. (See fines and late fees.)
- Payment of such assessments will be as discussed under violation policy.

EXCESSIVE NOISE, LIGHT OR ODORS

- Thoughtfulness and good judgment should be used in controlling noises that could be offensive to others. Homeowners shall prevent their dogs from excessive barking, keep the sound level of televisions, stereos, radios, etc., at a level not to disturb neighbor(s).
- No unreasonable bright light will be allowed to be emitted from any lot.
- No offensive or noxious odors will be allowed.

TRASH

- No garbage, refuse, rubbish, or cuttings shall be deposited on any street, the common area, or any lot, unless placed in a suitable container (solely for the use of garbage pickup) and suitably located. All equipment for the storage or disposal of such materials shall be kept in a clean and sanitary condition.

PETS

- No animals, livestock, poultry, or insects, of any kind shall be raised, bred, kept, or boarded in or on the property. The owner of each lot may not keep more than a total of three (3) household pets, but not more than two (2) dogs as long as not kept for any commercial purpose and do not create a nuisance to any resident. The owner of a pet shall be responsible to pay for any damage caused by such pet or pets, as well as any costs incurred by the Association as a result of such pets.
- Dog owners are required to keep their pets on leashes, in accordance with the city's leash laws, at all times when outside the fenced area. Dog owners must be mindful of health hazards and properly dispose of animal droppings. (Do do your dog's doo-doo. *In other words, scoop their poop!*)
- Pet owners must keep pet noise from annoying other unit occupants and be responsible for damages caused by their pets.

LOTS TO BE MAINTAINED

- Each lot, at all times, shall be kept in a clean and wholesome condition. No items, trash, litter, junk, boxes, containers, bottles, cans, implements, machinery, lumber, or other building materials shall be permitted to remain exposed upon any lot so that the same are visible from any neighboring lot, the common area, or any street, except as necessary during a period of construction. Generally, the lots are not to be used as storage areas.

TEMPORARY, MISCELLANEOUS STRUCTURES, WINDOWS, AND STORM/SCREEN DOORS

- No structure of a temporary character including, but not limited to a house trailer, tent, shack, or outbuilding shall be placed or erected upon any lot.
- No advertising or signs of any character shall be erected, placed, permitted, or maintained on any lot *other than* a name plate of the occupant, an address number, a "For Sale," "Open House," or "For Rent" sign not to exceed five (5) square feet.
- All types of refrigerating, cooking, or heating apparatus shall be concealed.
- Except as may otherwise be permitted by the Architectural Protection Committee, all antennae shall be installed inside the residence.
- No clotheslines shall be installed, except retractable clotheslines with the regulation that clothes are to be removed within a reasonable drying time and the clothesline retracted.
- No dog runs, drying yards, service yards, wood piles or storage areas are to be located on any lot as to be visible from a street, another lot, or from a common area.
- Owners and tenants are encouraged to maintain curtains and screens in a neat and orderly manner. Replacement of window panes and screens that are missing or in need of repair or replacement must be done at the owner's expense.
- Storm, screen, security doors, or windows may be installed with approval of the Architectural Protection Committee and the Board of Directors. Such doors are to be metal and the color approved by the Architectural Committee as suitable for the building, exterior door, and trim colors.

RESIDENTS

- For personal safety and protection and the safety and protection of others and their property, we discourage activities in the streets. No throwing of snowballs, baseballs, rocks, etc. is permitted in any manner as to harm residents or their property.

ARCHITECTURE AND LANDSCAPING

- Plans for any modification to the exterior and any significant modification to the internal structures must be submitted to the Architectural Protection Committee for their approval and the approval of the Board of Directors. Modifications must conform to the city's building codes. After Committee and Board approval, it is the owner's responsibility to obtain a building permit.
- Owners are to repair promptly, at their expense, all maintenance work for which they are responsible. If such repairs are not completed in a timely and professional manner and the appearance and aesthetic integrity of the community is affected, repairs will be completed by the Association and the owner will be assessed for the entire costs. (See fines and late fees below.)
- The Architectural Protection Committee must be informed and must approve significant additions or deletions in landscaping.

ASSOCIATION DUES, DELINQUENCIES AND VIOLATION FINING POLICY

- The monthly Association maintenance fee is due and receivable on or before the first day of each month. The Board of Directors has the responsibility of taking prompt action to collect delinquent fees. (See fines and late fees below.)

  ☆☆☆☆ Be a true, four-star neighbor. If you see a violation of the Rules and Regulations, first discuss it with the violator. The neighbor may not realize that he or she is in violation. Help your neighbors avoid notices and subsequent fines. ☆☆☆☆

  - Report violations in writing to the Service Representative. Such violation notice is to include whether you first spoke with your neighbor, the results of speaking with your neighbor, the name and address of the violator, the violation, date, time, place, and any other essential data. All reports must be signed by the reporting party. The name of the reporting party will not be disclosed unless required by law.
  - After investigation of the validity of a violation by the Service Representative or the Board a phone call will be made and followed up with a letter (first notice).
  - If the violation continues another letter will be sent stating a time period for correction of the violation (second notice).
  - If corrections are not made within the given time period, a third notice will be sent. A fine may be assessed to the violator. (See fines and late fees below.)

FINES AND LATE FEES

- All fines and late fees will be satisfied first from the maintenance fee payment. If this results in a shortage of the regular maintenance fee due, notice will be sent and a $10 late fee will be assessed each month until the proper amount of maintenance fee is satisfied by the 10th day of the month due. Voting rights may be denied for all delinquencies over sixty (60) days old.
- The fine for the first offense will be $25, the second fine for the same offense will be $50, and the third fine for the same offense will be $100.
- Following the third delinquency notice of fees, fines, and late charges the Board of Directors, as appropriate, may utilize the services of a collection agency, seek satisfaction through legal actions, and place a lien on the property.
- Prior to assessing a fine against any homeowner (with the exception of a late fee for delinquent dues), the owner will be sent (via certified mail) a notice of the homeowner's right to request a hearing, within ten (10) days of receipt of the notice, with the Board and Service Company Representative if the owner disagrees with the violation or has valid reasons to object to the fine. If a hearing is not requested by the owner, all fines can be assessed and are due and payable the following month.
- If the owner doesn't correct the violation and the Association needs to do any repairs to rectify the object of a fine, an additional ten (10) day hearing letter will be sent prior to the Association doing the repairs and charging the owner for the expense. Prior to subsequent fines being assessed, the same procedure will be followed.
- The homeowner will be liable for any attorney's fees required to settle the violation(s). If there is a lawsuit the prevailing party shall be entitled to recover its reasonable attorneys' fees, associated costs, and expenses incurred in connection with any legal proceedings.

Index

A

APPRECIATION, 22

B

BASIC INFORMATION

All communities with DABs, an HOA, and a BOD are CCCs, 36

All communities with restrictive covenants and a homeowner association are covenants-controlled communities, 35

All covenants-controlled communities have restrictive covenants, 34

Not all CCCs with restrictive covenants have DABs, an HOA, or a BOD, 37

The boring, but necessary basics, 34

What is a covenants-controlled community?, 34

BIDS FOR MAINTENANCE AND REPAIRS

Procedures to avoid

A sketch of what can happen, 119

All along, hanging in the wings, 120

Another sketch of what can happen, 119

BOARD OF DIRECTORS

Funds from developer to the HOA

Look who's in charge now, 40

Liability

Boardroom Discussion agrees, 178

Boardroom Discussion and *Managers Report* agree, 179

Take responsibility, but don't step in hazardous territories, 121

National survey

Sizing up board members, 192

Nefarious

Does LovingWay's BOD make Watergate-like decisions?, 131

LovingWay homeowners, look at the minutes to see how decisions are made, 132

Stories trickle in on a worst case scenario, 69

New BOD members

Scenario 1, 180

Scenario 2, 180

Now what do you do?, 172–174

Procedures to avoid

Another road kill story, 139

Board type A (strict), 187

Board type B (lax), 187

Does LovingWay's BOD make Watergate-like decisions?, 131

Don't be guilty of breaching your responsibilities, 188

Dull–witted moments continue, 192

Sometimes, as one problem ends the next one begins, 134

BOARD OF DIRECTORS (continued)

Procedures to avoid

You'll never reach the peak going downhill, 186

Your choices (for community attitude), 187

When common catastrophes occur, 124

When regular maintenance is needed, 124

Procedures to follow

A good plan (with management/service companies), 104

A happy community that uses homeowners dollars wisely, 80

Boardroom Discussion agrees, 178

Boardroom Discussion and *Managers Report* agree, 179

Conflict of interest procedures and a code of ethics for Board members, 189

Dec test, 54

Does LovingWay's BOD make Watergate-like decisions?, 131

Good points for the BOD and homeowners to remember, 113

Good public relations with your community is imperative, 176

If you're at the peak, stay there, 186

Minutes of all meetings should be available, 136

More reports like this one would be refreshing, 56

Now what do you do?, 172–174

Parliamentary procedures, VI

Reasonableness test, 181

Significance test, 148

Some BODs are from a friendly planet, 140

The BOD has responsibilities and duties to the association, 188

Turning BADs back into DABs, 180

Use ethics, empathy, and compassion, 171

Your choices (for community attitude), 187

Qualifying

Associations can get mired down in politics, 102

Information needed from BOD contenders — ask these questions, 103

Look for the responsible person who doesn't want to be on the board, 102

The profile of those who belong on the board, 99

The profile of those who do not belong on the board, 100

Responsibilities and involvement

A friend (a neighbor) 146

A preferable scenario, 76

A sketch of what can happen, 119

Another sketch of what can happen, 119

BOARD OF DIRECTORS (continued)
Responsibilities and involvement
Board members are not community flunkies, 76
Don't be guilty of breaching your responsibilities, 188
Is the board of directors real or let's pretend?, 117
Recognize the real problem, is it them or you?, 139
Some HOAs try a little of everything to keep raising the dues, 133
The BOD has responsibilities and duties to the association, 188
Work is relevant in any scenario, 180

BUYING IN A CCC
Benefits
From developer to dream, 148
The board of directors of the association cares and understands, 26
The dream, 23
The dream comes true, 25

Cautions
A few popular, old, canned rules, 195
An urgent need, 167
Be careful of complexes that were built pre-1980s, 90
Dumb and dumber moments, 142
From developer to disaster, 148
Further words of caution, 91
Let it be known, let it be said, let it be written, 201
Look for the provision to modify the Decs, 85
Melt away the tip and reality may be exposed, 38
No backyards in sight, 143
No For-signs allowed, 142
Sometimes it takes a while for the real stuff to smack the fan, 13
The benefits, according to advertising, 29
The nightmare, 24
There's more than one way to spread the word (buyer beware sign), 143
Thirty-year-old whiskers are growing on today's Docs, 37
Thoroughly investigate before you buy, 88
Which way to Utopia?, 30

Procedures to follow
If you're considering a move to a covenants-controlled "dreamland", 84
Know who's in charge — the enforcers, 83
Required reading — the documents, 83

Responsibilities and involvement
An outlook that truly allows dreams to come true, 27
What if a neighbor drizzles on my dream?, 26

C
CONDOS (condominiums)
Is it a bird, a plane, a condo, or a . . . ?, 34
COUP D'ÉTAT
By the end of the special meeting, 19
Don't go to the meeting one vote short!, 96
Don't leave without a signed proxy!, 95
How to organize your coup d'état, 93
Sample of the petition we used, 94
Set the stage, 14
Sometimes things happen because they need to happen, 16
The special meeting, 19
Time to organize a coup d'état, 18
You don't have to be a homeowner to organize a coup, 96
Survey (a poll)
How to organize your coup d'état, 93
Responses from the residents to that question, 17
Time to organize a coup d'état, 18

D
DEC TEST, 54

DEVELOPERS
Documents, developers, and attorneys can be friendly, 39
Dumb and dumber moments, 142
Look who's in charge now (funds from the developer to the HOA), 40
No backyards in sight, 143
No For-signs allowed, 142
Nefarious
Check who's controlling the votes, 107
Stories trickle in on a worst case scenario, 69

DOCS
Documents, developers, and attorneys can be friendly, 39
Fuzzy mold is taking hold, 42
Let it be known, let it be said, let it be written, 201
Thirty-year-old whiskers are growing on today's Docs, 37
Amend
A real struggle to reach a happy ending, 66
Another verse of the "Amend the Rules" song, 191
Let's sing the "Amend the Rules" song, 190
Look for the provision to modify the Decs, 85
Rules can be changed, 50
Your Decs may need amending, but it isn't easy, 166

DOCS (continued)

Discriminatory

Take a close look at this (discriminatory covenants), 167

Governing

Another culprit at the base of HOA problems is exposed 168

What's in a name?, 108

Inception

The primary purpose, 38

Thirty-year-old whiskers are growing on today's Docs, 37

DUES

A happy community that uses homeowners dollars wisely, 80

All along, hanging in the wings, 120

Another plot (everything covered in the dues), 120

Another sketch of what can happen, 119

Another way homeowners can save money, 123

Beware of excessively high dues, 125

Beware of phony low dues, 125

Group rates can save the HOA money, 122

HOA fees seldom cover everything, 77

How not to keep dues low, 123

It's about HOA fees, 77

Read the projected budgets and the statements of actual expenditures, 80

Some HOAs try a little of everything to keep raising the dues, 133

Speaking of money, 78

The real world, 121

There's more than one way to create undisclosed dues, 125

When common catastrophes occur, 124

When regular maintenance is needed, 124

F

FAIR HOUSING

What about the fair housing laws?, 63

FCC

Congress and the FCC step on the "No Satellite" restriction, 51

H

HOMEOWNERS

Procedures to avoid

Board members are not community flunkies, 76

Expect neighborliness, be neighborly — not nosy, 145

Good points for the BOD and homeowners to remember, 113

"Learn to work together, not against each other", 145

Overheard at a community holiday open house, 144

Talk about nosy neighbors, 145

Terrible trash terrorizes, 15

HOMEOWNERS (continued)

Responsibilities and involvement

A friend (a neighbor), 146

A happy community that uses homeowners dollars wisely, 80

An outlook that truly allows dreams to come true, 27

Arlene discovered unhappiness can strike even contented communities, 59

Associations can get mired down in politics, 102

Boardroom Discussion agrees, 178

Boardroom Discussion and *Managers Report* agree, 179

Check who's controlling the votes, 107

Does LovingWay's BOD make Watergate-like decisions?, 131

Expect neighborliness, be neighborly — not nosy 145

Get involved!, 75

HOA fees seldom cover everything, 77

Homeowners' involvement produces another happy ending, 62

If you happen to get romanced into a sub-happy community, 92

If you're at the peak, stay there, 186

If you're not going to get involved, at least cooperate!, 96

Important step, 106

Information needed from BOD contenders — ask these questions, 103

Is the board of directors real or let's pretend?, 117

It's about HOA fees, 77

"Learn to work together, not against each other", 145

Let it be known, let it be said, let it be written, 201

Look for the responsible person who doesn't want to be on the board, 102

LovingWay homeowners, look at the minutes to see how decisions are made, 132

More about votes and proxies, 105

Motivational trees, 97

Our community is now running smoothly, 20

Read the projected budgets and the statements of actual expenditures, 80

Required reading — the documents, 83

Responsibility demands the four-letter "W" word. Work can bring a happy ending, 61

Same scenario — different dictators, 106

Sample of the petition we used, 94

Speaking of money, 78

Some HOAs try a little of everything to keep raising the dues, 133

Step down from that soapbox and onto the next, 61

Take responsibility, but don't step in hazardous territories, 121

HOMEOWNERS (continued)

Responsibilities and involvement

Talk about nosy neighbors, 145

The power of votes and proxies can authorize a dictatorship, 105

The profile of those who belong on the board, 99

The profile of those who do not belong on the board, 100

Two constantly outvoted BOD renegades and an attempt to control proxies, 104

Volunteer isn't a four-letter, obscene word, 80

What if a neighbor drizzles on my dream?, 26

You'll never reach the peak going downhill, 186

I

INSURANCE

A little about insurance, 127

Add this coverage to your insurance policy, 127

Boardroom Discussion and *Managers Report* agree, 179

L

LEGAL

A point of law (differing opinions from two attorneys), 65

A wee pause for a moment of attorney levity, 164

Another road kill story, 139

As we creep back to the serious side, 164

Benefits the legal profession offers — according to rumor, 149

Conforming to the old, dusty Docs causes conflict, 150

Dec test, 54

Documents, developers, and attorneys can be friendly, 39

Is the fox in charge of guarding the chicken coop?, 162

It may be easier, but for whom, 25

Karen Abbott interviewed an attorney, 152-155

Now choose the right attorney, 151

Only hire a specialist, 160

Reasonableness test, 181

Significance test, 148

Step down from that soapbox and onto the next, 61

The HOA doesn't always win, even when it should, 164

The Judge judges. Who judges the Judge?, 158

LEGISLATION

Take a close look at this (discriminatory covenants), 167

Summary and additional suggestions for developers, the legal profession, document modification, and legislation, II

Well, maybe it will come state by state through legislation, 52

LENDERS

Lenders need cooperation, too, 68

Approval

A real struggle to reach a happy ending, 66

M

MANAGEMENT COMPANIES
(also see **Service companies**)

Bids

A sketch of what can happen, 119

All along, hanging in the wings, 120

Another sketch of what can happen, 119

Check signing

A good plan, 104

Nefarious

A classic example of how negligence and a management company's dictatorship can cause special assessments and raise the dues, 128

Stories trickle in on a worst case scenario, 69

Procedures to follow

Example of a declaration of being a service company, 110

Example of a good service company's approach, 114

Good points for the BOD and homeowners to remember, 113

Qualifying

Basic services performed by service/management companies can include the following and more, 112

Indeed, what is in a name?, 109

Management companies, 111

Some questions for the BOD to ask the company's representative, 113

Words do have power, 109

Responsibilities

Example of a good service company's approach, 114

MEDIATION

Mediation can solve problems, 156

MEETINGS

LovingWay homeowners, look at the minutes to see how decisions are made, 132

Meetings are supposed to be open to all homeowners, 108

Minutes of all meetings should be available, 136

P

PETITION

Sample of the petition we used, 94

PROPERTY VALUE

Pride of ownership cannot be legislated, 73

Pride of ownership is the quality that creates better subdivisions, 103

PROXIES AND VOTES

Don't go to the meeting one vote short!, 96

Don't leave without a signed proxy!, 95

PROXIES AND VOTES (continued)

How to organize your coup d'état, 93

Important step, 106

More about votes and proxies, 105

Same scenario — different dictators, 106

Sample proxy with a date limit, 106

The power of votes and proxies can authorize a dictatorship, 105

Then hostile happenings started to happen, 14

Time to organize a coup d'état, 18

Two constantly outvoted BOD renegades and an attempt to control proxies, 104

You don't have to be a homeowner to organize a coup, 96

R

REAL-LIFE SCENARIOS

A case where mediation, instead of litigation, would have benefited both the HOA and the homeowner, 157

A happy community that uses homeowners wisely, 80

A potpourri of information from residents of LovingWay Condos, 128

A real struggle to reach a happy ending, 66

After three and a half years, the suit and the dust finally settled, 160

Another road kill story, 139

Arlene discovered unhappiness can strike even contented communities, 59

Associations can get mired down in politics, 102

Check who's controlling the votes, 107

Covenants aren't the magic wand that bestows happiness, 30

Expect neighborliness, be neighborly — not nosy, 145

From hostility to happiness, 13–22

Further words of caution, 91

Homeowners' involvement produces another happy ending, 62

"Learn to work together, not against each other", 145

Look for the responsible person who doesn't want to be on the board, 102

Management companies, 111

More reports like this one would be refreshing, 56

Responsibility demands the four-letter "W" word. Work can bring a happy ending, 61

Rules can be changed, 50

Some HOAs try a little of everything to keep raising the dues, 133

Sometimes, as one problem ends the next one begins, 134

Speaking of money, 78

The HOA doesn't always win, even when it should, 164

Thoroughly investigate before you buy, 88

REAL-LIFE SCENARIOS (continued)

Two constantly outvoted BOD renegades and an attempt to control proxies, 104

You don't have to be a homeowner to organize a coup, 96

REASONABLENESS TEST, 181

RECORDS

BODs cannot arbitrarily deny inspection of the records, 135

LovingWay homeowners, look at the minutes to see how decisions are made, 132

RULES

Abandonment

A covenant and an ACC that should be abandoned, 184

Covenants can be abandoned, 183

Ambiguity

A point, 60

Some rules don't hold water, 191

"State-of-the-ark" hasn't been reached, let alone "state-of-the-art", 191

Amend

A real struggle to reach a happy ending, 66

A suggested solution to a silly problem, 54

Another verse of the "Amend the Rules" song, 191

Congress and the FCC step on the "No Satellite" restriction, 51

Helpful off-the-rack rule, 173

Let's sing the "Amend the Rules" song , 190

Look for the provision to modify the Decs, 85

Rules can be changed, 50

Development

A few popular, old, canned rules, 195

A prefab rule that can be friendly or possibly open up a bag of worms, 151

An urgent need, 167

Example of a canned, too vague or too strict, archaic rule, 51

Example of a ridiculous, ready-made rule, 151

Example of a tie-your-hands-behind-your-back, off-the-rack rule, 39

Excerpt from "today's" legalese Decs, 150

From developer to disaster, 148

Dec test, 54

From developer to dream, 148

Fuzzy mold is taking hold, 42

Helpful off-the-rack rule, 173

Let it be known, let it be said, let it be written, 201

No backyards in sight, 143

No For-signs allowed, 142

RULES (continued)

Development

Reasonableness test, 181

Significance test, 148

Take a close look at this (discriminatory covenants), 167

The primary purpose, 38

There's more than one way to spread the word (buyer beware sign), 143

Enforcement and involvement

A case where mediation, instead of litigation, would have benefited both the HOA and the homeowner, 157

A position of strict enforcement not only endangers happiness, it has the potential to kill!, 18

A suggested solution to a silly problem, 54

Another road kill story, 139

Another verse of the "Amend the Rules" song, 191

Arlene discovered unhappiness can strike even contented communities, 59

Cities shouldn't be arbitrary and capricious either, 56

Covenants can be abandoned, 183

Don't be guilty of breaching your responsibilities, 188

HOAs need to be reasonable, 176

Ignoring one rule doesn't dump the rest, 197

In midstream the BOD changed the advertised game plan, 158

It may be easier, but for whom?, 25

Kids too, 27

Know who's in charge — the enforcers, 83

Let's sing the "Amend the Rules" song, 190

Mediation can solve problems, 156

Meetings are supposed to be open to all homeowners, 108

Melt away the tip and reality may be exposed, 38

Might these decisions have a bearing?, 153

More about signs, 143

Pride of ownership cannot be legislated, 73

Pride of ownership is the quality that creates better subdivisions, 103

Some BODs are from a friendly planet, 140

Some rules don't hold water 191

Sometimes the rules change, 157

"State-of-the-ark" hasn't been reached, let alone "state-of-the-art", 191

Step down from that soapbox and onto the next, 61

The nightmare, 24

What's in a name?, 108

Which way to Utopia?, 30

RULES (continued)

Enforcement and involvement

You want to have a garage what?, 54

S

SERVICE COMPANIES
(also see **Management companies**)

Check signing

A good plan, 104

Procedures to follow

Example of a declaration of being a service company, 110

Example of a good service company's approach, 114

Qualifying

Basic services performed by service/management companies can include the following and more, 112

Good points for the BOD and homeowners to remember, 113

Indeed, what is in a name?, 109

Management companies, 111

Some questions for the BOD to ask the company's representative, 113

Words do have power, 109

Responsibilities

Example of a good service company's approach, 114

SIGNIFICANCE TEST, 148

SINGLE-FAMILY DETACHED HOME

Is it a bird, a plane, a condo, or a . . . ?, 34

SOLUTIONS

A suggested solution to a silly problem, 54

You want to have a garage what?, 54

Coup (also see **Coup d'état**)

Don't go to the meeting one vote!, 95

Don't leave without a signed proxy!, 95

How to organize your coup d'état, 93

If you happen to get romanced into a sub-happy community, 92

The special meeting, 19

Time to organize a coup d'état, 18

You don't have to be a homeowner to organize a coup, 96

Responsibilities and involvement

A real struggle to reach a happy ending, 66

A suggested solution to a silly problem, 54

Homeowners' involvement produces another happy ending, 62

If you're not going to get involved, at least cooperate!, 96

Motivational trees, 97

Responsibility demands the four-letter "W" word. Work can bring a happy ending, 61

SOLUTIONS (continued)

Survey

　Responses from the residents to that question, 17

SPECIAL MEETINGS (also see **coup**)

　By the end of the special meeting, 19

　Sample of the petition we used, 94

　The special meeting, 19

T

TOWNHOMES

　Is it a bird, a plane, a condo, or a . . . ?, 34

TRADE COMPANIES (vendors)

　Companies don't know how to charge less for fewer services, 127

　Companies know how to charge more for more services, 127

W

WARRANTIES

　Warranties can vanish!, 120

WORDS

　Words <u>do</u> have power, 109

　42, 73, 102, 103, 106, 107, 141, 165, 167

Articles

A

Association neighborhood bully? Battle over pickup costs homeowner thousands in legal fees [*Rocky Mountain News* Marlys Duran 10/6/96], 199

Audit: Homeowners' fees were misused. Association at Meadows considers settling for less than full payment; deal would clear way for ownership transfer [*Rocky Mountain News* Shelley Gonzales 10/29/96], 71

B

Behind Closed Gates [*USA Weekend* David Diamond 1/31–2/2/1997], 169

Big neighbor is watching. Covenants have their place — but when enforced too zealously, the rules can make residents feel like they're living in a police state. [*Rocky Mountain News* Karen Abbott 2/8/94], 44

C

Conversation heard over the backyard fence [*Rocky Mountain News* Karen Abbott 2/8/1994], 38, 48–49

Covenant pettiness peeves Parker couple [*The Denver Post* Ginny McKibben 5/8/91], 137

Covenants rankle residents [*Rocky Mountain News* Shelley Gonzales 7/28/1996], 192

Articles　(continued)

Covenants: altering the landscape. A horse too many spurs legal battle in Douglas [*Rocky Mountain News* Marlys Duran 10/21/96], 197

Covenants: altering the landscape. Proposal would trim power of subdivisions over their homeowners [*Rocky Mountain News]* Marlys Duran 10/21/96], 52

D — H

Developer takes homeowner off board. Removal causes uproar at meeting of residents of Castle Rock subdivision [*Rocky Mountain News* Shelley Gonzales 2/28/1996], 70

Have the covenants police come after you? [*Rocky Mountain News* Karen Abbott 2/8/1994], 21

Hi-Riser [a Florida paper 11/3/94], II

Hung up: covenants can be all wet [*The Denver Post* Ann Schrader 7/16/1995], 64

M — O

Meadows settlement reached [*Rocky Mountain News* Shelley Gonzales 10/30/1996], 73

Out of time. Stolen Rolex marks change in meadows [*The Castle Rock Chronicle* K.T. Kelly 4/2/1996], 71

R

Read the rules before moving in [*Rocky Mountain News* Karen Abbott 2/8/1994], 152–155

Residents look for new management [*The Castle Rock Chronicle* K.T. Kelly 2/21/1996], 69

S — T

Subdivision gives up fussy rules [*Rocky Mountain News* Tillie Fong 8/7/1996], 194

Trouble on the Home Front? [*Woman's Day* John Grossmann 11/1/1996], 39, 157, 162, 169

Memorable quotes

Albert Einstein, 62, 93

Ancient Chinese Proverb, 88

Anonymous, 100, 144, 146, 150

Arnot L. Sheppard, Jr., 55

Benjamin Franklin, 30, 97

Confucian Curse, 201

Frank A. Clark, 132

George Eliot, 146

Grover Cleveland, 202

Harlan F. Stone, 150

Henry M. Robert, XIII

Lawrence J. Peter, 76

Margaret Thatcher, 62

Mark Twain, 187

Martin Luther King, Jr., 81, 202

Murphy's Law, 156

Sam Ewing, 97

Wendell Phillips, 162

Newsletters

A — B

Ambiguous language construed against association, 191

Amending your documents, 191

Are your architectural guidelines unclear? 191

Associations should act reasonably, 176

"Buyer beware", 143

C — D

Conflict of interest procedures and a code of ethics for board members, 189

Court holds garbage collection policy unconstitutional, 56

Dealing with two-legged pests, 190

Developer breaches fiduciary duty by not properly funding reserves, 40

Directors and officers liability insurance is a board member's last line of defense, 179

"Disability" suits, 153

E — F

Embezzlement, 79

Fiduciary duty, 188

For success, examine the advice of others, 188

H — I

Have your covenants been abandoned?, 183

Is our association exposed to liability if we use volunteers?, 121

Is Silverado a role model?, 136

L — M

Limit the board's liability, 178

Loss assessment insurance coverage, 127

Mediation and conflict in associations, 156

N — P

No lemonade stands allowed?, 27

Owner's right to inspect association books and records, 136

Pet restrictions, 191

Preparing board minutes, 132

R

Real estate sign ordinance, 143

Reasonableness test applied, 157

Releasing reports, records, and lists, 135

S — T

Sizing up board members, 192

Some BODs are from a friendly planet (Fly the American flag), 140

Some FHA violations, 63

Ten ways to make unhappy people happy, 176

The declaration says what???, 166

Newsletters (continued)

U — W

Unanimous decisions can lead to trouble, 131

Using mediation to resolve disputes, 156

Warranties can vanish! (legal tip), 120

Relevant reading

Caveat Emptor: Before You Buy That California Condo Frederick L. Pilot, 164

Finding the Key to Your Castle Grimm and Lane, 164

Managers Report Magazine, 179

Privatopia: Homeowner Associations and the Rise of Residential Private Government Dr. Evan McKenzie, 168

Problems of Long-Standing Homeowner Associations Jim Winzenburg, 163

The Complete and Easy Guide to All the Law Every Home Owner Should Know The American Bar Association, 164

Samples and examples

Bill for voluntary dues and request for committee volunteers, 81

Bulletin to allow garage sales, 55

Example of a declaration of being a service company, 110

Form for lender's approval, 67

HOA's newsletter with a friendly overtone, 74

Homeowners' questionnaire, V

Newsletter from a homeowner, 62

Sample of the petition we used, 94

Sample proxy with a date limit, 106

The first letter (from the HOA), 57

The second letter, 57

After the resident has complied, 58

Glossary (acronyms and abbreviations)

ACC — Architectural Control Committee

BAD or **BADs** — Bylaws, Articles of Incorporation and Declarations

BOD or **BODs** — Board of Directors

CAI — Community Associations Institute

CCC or **CCCs** — Covenants-controlled Community

CC&Rs — Covenants, Conditions, and Restrictions

CCIOA — Colorado Common Interest Ownership Act

CIC — Common Interest Communities

CID — Common Interest Development

HOA — Home Owner Association

DAB or **DABs** — Declarations, Articles of Incorporation, and Bylaws

Decs — Declarations

Docs — Documents

Regs — Rules and Regulations

UCIOA — Uniform Common Interest Ownership Act

About the author

Joni Greenwalt had never expected to become a writer. Born in Gary, Indiana, she began her working career at a Denver television station.

In the 1950s she was the media director at a large advertising agency for a number of major Hollywood film companies.

She established Student Film Programs, Inc. in 1967. Her company presented major-studio educational films to students in grade, middle, and high schools in Colorado, Kansas, Oklahoma, Washington, and Oregon. She sold her business in 1979 and began her career in real estate.

This book is an outgrowth of Joni's varied experiences along with living in a community under the rule of an association.

She gained valuable knowledge from her career in real estate, leading her community from discord to harmony, and serving as president of her association for over five years.

I've known Joni since 1959. She is dedicated to helping others succeed.

Phill Dreckman, Vice president
Wodell, Iltis, Sherman Associated, Inc.
(advertising, public relations, marketing and
publicity of major Hollywood film companies)

For single book orders or for quantity discounts
Cassie Publications, Inc.
P.O. Box 261368
Denver, CO 80226
303-274-0208 or Toll Free 888-683-9550
www.homeownerassoc.com

For consultation on specific HOA questions
303-422-6277 or Toll Free 866-422-5224 to make an appointment
Monday through Wednesday – 9:00 A.M. to 5:00 P.M. Mountain Time
www.angelfire.com/ok/homeowners/free.html